DRINKS ALL ROUND

DRINKS ALL ROUND

KEVIN DRINKELL
WITH SCOTT BURNS

BLACK & WHITE PUBLISHING

First published 2010
by Black & White Publishing Ltd
29 Ocean Drive, Edinburgh EH6 6JL

3 5 7 9 10 8 6 4 2   10 11 12 13

ISBN: 978 1 84502 327 0

Typeset by Ellipsis Books Limited, Glasgow
Printed and bound by MPG Books Ltd, Bodmin

CONTENTS

FOREWORD
BY GRAEME SOUNESS

I ONCE famously said that if I had 11 Kevin Drinkell's in my team then I wouldn't have to do much of a team talk. I stand by that. Kevin was one of the most professional and dedicated players I have worked with in all my time in football.

Kevin was a manager's dream. He was the type of guy who could not only score goals and lead the line but would also run through brick walls for the team. That was shown at every club he played from Grimsby right through to Stirling Albion.

I know a few eyebrows were raised when I signed Kevin for Rangers, although it had nothing to do with his ability but the fact I was taking him from Norwich City, who weren't one of the most fashionable sides in England at that time.

I knew that I was getting a top striker and a really good professional into the bargain because he had been on Rangers' radar for some time. I had actually approached Norwich a year earlier but they wanted £1 million.

I seriously thought about paying the money but I needed to strengthen two or three other positions and decided to put things on the back burner.

The following season I knew I needed somebody to partner Ally McCoist and Kevin was the man at the top of my list. Fortunately, by then Norwich had dropped their asking price and I ended up getting Kevin for somewhere in the region of £500,000. I knew as soon as the ink on the contract was dry that we had done a decent piece of business. I believed Rangers had got themselves a real bargain and Kevin showed that in his time at Ibrox.

He scored on his Old Firm debut and I think that 5–1 win went a long way to helping him become a big favourite with the Rangers fans. After that he never looked back and I also knew that when it came to the big games Kevin could and would deliver.

I genuinely believe that in that first season of our nine-in-a-row charge Kevin was one of our biggest players. He finished as our top scorer but it wasn't just his goals it was his work rate and his unselfishness. He wasn't interested in being the big star. Success for him was seeing the team do well rather than chasing any personal glory. That in football is very much a rare commodity, especially these days.

Kevin was a great professional who gave everything whenever he crossed that white line and was an inspiration to others around him. If you ask anyone who played with Kevin at Rangers they will all tell you what a great asset he was to the team. I am sure that was the case at every club he played at throughout his career.

He was a good level-headed guy to have in your dressing room. By the time Kevin arrived at Ibrox he was already vastly experienced. He was always quite quiet off the pitch but had a real dry sense of humour. He was always quick to slap down Ally McCoist and Ian Durrant with his cutting one-liners. That was always worth watching because from time to time they needed to be put in their place. Drinks had been around the block and knew how to handle himself on and off the pitch.

I know a lot of the Rangers fans were unhappy when Kevin was sold to Coventry. I was also reluctant to let him go but he was frustrated that I planned to rotate my three strikers, Ally McCoist, Mo Johnston and Kevin. He wanted to play every week and wasn't too comfortable about having to sit out from time to time.

In the end Coventry City came in with an offer, which for Kevin and Rangers was just too good to turn down. I knocked back several approaches from John Sillett but he kept coming back and in the end the deal was too good to turn down and we both had to consider it.

Kevin achieved so much throughout his career and went on to make his mark on both sides of the border after he left Rangers. He was a credit to himself throughout a really distinguished career. He can look back on his playing days with great pride. I just wonder what more he could have achieved if it hadn't been for the 150 cigarettes a day!

JUST BEFORE we kick-off there are a few people I would like to mention. My Dad, John Drinkell, was a major driving force behind my football and my life and I would like to dedicate this book to him. Unfortunately, he passed away a few years ago and is sadly missed but will never be forgotten. He, along with my mother Betsy, ensured that my brothers and I wanted for nothing and gave us all a wonderful start in life.

My wife Andrea has always supported my sometimes-selfish decisions, she has been a wonderful companion as well as giving me two fantastic daughters along the way.

There are so many other people I have met and come across in my time in football, too many to do justice to in a single book (the publishers wouldn't let me have a second volume!) and I acknowledge them here. They know who they are.

I hope you enjoy reading *Drinks All Round* and that it brings you as much enjoyment as football has given to me.

Kevin Drinkell

ACKNOWLEDGEMENTS

Kevin and Scott would like to thank: Robert Briggs, Jim Brown, Ken Brown, Steve Bruce, Stuart Darroch, Ian Dawson, Kevin Gallacher, Roger Harris, Michelle Hurst, Jim Jefferies, Ally McCoist, Robert McElroy, Steve Ogrizovic, Alan Poole, Billy Reid, Graeme Souness, Ray Stewart, Willie Vass, David Weir, Trevor Whymark, Paul Wilkinson, Aileen Wilson, Chris Woods for their invaluable help in making this book possible. We would also like to thank DC Thomson, *Coventry Evening Telegraph*, *Grimsby Evening Telegraph*, SNS pix, Wylies Pictures (Stirling), Photoaction and *Scottish Daily Express* with regards to the picture section.

1

FOLLOWING IN THE FOOTSTEPS
OF JOHN CHARLES

FOLLOWING in the footsteps of John Charles was always going to be a bit of a challenge. The legendary Welshman, who starred for Leeds and Juventus, was the ultimate footballer in the Drinkell household.

Charles may not have had much of a connection with Grimsby but to my dad, John Drinkell, he was almost untouchable because of the way he played the game.

So much so that my parents called their first son John Charles Drinkell, born 2 October 1957 after him, although I am not sure how much say my mum, Betsy, actually had in the matter.

My dad loved the game and was a decent footballer in and around the Grimsby area. He was a striker and actually turned down the chance to sign professional forms with Derby County, who were a top-flight side at the time.

The Midlands were only a few hundred miles away but it might as well have been on the moon as far as my parents were concerned. Dad was a local lad through and through and proud of his roots. He was a real family man and the people around him were important to him. Those reasons along with my mum were enough to convince him to turn his back on the big time with Derby.

Dad, who had just returned from his national service, felt he would be better carving out a career for himself down the docks and playing football for fun.

Maybe he thought he might get the chance to turn professional again but that dream was cruelly crushed at the tender age of 22 when he suffered a career-ending knee injury.

The fact he couldn't fulfil his own playing ambitions certainly didn't quell his love for the game. He watched football whenever he could, especially if it involved his boys, whether it be at Grimsby Town, a local amateur game or just a simple kick-about in the park.

He was a football purist. He liked to see the game played in the proper manner, good attacking play with the ball stroked around the deck. Dad was an advocate of the old 'W formation', which included two wingers in a five-man attack. That is why he loved to watch guys like Johnny Haynes and Kevin Keegan, who was born just up the road in Scunthorpe, but his all-time hero was Charles.

It wasn't long before John Charles 'Mark II' was out and about with a ball at his feet. He had about three years to hone his skills before his brother, a certain Kevin Smith Drinkell, made his debut appearance on 18 June 1960.

With a dad and brother who both lived and breathed the game it wasn't long before I would be out kicking a ball. I soon picked up the nickname of 'Baggy' but it was nothing to do with my art of finishing. It was down to my mum. It didn't matter how well she turned me out because within minutes I always looked like I was wearing a bag of rags.

I was always out in the back garden running about with John and his pals, even though they were a few years older than me. As the older brother I always looked up to him. John was the first one into the primary and secondary teams and was a stand-out for the local boys clubs.

John continued to progress and his talents saw him sign professional forms with Grimsby Town. From those earliest years I longed to follow my big brother into the senior game.

Unlike him, I wasn't interested in beating a man and playing a beautiful pass. I just wanted to get the ball and smash it into the net. I got my buzz from scoring goals – there was no greater feeling.

My parents celebrated the birth of their third son, David, on 30 April 1963.

A couple of years later I started school at Yarborough. It probably won't be a surprise to know that although I wasn't too bad academically football always took centre stage at the Yarborough School.

Playing with my brothers and their pals gave me an obvious advantage when I played with my peers. It wasn't long before I was in the school team and playing for my local boys club, Grimsby Colts.

I enjoyed school and the highlight for all budding footballers was the end-of-term Teachers versus Pupils match. It was a big thing because all the senior boys wanted to play before they headed off to secondary school, and it was their chance to finally put one over the teachers.

I was no different. I was desperate to play until a silly schoolboy prank almost cost me my place. I used to help my cousin, Tony Drinkell, do his paper round on Sunday mornings. We used to get up early and start around 5am. By 7am the milk would start to be delivered. We used to wait until there were two bottles on a doorstep. We would deliver the paper, pick up a bottle and run round the corner to drink it.

Not the sort of behaviour you would expect from somebody of my standing in the school; I was head boy of the infants, captain of the football team, monitor, prefect and a librarian.

That was until one Monday morning when my whole world came crashing down around me. I walked into the school and was dragged straight into the headmaster's office. I wasn't aware I had stepped out of line but unbeknown to me it had been the headmaster's bottle of milk I had downed the previous day.

I was publicly humiliated in front of my entire class, as the furious headmaster ripped my monitor and prefect's badges off me. He also stripped me of all the other special privileges I used to enjoy.

To further my humiliation my mum and dad were also called to the school. That was the ultimate punishment, especially as you never wanted to get on the wrong side of my dad, he was a stickler for discipline.

I had seen it as a stupid schoolboy prank but looking back now it was petty theft. I regretted doing it but the worst possible punishment was still to come.

The headmaster told me I was no longer allowed to play for the school team, which included the end of season game against the teachers. I was absolutely gutted.

Match day came for the teachers' game and I remember being a rather frustrated spectator. The teachers were 2–0 up and were all over us. I thought if only I hadn't stolen that pint of milk I could have been out there making a difference. Then at half-time the headmaster came up to me and said: 'Go and get your boots on and get out there for the second half.' I went on and scored a hat-trick, helping the pupils to win 3–2. I walked off the park proud as punch but at the same time I had learned an important lesson.

I was quite fortunate because whether I was playing for the Yarborough School or with the Colts we won most of the tournaments on the local scene.

It was the same when I moved up to the new Whitgift School. It was a state-of-the-art facility with theatres, swimming pools, sporting pitches and even a cinema. There was plenty to do and see but, for me, nothing beat kicking a ball about.

My PE teacher, Gordon Royston, who has now sadly passed away, was a big influence on me. He kept me on the right track and stood up for me, especially when it came to school sports.

Like my brother, John, I was a budding sportsman who would try everything but that caused us both unnecessary grief.

John played for the football and cricket teams and also ran cross-country for the school. Trying to make time for all three was a major issue and so he decided to drop the cricket. He felt it would help his football but the school didn't see it that way and banned him from playing all sports for a year. It was all a bit over the top.

I found myself in a similar situation. I was in the basketball team, running cross-country in Lincoln on a Saturday and then trying to get back to play for Grimsby Colts in the afternoon.

It was too much and these days you would never be pushed like that. I decided to stop my running because I couldn't do myself justice doing all three sports. The headmaster was furious and also tried to ban me from playing football. Thankfully Mr Royston, who ran the football team, fought my corner and eventually I got back kicking a ball.

I really appreciated what Mr Royston did and whenever I went back to Grimsby I used to pop into the Notts Bar, his local, to have a pint and catch up with him and some of his old pals.

If I wasn't playing football then I was watching it. My earliest memories were being allowed to stay up and watch the 1970 World Cup final before my dad headed out on nightshift. It was great seeing top stars like Rivelino, Jairzinho, Pele and Gigi Riva in their prime.

Closer to home, I was a fan of Derby County and my favourite player was Colin Todd. He was a cultured defender in the mould of the legendary Bobby Moore.

A few years later I became a fan of Bobby Robson's early Ipswich Town teams, which included the likes of David Johnson, Alan Hunter and Trevor Whymark.

The latter was a player I always looked up to as a fellow centre forward and often tried to emulate. It was quite ironic because I ended up playing alongside Trevor and became good friends with him several years later. Locally, Grimsby were also doing well and when I was only 10 or 11 they won the old Fourth Division. That team had legends, who are still revered today, like Matt Tees, Dave Boylen, Stuart Brace and Jack Lewis. My dad would sit me on the fence behind the goal in the Pontoon Stand where I would cheer on the local heroes. Unbeknown to me at that time, I would get a slightly closer look at the same Grimsby players three or four years later.

I was dedicated to my football but there was one particular vice that didn't help my cause. Off the pitch I was quick on the draw of another kind – smoking.

My mum actually caught me hanging out of our bedroom window one day. That was when my cover was first blown. She threatened to tell my dad unless I promised to stop, although he also smoked. It was a bit of a generational thing. It certainly wasn't as taboo as it is today.

For whatever reason, much to my relief, my mum never told my dad. So I continued to smoke although I made sure I never got caught again, but I'm sure my dad still had a fair idea.

That was down to the fact I used to wait until he left the room and then I would light his tab to get the last few draws of tobacco out of it.

Looking back I wish he had caught me or my mum had told him because it might have forced me to stop what has now become a major habit.

But your parents can't be there to look over you 24 hours a day although my mum and dad gave all three of us everything we ever needed, especially when it came to our football.

My dad worked hard on the docks and would regularly do extra shifts while my mum would turn her hand to anything: working in factories and local shops to get our boots or whatever we needed.

Our main interest was kicking a ball about but my dad also knew the importance of having a good education, especially the way his own sporting career had vanished into fresh air.

He might have been from a working-class part of Grimsby but he was also a really intelligent guy. He had won a scholarship for the private Wintringham School. He was always a man who had his head screwed on although he also took great pride in his sons' careers.

My older brother John signed professional forms while I was

6

still playing in the juvenile ranks. I was playing for the school and for Grimsby Town's youths. It saw me up against guys like Gary Briggs at Middlesbrough and Mick McCarthy, who was a promising central defender at Barnsley.

I continued to play well and eventually broke into the reserves at Grimsby, where I played alongside John. It also looked like I might get one of the two annual professional contacts handed out to youth players.

I have to hold my hands up and say John was a technically better player than me but he didn't have the same luck. When I was pushing to turn professional he was hit with the hammer news he was to be released.

He was told around the Christmas and was devastated but it seemed to take a huge weight off his shoulders.

He no longer cared what the manager thought and just went out and enjoyed his football. He played out of his skin and by the end of the season the club had changed their mind and tried to offer him a new deal. By then the damage had been done and he told them to stuff it.

It had been such a knock to him and he wasn't prepared to put himself in that position again. So he walked away from the professional game at 18.

My dad was already working on the docks and helped John to get his ticket. He went on to become a docker and didn't actually play football again until two or three years later, when he turned out part-time for the likes of Skegness and Boston. John was a talented player and was always in demand at semi-professional level. He made a decent name for himself and played there for more than a decade.

Our younger sibling Dave was a similar player to John but got the knock at a slightly earlier age. He was unlucky to miss out on a YTS contract at Grimsby and decided to follow John down the semi-professional road, with the likes of Boston and King's Lynn. Both could have easily stepped back up the levels but were happy and enjoyed their football at that level.

I, however, decided to take my chances when I was offered schoolboy forms at Grimsby, although I didn't sign them right away. I would have jumped at it but dad wasn't as eager. I was still training and playing for the youths and he didn't see why I had to sign a form to do that. Then in the second year the club told us if I wanted to go on to a YTS contract I would need to sign schoolboy forms. I was 15 when I finally committed myself to the club. There had also been interest from Derby and Nottingham Forest but I decided Blundell Park was the best option.

I knew youth got its chance at Grimsby; after all I had already played for the reserves as a schoolboy and believed I would soon be knocking on the first-team door. I signed for the princely sum of £14-a-week plus £2 digs money, which went straight to my mum.

2

THE GRIMSBY GANG
RISES FROM THE ASHES

I WAS taken on at Grimsby with one of my best mates, Dave Moore, a dogged right back, who I had played alongside from an early age. His older brother Kevin, along with Tony Ford and Shaun Mawer, who the club had taken on as apprentices the previous year, were already at the club. We had played most of our juvenile football together although Shaun and 'Fordy' were slightly older.

We all got on really well on and off the park. We knew each other's games inside out and I was almost telepathic with Fordy. He was a talented winger, I knew whenever he ran up the flank just where he was going to land the ball. It proved to be a regular outlet for many of my goals throughout my early Grimsby career.

I quickly found that turning professional wasn't as glamorous as I dreamt it was going to be. I was up at the crack of dawn to get the first-team kit ready and then after I'd done my own training I would have to get everything cleaned and tidied for the next day. I enjoyed my second year a lot more because we became seniors and had a bit more power. I volunteered to take charge of the kit because it was a cushy number.

There used to be an old boiler room up at Blundell Park. It was kitted out with long poles along the top where we used to dry the towels and kit. It was also the perfect spot for a sly puff. I would sneak up there and have a quick smoke or a short nap after training. Dave Moore or one of the younger boys would then come in and say 'that is the place tidied can you go and ask the physio, John Fraser, if we can get away?'

That became a regular habit until I came in one morning and the boiler room had been burnt to the ground. I was struck by fear when I saw the remains. My initial thought was maybe I had been to blame. Had I left a burning cigarette butt up there? I was panicking for days until it emerged the fire had been down to faulty wiring.

It was a major relief, although my professional dream also looked like it could end up in smoke. My progress towards the first team had started to stutter and stall. I was a full-time professional but there were times when I couldn't even get a game for the reserves, even though I had been playing at that level a year before, when I was still a schoolboy.

That was under the management of Tom Casey but, fortunately, things were to change when the Irishman was sacked in November 1976.

The Exeter boss John Newman was brought in to replace him and before the end of that season my career was back on track.

The team looked doomed before Newman took charge. The pressure was off and he could afford to give the younger boys, like myself, a chance. He eventually went on to promote six or seven of our successful youth side, all guys who had played together from schools level right up to the reserves. There was Fordy, Mawer, Kevin and Dave Moore, Terry Donovan, Nigel Batch as well as myself. They were great days, living the dream of playing professional football with a bunch of pals I had grown up with.

It was a remarkable feat to have so many local, young, talented players come through the ranks at the same time. It is unlikely to happen at a club the size of Grimsby again.

The game has changed so much these days. The top clubs are getting richer and the smaller teams are getting poorer and poorer.

The gulf is bigger than it ever has been. Now even if clubs like Grimsby do have a promising youngster they are cherry picked by Premier League teams before they have even kicked a competitive ball. I find that sad because many players are missing out on so much by going straight into academies, knowing they might never make the breakthrough.

I could have gone elsewhere like my friend Paul Bartlett, who joined Derby, but looking back I believe I made the right choice joining my local club, where I was able to learn my trade.

Now some young players are earning lots of money but their careers are over before they are even out of their teens because they have failed to live up to the hype or expectation. It is such a waste!

On the subject of the 'scrapheap', there was one particular night when three young, rising stars ended up on it. Yet it had nothing to do with our football.

Dave, Bartlett and myself, who were as thick as thieves off the park, would go everywhere together, whether it be round the pubs of Grimsby or the local disco, Tiffany's.

One night we were all a little worse for wear when we decided to walk back to Dave's house from Tiffany's and we all ended up asleep in a skip. Don't ask me how it happened!

All I remember was waking up a few hours later and birds (the feathered variety) were squeaking in our ears, giving us an early morning alarm call, which was the last thing we needed after such a heavy session. It wasn't the sort of behaviour you would expect from professional athletes but we were fortunate our managers never found out or we could have found ourselves back on the scrapheap.

That night certainly wasn't a one-off. We definitely enjoyed our youth but we were serious about our football and determined to make names for ourselves. We didn't have to look far for role models because Fordy and Kevin Moore were already established in the first team.

Fordy made his debut first, becoming the club's youngest ever debutant in the process back in 1976. He was black and actually came through before more high-profile guys like Cyrille Regis and Viv Anderson came to the fore.

Tony did take a fair bit of stick but it was more from the away stands because the Grimsby fans loved and adored him. He took a lot of racial abuse and I really felt for him but Tony always let his football do the talking.

Tony deserves enormous credit for the way he handled himself and forged such a distinguished career. For some people it might have been too much but he showed great character and determination. He went on to play more games than anybody else and broke Terry Paine's outfield league record, making over 1,000 senior appearances. He was still playing for Rochdale at 40 – that shows some dedication. He was a fantastic player and a real example for any budding professional. He got a well-deserved MBE for his services to the game. It was a great accolade for a guy who had to overcome so much to achieve what he did.

Kevin was slightly different because he actually played with Grimsby while at college. He decided to finish his education and qualified as a surveyor before he turned full-time.

It was good having guys like that around us. They were friends and kept us grounded. In our dressing room there was no chance of anyone getting too big for their boots because they would be quickly slapped down.

There was one day when, as a young apprentice, I was cleaning the dressing room and I started to dish out some stick to Kevin. He might have been a senior player but I classed him as a mate and saw it as a bit of friendly banter.

I failed to notice our experienced midfielder Phil Hubbard standing behind me. His big hand came out and gave me a clout around the ear. I looked at Phil, as if to say 'what was that for?' He turned to me with this no-nonsense stare and said: 'You don't speak to full-time professionals like that and if I hear you do it again you will get more of the same.' It was all about respect and I was put firmly in my place.

After that I kept my head down and longed for my first-team chance. I still remember the day it finally arrived. It was Saturday, 11 April 1977 when I was told I would be making my Mariners debut. I actually thought the physio, Fraser, was pulling my leg when he broke the news.

I was hanging the No. 9 shirt up on its peg he said: 'Look after that, son, because you will be wearing it this afternoon.' I thought it was a joke and laughed it off.

I continued with my chores and went to find Mawer, who used to give me a run home prior to the home games. We jumped in his Mini and made our way across town when old 'Fraz' started to tail us and flash his lights until we pulled over. He said: 'I'm not kidding you. You are making your debut this afternoon.' Then I knew it was for real.

I rushed into the house to tell my mum and dad and they just looked at me as if I was mad. They quickly realised I was deadly serious and made a mad rush of phone calls to get family and friends down to the game.

I stepped out against Gillingham as a rookie 16-year-old although it was hardly a debut to remember. The game passed me by and was a rather lifeless 0–0 draw. It certainly wasn't how I had dreamed my first-team debut would go.

I remember more about after the game than the match itself. I hadn't even got my boots off when Harry Wainman, our goal-keeper, started to hand the cigarettes around the dressing room, to guys like Dennis Booth and Clive Wigginton. Smoking was pretty much a part of the culture back then but thankfully foot-ball has moved on and most top professionals wouldn't even consider putting a cigarette to their lips now.

Looking back now I actually have to laugh. There was even a period when the smokers, who outnumbered the rest, tried to be more sociable when we agreed to smoke pipes rather than ciga-rettes on the team coach. It is fair to say it didn't last long, but at least we made the effort!

Drinking was another vice that was very much part of the

scene. I remember going into my local pub, The Valiant, on the Willows estate, the evening after I had made my debut.

The owner knew I was under-age but he never said anything. I walked up and ordered a pint. He put my beer down and said: 'Have you seen the paper, Kev?' and laid it down in front of me. There was a big picture of me on the back. It read: 'Drinkell, 16, makes his debut.' Fortunately all he asked me for was the price of the pint and not proof of ID.

Things got even better the following week when we went to play Wrexham. We lost 3–2 but I scored twice to open my senior account – even though I can't remember much about them!

I went up for a high ball and clashed heads with a defender. I was still dazed when Dave Boylen put me through on goal. I fuzzily recall hitting this shot which somehow slipped through the keeper's legs for my first Grimsby goal. I turned around and tried to focus on the big turret stand they used to have at the Racecourse Ground but everything was just a massive blur. It was like that for a good 20 minutes. When I finally regained my senses I netted my second with a classic header.

Boylen had been the architect for my first senior goal. He also claims the credit for getting me my big break at Grimsby. He says he went in and told the manager that I should be playing. To this day I still don't know if that conversation really took place, but if it did then I would like to go on record and personally thank him.

I played another couple of games before injury prematurely ended my season. By that time Grimsby had already been relegated to the bottom tier of English football, so the only way was up. It was a fresh start and the manager was ready to build his team around the club's youth policy.

3

ELTON AND THE GRIMSBY
ROCKET MEN

BY THE time the new season came around I was desperate to become a first-team regular. I had been given a taste and wanted more. I also had to justify my hefty wage rise, which saw my weekly income jump to £20-a-week and my dig allowance to £3.

Being a youngster, the step up took a bit of adjusting to and I have to admit I was easily influenced. I was often dragged for a pint by some of the more experienced players. Dave Boylen was always the one assigned to get me home because he lived closest to my parents. It always came down to the same old routine, without fail. He would say: 'I'll drop you off but you have to come with us so we can get a couple of pints first.'

I used to sit in the corner of the pub and have a soft drink. Then as I came out of my shell I would be standing next to them with a pint in my hand. Those late-night sessions helped the players to bond and the team spirit to blossom.

On the park, things were going well. I was in the team and scoring goals. I played the first two or three months, getting valuable experience at less fashionable outposts like Stockport, York and Newport, while I pitched in with an early goal against Southport.

I followed that up with a goal at Hartlepool, but that day, 16 August 1977 somebody else made the headlines. We were on the coach travelling back from the North-East when it came on the radio that the King had died! I thought, 'We don't have a king,' and then the news broke that Elvis Presley had passed away.

Our assistant manager, George Kerr, immediately ordered the bus driver to pull over at the next village pub. We wondered what he was doing, I don't know if he was a big Elvis fan or not but he wanted us to pay our respects by going for a drink in his honour.

On the field, we continued to leave the opposition all shook up, as John Newman added some experience to his young squad. He brought in Gary Liddell, who was a good player but always found himself 12th man in Don Revie's legendary Leeds United side, and Michael Lester from Manchester City. Another young protégé and close friend of mine, Nigel Batch, also got his chance when Harry Wainman broke his wrist.

We were holding our own in Division Four but the real glamour came in the League Cup when we drew Watford at Blundell Park. The legendary Elton John was the chairman. It was a bit of a story back then because he was one of the biggest stars around.

I remember being really excited about the prospect of meeting Elton because he was a real-life superstar and showman into the bargain. He didn't disappoint. Elton turned up in this full-length mink coat, which would have cost more than I earned that year.

I also remember going out on to the pitch saying to myself: 'Elton, you don't know who I am but by the time I am finished you will be well aware of the name Kevin Drinkell.' Unfortunately, I put on a damp squib of a performance in front of the Rocket Man. I struggled to make an impact and we lost 2–1.

But it is fair to say that particular night in Grimsby made an impression on Elton. It later inspired him to write a song about the town. It is on his *Caribou* album and it goes something like 'Grimsby, one thousand delights that couldn't match the sweet sights. La la Grimsby.' I hope it was a positive reflection of his visit to my hometown and the bright lights of Cleethorpes rather than the great man being mischievous about Grimsby.

The burden of playing every week and being in the spotlight was beginning to take its toll and my performances began to dip. I found myself in and out of the team, as the manager was careful not to burn me out.

My first full season hadn't gone the way I had hoped and then injury saw me miss the last two months of the season. I scored my final goal of the campaign in our win at Rochdale but by the end of March my season was done and dusted. I had to watch from the stands as we finished sixth, some way behind Elton's champions Watford and runners-up Southend.

It wasn't a bad attempt for such an inexperienced squad and at least the foundations had been laid. I could be relatively pleased because I had been involved in 26 games and 20 of those had been starts. I had scored six goals, so I wasn't too disappointed and it gave me something to build on.

Over the summer I put on a few pounds and went through my rebellious stage, where I decided to grow my beard. My parents just looked at me and shook their head as if I was some sort of scruffy nuclear protester. Ironically, this was when I met my future wife, Andrea, for the first time. She insisted I wasn't exactly a great catch but we are still together today so I couldn't have been that bad!

We had some fun around that period. We would all go out together, Tony Ford, Dave Moore and all our girlfriends. Those were carefree days and my disposable income was boosted again when I was rewarded with my first, full professional contract. I was no longer a YTS and now I was up to £50-a-week on a 12-month contract with another year's option.

I felt like I had won the lottery because I also got a £500 signing-on fee. Half of it went to the PFA's benevolent pension fund and the other £250 was due to me over the next three years.

I returned fully fit for pre-season to the 1977–78 campaign. I might have been coining it in but on the park I was beginning to feel short-changed. I didn't even feature on the subs' bench for the first half dozen games. I was disappointed but what could I say? I was still only 18, filling out, growing, and a simple boy adapting to a man's game.

Fellow Blundell Park starlet Terry Donovan became the main striker along with Lester. Terry, a Republic of Ireland under-21 international, scored three goals in his first four appearances and ended up getting a move to Aston Villa in my absence. He made the switch for a then club record fee of £75,000.

His departure gave me my chance to get back in. The team had already made a solid start. We kept ourselves in the top six. I was doing okay but I had to wait until late October to open my account, when I hit two goals in a 4–3 win over Northampton.

That gave me a much-needed shot in the arm and I netted four goals in the next five games although niggling injuries stopped my season from really taking off.

I had still shown enough promise for the club to hand me another improved deal. It came as a welcome Christmas present. They offered me £140-a-week in the first year, £180-a-week the second and £220 in the third. I was also due a £1,500 loyalty bonus for every season I was there. I didn't need to think twice about signing it. It also showed the club rated me.

On the field, I just couldn't shrug off my injury problems although the team were doing well without me and hit the top with a 3–1 win against Wigan.

I was desperate to play my part and came back for the local derby with Scunthorpe. The derbies against the likes of 'Scunny', Hull and Lincoln were always massive. They were big because, as a local boy, I knew what they meant to the fans. They always guaranteed decent crowds and Grimsby would regularly boast attendances of 12,000 or 13,000 in the old Fourth Division for these games.

I scored but we had to settle for a share of the spoils. A couple of days later I got in on the act again when I netted against Bradford. We followed that up by beating Barnsley to go top. Almost 16,000 fans crammed into Blundell Park for that game to see us jump back above our main rivals Reading and Wimbledon.

We kept our noses in front at Northampton but left ourselves needing snookers after we dropped a point at Newport. The fans that day were more interested in a very different ball game. They were glued to the final of the World Snooker Championships.

All the locals were rooting for fellow Welshman Terry Griffiths. Hundreds of Newport fans were watching the match in the adjoining social club rather than us playing Newport. Fortunately, for them, he made it a weekend to remember – although it is one everyone in Grimsby would rather forget!

I know Terry now, through Ian and Lee Doyle working at 110 Sport, and I still say to him that I was in his homeland the day he became world champion.

But our Welsh miscue saw us drop back to second and needing championship snookers of our own going into the final two games. It never happened.

We lost at home to Doncaster and to Barnsley, who were also pushing for promotion, on the final day, to let Reading walk away with the title.

That last game was a real anti-climax because more than 21,000 crammed into Oakwell hoping to see some silverware.

We, at least, had the consolation of promotion. We were disappointed but the most important thing for the club was getting out of the Fourth Division.

We had a civic reception in the town hall to mark our achievement. I was still 18 and so it was really something to savour, seeing the celebrations and all the fans out in the streets.

It was a new experience for me and at one stage I was actually seen up on the balcony giggling. I didn't really take it all in because you think occasions like that are going to be a regular occurrence.

I finished the season with seven goals, although I was still some way behind our top scorer, Tony Ford.

On the back of my new contract I decided to treat Andrea to a luxury, foreign holiday. I took her to Mallorca and we checked into this really nice hotel.

I was beginning to think I had made it. I was the local hero at Grimsby and a string of big clubs had been linked with me. I was walking around as if I was Kevin Keegan rather than an up-and-coming youngster ready for his first crack at Division Three.

When I got up that first morning I said to Andrea: 'Why don't we go for a cappuccino?' being the sophisticated footballer. I was walking up the street as if I was the main man when this chocolate brown Rolls Royce pulls up next to us. I just stood and looked as this bronzed and well-groomed guy stepped out of the driver's seat and took some buckets and spades out of his boot for his kids.

A clearly impressed Andrea said: 'Is that Graeme Souness over there?'

Needless to say he never recognised Kevin Drinkell and maybe had never even heard of him! That snub well and truly put me in my place. I knew there and then I had a long way to go before I could say I had made it.

I got just as big a shock when I returned for the 1979–80 season to learn we had lost our promotion-winning boss. Newman decided to quit to become to become Colin Addison's No. 2 at Derby County. He was replaced by his own assistant George Kerr. He was a tough Scot, who had played for our rivals Scunthorpe and been part of the management team at Lincoln.

I gave Kerr an early headache when Middlesbrough bid £300,000 for me. George pulled me in and said, 'We have had an offer from Boro' but you aren't for sale.' I was fine with that because I had never even thought about leaving, even though Boro' were and still are a massive club.

The speculation hit the local press but I was happy and settled in Grimsby with Andrea. It wasn't until a few years later that Dave Hodgson, who had been at Boro', told me how much I could have earned if I had made the move. He was pocketing 10 times more than what I was on with the Mariners. If I had known that I might have chapped the door but I had no idea and Grimsby had also rewarded me with a new contract of my own.

20

I was buzzing and ready to start the season when another niggling injury curtailed me again. It left Kerr short of firepower and he went out and paid a £60,000 club record fee to sign Kevin Kilmore from Stockport.

He made a real, early impression and to be fair Kevin was a good player. A lot of nice things were said about him and at one stage there was even talk of Liverpool being interested. The story was KK was being lined up to replace somebody of the same initials – in Kevin Keegan!

I was more interested in trying to grab my first-team slot back. By the October I was fit enough to make a couple of substitute appearances although I was still playing catch-up after missing most of the pre-season.

I just kept my head down and continued to give my all. I was determined to get back in the starting XI. Kilmore had already bagged a few goals and I felt we could become a decent partnership.

We made a decent fist of things in the League Cup. We saw off 'Scunny', Huddersfield and Notts County before we faced our biggest challenge, in Everton.

The Toffees were a massive club and had top players like Mike Lyons and Brian Kidd. That was a big thing for me because I was a fan of Brian but there was no room for sentiment and we managed to spring a major cup shock.

Mike Brolly, who was a smashing guy, was our hero scoring both our goals. He was a decent left winger, who I always felt was under-rated. His enthusiasm for football was unmatched. He loved being out on the training pitch. He was always the first one out even in the middle of winter when it was snowing and the rest of us were in hiding.

It was good for him because Mike was normally the one supplying the ammunition and this time he was able to grab the headlines.

That famous scalp helped to put Grimsby back in the spotlight. It proved we had a talented side, who could take the step up.

21

The Everton win set up an epic fifth-round clash with Wolves. It was another big draw because they had Emlyn Hughes, Andy Gray, Kenny Hibbitt and big George Berry.

The initial game ended goalless, at a packed Blundell Park, although we should have won. We had been the better team and Kevin Moore had a chance to win it with a header but his effort came back off the bar.

It went to a replay the following week at Molineux.

Wolves were favourites but, once again, we rose to the occasion and had the better of the exchanges. Gray put them in front and we pulled it back thanks to a rather fortunate own goal.

The tie was eventually decided by a second replay at Derby's Baseball Ground a week later. By that time our chance had gone. We had missed our opportunity and never got going.

Wolves went on to win the tournament by beating Swindon in the semi-final and the holders Nottingham Forest in the final, with Gray scoring the only goal of the game.

It was hard to watch Hughes lift the trophy knowing we really should have put them out. 'Crazy Horse' had a glittering career but he was a guy I lost a lot of respect for later in my career.

It was when he went on to become manager at Rotherham two or three seasons later. He was still their player-boss when Grimsby travelled to Millmoor for a game.

I was seen as one of the more promising up-and-coming strikers in the English game and I had been linked with a few top teams like Everton, Stoke, Leeds, Manchester City and Middlesbrough.

The ball was booted up to the other end of the pitch when he turned and snarled at me: '£200,000 to Stoke. I wouldn't even pay £2,000 to take you here!' There had been no previous bad blood, so he didn't need to say anything. This was a guy who had probably won more medals than I had scored goals. I just looked at him but never said anything. From that moment on I lost all respect for him. He had played at the top level and didn't need to stoop that low.

I don't know if he thought he might struggle against me because he was coming to the end of his career and didn't have the same legs. I don't know. I had the last laugh when we left with the points.

I also got the chance to silence another footballing legend when I netted in our win at Sheffield Wednesday. I took a great deal of delight from that goal.

I had been linked with a move to Wednesday, who had Jack Charlton in charge at that time. The build-up had all been about me possibly going there, but before the game Charlton had said: 'Drinkell wouldn't even get in my team!' Needless to say I didn't need much of a team talk. I scored my goal and, for me, that was the perfect way to respond to Mr Charlton's cheap and needless jibe.

It was also a big win for the team. It kept us away from the relegation zone and allowed us to consolidate. The squad was bolstered by the signing of the experienced striker Trevor Whymark. The club broke their record transfer fee when they agreed to pay £80,000 for the former Ipswich and Vancouver Whitecaps forward.

Trevor was a player I really admired. When I started to play alongside him he didn't disappoint. Trevor was a real class act. Everybody could see he had played at the top level, he was so comfortable on the ball it could be blasted at any part of his body and he would kill it stone dead. His touch was amazing and he always knew where he needed to be on the pitch. You never saw him haring after a ball, like me, because he was always in the right place at the right time. I learned a lot from him and playing with Trevor helped me improve my game immensely. Trevor was also a great guy away from the ground and we became good friends. Andrea and I became really close to Trevor and his wife Rita and, when we all moved into the same Wybers Wood estate in Grimsby, they became godparents to our eldest daughter, Alexandra.

Trevor helped the team to bed in after a difficult start although we were given a real going over by the European Champions Liverpool in the FA Cup.

We had seen off Chesterfield and Sheffield United in the earlier rounds but Bob Paisley's legendary team were a class apart.

They boasted the might of Kenny Dalglish, Phil Neal, Alan Hansen, Souness, Jimmy Case and Terry McDermott. It was such a big game even Andrea went to Anfield. She didn't really like to go to away games and it proved to be one of her last and it had nothing to do with the trauma of seeing her boyfriend and his team publicly humiliated.

The game was a sell-out, in front of more than 49,000 fans, and for many of us it was the biggest crowd we had ever been involved in. Andrea was in the terracing but was so shaken by the size of the crowd and the constant swaying that she didn't go to many away games after that.

We headed to Merseyside confident we could give them a game although we were well aware of the magnitude of the task. The good thing about that Liverpool team was that it didn't matter if it was Grimsby or Bayern Munich, they played the same way. They had high standards and never let them slip.

I was up against Hansen and Phil Thomson and it was a challenge I was looking forward to, but in the end I came up very much second best. We were thrashed 5–0 with a Craig Johnston hat-trick and goals from Souness and Case putting us to the sword. It was a painful lesson and showed we still had a long way to go.

That result acted as a wake-up call for the league. At the turn of the year we put an unbelievable run together.

I played my part with 13 goals in our final 18 games. Amongst those goals the one in the 2–2 draw with Hull really stood out because they were our big rivals and it was always good to get one at Boothferry Park.

Going into the final run-in we were always within the top two places. We were also well aware of our late slip the previous season and this time we wanted to finish the job.

We hit the top in late March and stayed there, putting together a 15-match unbeaten run of 10 wins and five draws.

The season finale came down to our last game of the season

against Sheffield United at Blundell Park. There was a big, big crowd, even though United had been top earlier in the year but had fallen badly away. Their main rivals, Mr Charlton's Wednesday, had since emerged as the main threat to our championship ambitions.

We made a good start when I scored an early goal and things just snowballed. Joe Waters added a second and I grabbed another couple to complete my hat-trick. We ended up cruising to an easy 4–0 win to clinch the title and my first senior medal.

The scenes at the final whistle at Blundell Park were absolutely amazing and just a vision of sheer joy. I am sure a few visiting fans were also heavily involved in the celebrations, knowing that Sheffield Wednesday had missed out on the title.

The manager showed a nice touch after the game when he went and rescued the match ball for me. George wrote a touching message on it, paying tribute to my exploits that season, before he passed it over.

I later gave the ball to my dad. He kept it above his wardrobe for years until the club got in touch and asked if they could put it on display at the park.

They built a restaurant called Inn at the Park, in one of the stands, and wanted to put some memorabilia, old shirts and pictures out. I thought it was a good idea and cajoled my dad into giving up his prized possession. We agreed to hand the ball over on the proviso we got it back when it was no longer needed.

A few years later I bumped into the club's commercial manager Dave Smith, who I played with at Coventry. I asked him about the ball and he said that nobody at the club had a clue where it was. That is something that really disappoints me because it meant a lot to my dad and it looks like we will never see it again, although I still live in hope.

The Grimsby fans flooded on to the pitch and we had to scramble up to the directors' box for the ceremony because we couldn't get onto the pitch. The champagne was popping and there were smiles everywhere.

25

I was delighted for my team mates but the key for me was seeing the joy the title brought to the Grimsby fans, my friends and family. My dad was a dedicated follower, along with my uncles, Tony and David, and it was great to give them something to celebrate.

That had always been the big motivation for me rather than personal glory. I knew what it meant to them because the Grimsby people love their football. It was their release from pressure of the docks and the factory floors. We were living a different lifestyle but our manager, Kerr, was always one for keeping our feet firmly on the ground. He would quite often take us down a peg or two by taking us to the docks to see people work at 5am. These were the people who paid our wages and George wanted to drum that into us. It was a real eye-opener and it was good to give them something back.

These were the same guys I mixed with down the pub and at the local market stalls. They paid their hard-earned money to watch us so it was important they got something back in return.

I think that is lost from the modern game. That is sad because some players only care about the money rather than the people they are representing.

The Championship party turned out to be a brilliant night. It was another civic reception and open-top bus around the streets of Grimsby. All the roads were packed with punters, desperate for a glimpse of the Division Three trophy.

It was the perfect end to a near perfect season. Personally, I had done myself proud netting 16 league goals in 33 games. I was quite pleased. I had established myself as the No. 9 and Grimsby's main striker and although speculation continued to rage I was still more than happy to be a Mariner.

4

NOT ALL PLAIN SAILING
FOR THIS MARINER

DIVISION TWO was another step up and the question was whether we would continue to progress; It was the first time that Grimsby had played at that level in 15 years.

Now we really were in with the big boys, with Chelsea, Newcastle United, Blackburn Rovers, West Ham United and Bolton Wanderers. The fixtures, at least, were kind and broke us in gently. I grabbed the first goal of the campaign in our opening day draw at Shrewsbury Town although I still don't know how we escaped with that point.

The manager, George Kerr, used to allow us a couple of pints on the Friday night before away games. Bobby Cumming, Joe Waters, Nigel Batch and myself all went to this local pub just round the corner from the hotel. We had two or three pints and were just about to head back when the local *Grimsby Evening Telegraph* reporter John Kirby came in and bought us all a drink. It was only right we got him one back and so by the end of the night we had ended up downing six or seven pints each.

We headed back to the hotel and unsurprisingly missed breakfast. We were ordered down for our mid-morning training session, which we blundered through, before we returned to our rooms to sleep through lunch.

Fortunately we all made the match in various states of disrepair.

Shrewsbury gave us a real battering but 'Batchey' had an amazing game and kept us in it. My own thumping headache got worse when I took a kick in the head. I needed five stitches before I returned to score and get us out of jail.

The drinking crew all got back on the bus after the game and we realised we had been lucky and it was time to call time on our Friday night drinking sessions.

Confidence remained high within the squad thanks to our back-to-back promotions. We put together a four-match unbeaten run with three draws and a win against Wrexham.

Any thoughts of a third consecutive promotion were then put into perspective when we hit the skids. We picked up one win in 12.

By mid-November we were looking over our shoulders rather than above. We managed to stop the rot with a six-match unbeaten run that pulled us away from danger.

We really kicked on under George Kerr, as our young, hungry squad continued to develop. t was good because the likes of Fordy, the Moore brothers, Shaun Mawer and Batchey had all come through the youth ranks and were thriving on our diet of first-team football.

George was a good manager but a typical Scot. He would get really angry when players weren't giving it their all. To him it was never about individuals, it was always about the team. That was our great strength.

George worked hard on it and there were days where we wouldn't even train. He would come in and order us to take a walk down the sea front for a bacon roll and a cup of tea in a local cafe.

Nobody could argue because we were getting results. By the end of March we were on the promotion fringes, although West Ham were well clear in the title race. We still felt we could join them if we could show a bit of consistency over the last seven games.

I helped us to a point at Newcastle and nabbed a goal in our win against Sheffield Wednesday but we couldn't get the points we needed.

We ended up five points off the promotion spots and that left a fair bit of disappointment around the place. It had still been a decent achievement for a club like Grimsby, but at the same time, to come so close and miss out was hard to take. Personally, I was disappointed with my tally of seven league goals.

I was hoping the 1981–82 season would see me back amongst the goals more regularly. I scored in our opening day draw with Leicester City, who had just been relegated and were strong favourites to win the league. I played the first dozen or so games, but we showed very little in terms of consistency in the league.

We managed to put a decent run together in the Football League Group Cup – the current Football League trophy. We topped our section with three wins over Doncaster, Sheffield United and Chesterfield.

Not long after that I was stopped in my tracks by back troubles. It caused me to miss a large chunk of the season. It was down to a constant pain in my lower back. Some of my lower vertebrae had been pushed together and the discs were rubbing against each other. I was sent to see a specialist in Leeds.

I travelled to see him with our physio John Fraser and assistant manager Dave Booth. He looked at the scans of my back and Dave asked him if I would be back playing in a couple of weeks. The specialist turned and said: 'I can't say at this stage whether Kevin will be fit again in a fortnight or if he will be fit at all.'

We all just stood there in stunned silence. I didn't know what was going on. All he said was, 'Come back in a fortnight to get more treatment.' He never told me how bad the injury was. Needless to say I feared the worst.

I felt so bad we had to stop the car on the way home so I could be physically sick by the roadside. I really did fear my career was in the balance.

I remained in a lot of pain and after a few weeks of getting nowhere we decided to seek a second opinion. John was friendly with his counterpart at QPR and he recommended their osteopath Ron Johnson. We travelled down to London to visit Ron at his practice in Woking. He identified the problem within minutes. He did a bit of manipulation, performed some acupuncture and amazingly that brought an immediate relief to all my problems.

I continued to use Ron throughout the rest of my career, regardless of whether I was in Scotland or the Midlands. Psychologically, whenever I tweaked my back or had any other problems I knew he could get to the bottom of things.

After a couple of months on the sidelines I was ready to return. The team had started to struggle and that was when George Kerr's reign came to an abrupt end. It wasn't really a great shock to anyone at the club because he always seemed to try and test the patience of the board.

Things came to a head when the club tried to pay off some of the office staff but George felt they were part of the team and if they were sacked then he was going to walk with them.

I think over his two years in charge he offered his resignation three or four times and eventually the board became sick of his 'Brian Clough at Derby'-style antics and said cheerio. George was quite philosophical about it all because he knew it was time to move on.

His assistant Dave Booth was put in temporary charge. Dave had been a real Grimsby Town stalwart and was a popular figure at Blundell Park, where he had been an exceptional player. The former Mariners boss Lawrie McMenemy famously said the £5,000 he paid for him was pound-for-pound the best signing he ever made.

Booth's popularity at Grimsby had been shown when more than 14,000 fans turned up for his testimonial game against Derby County a few years earlier. There were a few supporters who were disappointed to see George go but most were delighted to see Booth get the job.

He had served his apprenticeship and had the respect of

everybody in the dressing room. The new boss also pulled off a masterstroke by appointing Trevor Whymark as his assistant.

Dave knew he had a tough job, especially as we continued to toil in Division Two. We did, however, manage to progress in the Football League Group Cup, where I scored in the quarter-final against Newport.

I got a brace in our 6–1 FA Cup demolition of Millwall and hit the winner at Newcastle. I kept things going with a double in our draw with Charlton and chipped in with goals against Cambridge and Barnsley.

My back problem flared up again and apart from a couple of brief cameo appearances I had to see out the season frustratingly from the stands.

It saw me miss out on more silverware, as the team beat Shrewsbury in the semi-final and then Wimbledon in the final to win the Football League Group Cup at Blundell Park. Cumming and a brace from Fordy gave us that famous 3–2 win. It was a major achievement for the team because we had gone through the entire tournament without losing a game. I also received a medal for my part in the early rounds, which was a nice touch from the club.

The league was more of a nail-biting affair, especially as I couldn't play my part. We were fighting for our lives and finally managed to stay up thanks to a Whymark double on the penultimate day, which handed us that all-important win at Leicester's Filbert Street.

It took the pressure off on the final day, as we lost at home to Cardiff. We finished in 17th position, two points ahead of Cardiff who took the plunge.

My own contract was up and despite my injury worries there was still a fair bit of interest. I had a few options but it would have meant a tribunal and that was still uncharted territory. Clubs weren't willing to take the gamble.

I was also due to marry Andrea and we were planning to buy a house, so I decided to sign a new three-year extension at Grimsby. I was on a basic of £190-a-week but it was topped up by a number of incentives. I received £25-a-game appearance money and another £150-a-week, as long as we stayed in the Second Division. If we were relegated that would go down to £50-a-week. I also received a club car, but the most important thing for me was the verbal agreement with the board that if a realistic offer came in then I would be allowed to go. I signed it because it was a decent contract and it gave me a bit of security although I firmly believed I would be leaving sooner rather than later. I thought the deal would benefit us both because I got a wage increase and Grimsby had more bargaining power when it came to demanding a fee. I thought it was a win-win situation for us both. It showed a bit of loyalty from both sides and it allowed me to concentrate on my own Match of the Day.

Andrea and I were married on 10 July 1982. The wedding was at St Michael's Church and after the reception I booked us into the Humber Royal Hotel for the weekend. It was too near the start of pre-season to go anywhere too exotic and so I decided we should stick close by. Andrea still gives me stick for that!

We had a really great day and it was topped off when we returned to the room to find my brother, John, had left a bottle of champagne. I thought it was a really nice touch, until we checked out and found John had put the champagne on my room bill! Thanks, John.

The next day we went to see my Nana and Grandad, who lived close by, before we returned for a romantic meal. It didn't take the new Mrs Drinkell long to realise she was going to become a foot-ball widow. The World Cup final was on and I kept disappearing off out to the main reception to watch the game. Marco Tardelli's goal may have won it for Italy but it was fair to say that I had strayed offside with Andrea less than 48 hours into married life.

It wasn't long before the honeymoon was over and I was back into pre-season. My back problems, thankfully, seemed to have eased. It was just as well because we knew we would have to be at our best to maintain our Division Two status.

Luton Town, Watford and Norwich were promoted and replaced

by Leeds United, Wolves and Middlesbrough, who had all come down from the top flight.

I concentrated on getting fit but at the back of my mind I believed I would be on the move. I didn't have an agent but there was a lot of speculation and interest from the likes of Everton, Manchester City and Ipswich Town.

I took Grimsby at face value and believed they would be true to their word over our gentleman's agreement. I quickly found out that wasn't going to be the case. I learned of two bids from two Division One clubs that were turned down although Grimsby never revealed their identities. That was annoying and frustrating because I felt the club had let me down. I had wanted to go but the club moved the goalposts.

Suddenly my definition of a realistic offer was slightly different from Grimsby's. There was no definite figure down in writing so they could demand whatever they wanted and they did!

Now, working as a football agent, I always make sure any agreement of that kind is down in writing so my clients don't get done in the same way I did.

What happened left a bitter taste in the mouth. I regretted signing that new deal. My anger wasn't at the fans or my team mates, who I would have done anything for, but the board of directors who I felt had sold me down the river.

The one thing I was determined wouldn't be levelled at me was a lack of commitment or determination to the cause. I continued to give my all.

We opened up the new campaign against Leeds and held them to a 1–1 draw. I netted a few as we beat Carlisle and again as we thrashed Blackburn and Shrewsbury.

We then gave our fans something to shout about by seeing off Scunthorpe in the League Cup. I scored both our goals in the home leg to see us through but in the league survival remained the name of the game. I got the goal that mattered against Cambridge but we lost heavily to Wolves, Fulham and Barnsley, before we drew at Oldham and thumped Crystal Palace.

We beat them 4–1 and I got a hat-trick. My third goal was the pick of the bunch. I was 30 yards short of the corner flag and bent one right into the far, top corner. It was fair to say it was one of my better efforts. We also beat struggling Burnley but remained inconsistent. I still pitched in with my fair share. I bagged another double in our draw with Newcastle and celebrated another hat-trick in the 3–3 cup draw with Sheffield United. Through the turn of the year we remained up against it. My double against Chelsea, along with our two points against Leicester City, gave us hope although 5 March 1983 turned out to be the blackest day of my professional career. It was the one and only time I was sent off. It came at home in a fiery match against Sheffield Wednesday.

Their defender, Pat Heard, who I had played football with at school and select level, caught me late. I stupidly retaliated and was shown a straight red card.

I was so embarrassed I couldn't watch the rest of the game although my mood was lightened when we took the lead. That joy, though, was short-lived when I tried to make a quick getaway and I heard the roars of Sheffield Wednesday's fans as they celebrated their team's late leveller.

My misery was compounded when I copped a three-match ban from the FA, which went down well with the manager, especially as we were already struggling. Losing his main striker was the last thing he needed. I felt guilty sitting in the stands and was determined not to put myself in that position again.

When I returned the team's confidence had gone. We couldn't buy a win and were plummeting towards the relegation zone. We didn't win a league game in those final three months. In the end, we only stayed up thanks to three draws against Bolton, Burnley and QPR.

We survived by two points, finishing above Rotherham, Burnley and Bolton who made the drop. It may have been a close-run thing but we had kept Grimsby in the league.

Personally, I felt I had done quite well getting 17 goals in the league and another five in the cup competitions, which wasn't bad for a team who had spent most of the season in the bottom half.

I knew it was time to move on at that point because I had served my time.

I had begun to feel a bit stale at Grimsby and maybe the fans started to feel the same way. I had been in the first team for seven seasons or so.

I had done well but supporters were looking for new heroes and I was no longer the golden boy. The fans also had their first sighting of Paul Wilkinson. Like me, he was a bustling striker. This time I was the experienced, if not so old, head trying to ease him in.

Paul was the apprentice responsible for cleaning my boots. I always used to ask him how the youth team had got on. He was doing well but then his confidence seemed to shatter. He stopped scoring and his strike partner, Gary Lund, become the main man.

There was a stage where I was concerned Paul wasn't going to make it, although I always tried to keep encouraging him. Fortunately, he started scoring goals again and more than fulfilled that early promise. I was delighted when he got into the first team because he was a good, young kid and a decent player, who could run all day and score goals into the bargain.

Lund was also a talented frontman, whose main asset was the way he could drop his shoulder and stick the ball in the back of the net. They both went on to represent England under-21s together, which was some achievement for Grimsby. It wasn't going to be long before they were both making their mark at Blundell Park.

5

THE DAMNED UNITED

THE 1983–84 campaign arrived and I was still at Blundell Park. The manager, Dave Booth, knew we needed to improve and his main priority was trying to tighten things up at the back. He tried to sign the experienced defender Chris Nicholl, who had played for Aston Villa and represented Northern Ireland, although there was one major stumbling block. Chris would only join us if he got the assistant manager's job into the bargain.

Booth knocked him back because he had Trevor Whymark but after a poor pre-season he bit the bullet and agreed to Nicholl's demands. This caused friction in the camp and led to Trevor walking out midway through the season. Dave had tried to operate with two assistants but it didn't work because Nicholl always tried to keep Trevor out of the loop. It was fair to say that hardly helped my situation. I wanted away and I didn't really want to play for Nicholl after he had pushed one of my best mates out the door.

I took my early frustrations out on Shrewsbury on the opening day. We got over our loss at Cardiff with wins against Leeds and Fulham and draws with Newcastle and Middlesbrough.

I scored a beauty against Leeds and it wasn't the usual run-of-the-mill Drinkell affair. I picked the ball up 35 yards from goal, looked up and rocketed the ball past David Harvey, the stunned

Leeds keeper. The manager Dave Booth was quoted after the game saying: 'Give Kevin an hour and he'll talk you through his goal.' Suddenly after entering the season looking at survival we were on the fringes of promotion.

Young Paul Wilkinson was finding his feet and pushing me all the way in the goalscoring charts, while Paul Emson also chipped in from the flanks. The goals started to flow and so did confidence.

We smashed Brighton 5–0 at home and I wasn't even playing! I came back in for the win against Crystal Palace and then claimed a brace at Derby to push us up to the dizzy heights of sixth.

We lost to Portsmouth but beat Charlton and Swansea. We then set off on this amazing unbeaten run from mid-November through to the start of March.

It was some sequence of results. We beat Oldham, Sheffield Wednesday, Chelsea, Cardiff, Shrewsbury, Newcastle and Derby and I netted five goals along the way, although the big one for me was the day we beat Newcastle 1–0 at St James' Park. I picked the ball up on the edge of our box and made towards the halfway line. Nobody in black and white came near me so I knocked it towards their box. By that time I was absolutely knackered. I just swung my left foot at the ball and watched it smash off the under-side of the bar and over the line.

Suddenly people were talking about tiny Grimsby in the same breath as Chelsea, Sheffield Wednesday, Newcastle and Manchester City.

Tony Ford backed that up when he scored the only goal at Crystal Palace to fire us up to third. Now promotion was a distinct possibility with only three months to go.

We dropped points against Portsmouth and at Charlton. I grabbed two goals as we drew at the Valley and still have the scars to prove it. I burst my shin. The Charlton doctor came in, stitched it and put sticky tape over the scar. He didn't even put a dressing on it!

As we made our way home my leg and ankle began to swell up like a balloon. I was in agony but thought it would be okay if I could get a decent night's sleep. There was to be no chance of that. I hardly slept a wink and ended up in tears because of the pain.

I went straight up to Blundell Park in the morning to get John Fraser to peel the tape off but he couldn't and had to take me to the hospital. The only way they could get the sticky tape off was to rip out the stitches, re-open the wound and stitch it back up again. I was still in pain for days but I was back in the team as we lost to Leeds, a result which killed off our plucky promotion push.

We slipped down to sixth and, although we beat Barnsley and Huddersfield, couldn't claw back the ground we had lost.

It didn't help that I failed to score in four consecutive games. I was still the top scorer but even the local media started to turn against me with headlines like, 'We don't need Drinkell anymore!' Whenever I was selected in front of Wilkinson or Lund the reports would question the manager's team selection and intimate that I should no longer be a first choice – even to the extent where one Friday night headline read: 'Drinkell's last chance!'

The story was along the lines of, if Drinkell's doesn't score then surely the manager has to drop him and go with Wilkinson and Lund. It was a real body blow and showed a real lack of respect. I was determined to go out the next day and prove my worth. I went out and scored a hat-trick against Swansea City. I thought I had silenced my critics only to pick up the Saturday night edition and it cheekily read: 'My warning to Drinkell inspired him to his hat-trick.' Yeah, so it did!

Draws against Cambridge and Carlisle and a win against Blackburn moved us up to fourth, but losses to Oldham and champions Chelsea saw us slip back down a place, on goal difference.

For a team like Grimsby, fifth was still a major achievement. We had a decent side with Kevin Moore, Tony Ford, Nigel Batch and myself as the nucleus along with Wilkinson and Lund. The Blundell Park youth policy had done the club proud and provided a real core for the future.

My dad always felt that if the directors had gambled and put a little bit more money in and made a couple of quality signings then we could have won promotion that year. Looking back if there was ever a time where Grimsby were going to get to the top flight then it was that season. Unfortunately we never took that step and I don't think Grimsby will ever be in that position again in my lifetime. We remained a small and unfashionable club run by local businessmen.

I finished third top scorer in the Second Division, behind Kevin Keegan and Kerry Dixon, with 18 goals in the league and three in the cups. I was pleased with the way things had gone for both myself and the team. We had dug ourselves out of the troubles of previous seasons.

Now was it a flash in the pan? Despite all my problems I wanted to go out and prove we were the real deal. I felt we could do that with Chelsea, Sheffield Wednesday and Newcastle all going up. They were replaced by the Midlands trio of Birmingham City, Wolves and Notts County.

Our opening matches suggested we could. We beat Barnsley and Charlton and thrashed Middlesbrough 5–1 at Ayresome Park. I grabbed a couple of those goals.

Consecutive defeats against Leeds, Blackburn and Oxford brought about another dose of reality.

In the Milk Cup we saw off Barnsley and Rotherham and the big prize was a mouth-watering tie with Everton, who went on to lift the Cup Winners Cup under Howard Kendall's guidance.

They had tried to sign me previously and I was desperate to play, to try and seal the deal.

Yet when Booth read out the team I was named on the bench. I couldn't believe it and childishly just sat there. Minutes before kick-off and I still hadn't got changed, while the rest of the boys were out warming up.

The manager had seen my petted lip and hauled me into the shower area. He said: 'The reason you aren't playing tonight is because Leeds United have been on. They are going to make an offer and I expect the deal to go through. There is no point in starting you if you are going to be away tomorrow.'

I said: 'I wish you had told me that earlier then I wouldn't have been so childish about things. I just couldn't find a reason why you would leave me out for this game.'

Young Wilkinson came in and scored the only goal while I came on in the last 20 minutes to help us hold on for our famous 1–0 win. I was happy thinking I had signed off my Grimsby career on such a high. How wrong I was!

I woke up the next day expecting the call giving me permission to speak to Leeds but it never came. I went to the Park but I couldn't get a hold of the manager or the chairman Dudley Ramsden.

I then turned on the local Viking radio station, which was broadcast from a studio at Blundell Park, and it came across on their sports bulletin that Grimsby had turned down Leeds' offer. The chairman claimed it fell short of their valuation and I wouldn't be going anywhere.

I was left bemused by the entire situation. I was the big loser. I had missed out on a move to Leeds and the chance to start in Grimsby's biggest game of the season, while Wilkinson had got the goal and that eventually helped him win his dream move to Everton. I was disappointed for myself but delighted for Paul because he was a decent player. He proved that at Goodison, then at Watford and Middlesbrough.

The good thing for Grimsby is we always had an abundance of decent strikers. Even after Wilkinson left we still had the attacking talents of Lund, Phil Bonnyman and myself. So we still had plenty of firepower.

Fortunately events off the park were keeping my own spirits up. The birth of our first daughter, Alexandra, on 5 December 1984 was a real high.

We had moved to the Wyber's Wood estate by then and I had disappeared to The Jubilee pub for a quick pint. I got a call at about 9.30pm to tell me to get home because Andrea had gone into labour. I rushed home and took her up to the hospital but this is where Andrea tells the story of how I deserted her. The real truth of the matter was the midwife told me the birth would still be a good few hours and I should go home and get a sleep. I did that and got a call from the hospital to come back in at 6am. Needless to say when I returned Andrea was far from happy with my disappearing act. Thankfully our beautiful little girl arrived a few hours later and took some of the heat off her under-pressure dad.

I now had responsibilities as a new parent and that was a major part of my thinking as my Grimsby contract was about to expire at the end of the season. Alexandra would be six months old and it was a difficult one because neither of our families had moved far away from Grimsby.

I knew to get the move I craved then I would have to keep amongst the goals. I got a few around the Christmas period, although it was to fall into another season of mid-season mediocrity. We went out of the Milk Cup to Norwich and in the league we slipped down to 12th. I claimed consecutive doubles in our wins over Notts County and Cardiff but we were too far off the promotion places.

The fans became pretty disgruntled we weren't up challenging, even though in most of the previous seasons we had struggled.

I got it in the neck from some sections and it centred round my contract situation. It was no secret that I wanted to leave. I continued to give my all but as far as I was concerned I was off in the summer.

I was still determined to go out with a bang and 13 April 1985 became a big day in my Mariners career, as we rattled Manchester City 4–1. I netted our second goal and it was a landmark strike. It was my 100th goal for Grimsby in all competitions. It was a tremendous milestone for a young boy who had come through the ranks. It was made even more special by the fact that it was scored at Blundell Park in front of my own fans.

The campaign finished with a mixed bag of results although I signed off my Mariners career with two goals in our final-day win over Crystal Palace. I think that showed my commitment right to the end.

6

RELEGATED AND BANNED
FROM EUROPE – WELCOME
TO THE BIG-TIME!

I HAD been loyal to Grimsby for the entirety of my contract but I wanted a new challenge. It now came down to which club really wanted me.

I had been linked with a number of clubs, including Manchester City, Everton and Celtic; now it was time to see who was prepared to risk a transfer tribunal. Being out of contract doesn't mean what it does today, with the Bosman ruling. When you were out of contract your club still held your registration and were entitled to a transfer fee. If the two clubs couldn't agree on a figure then it was set by an independent tribunal. That is why I have been delighted to see things swing the way of the player. It was a lot harder to move freely back in my day.

There were a few clubs who were interested but Norwich, who were in the top flight, were first off the mark. Their manager, Ken Brown, phoned and asked if I would meet up with him. I agreed and we met in King's Lynn, which is halfway between Norwich and Grimsby.

Ken was a very bubbly character and sold Norwich to me right from the start. It was the whole package he was offering. They had some top players and were a good footballing side. Ken was also a likeable character, he was a jovial guy and looked like he would be a good manager to work under.

Norwich were also a Division One team. They had just won the Milk Cup and were also about to play in Europe. It was a step up for me on the football front and Norwich certainly ticked all the boxes.

I went home and had a think about things. I had a chat with Andrea and then we drove down to Norwich to have a look around. Andrea and I spent a lot of our summers down in Great Yarmouth, so we knew the area quite well.

We liked what we saw and agreed to meet with Ken at Carrow Road. It was an impressive set-up and the city seemed a charming place.

Everyone was so laid back they were almost horizontal. I remember being driven about by Ken when we got stuck behind two cars at traffic lights. He turned and said: 'You realise this is a traffic jam for Norwich?' He was right but it was a place I felt I could call home.

Everything about Norwich felt right. It felt like the best move and the only stumbling block now was the tribunal. I had agreed terms with Norwich and they had agreed to sign me providing the fee was not too over-the-top.

A lot of Grimsby fans believed I wanted to go to Norwich for money but that was never the case. In terms of wages my contract at Norwich wasn't much better than what I had been on at Grimsby.

Grimsby offered me a new contract but the way they had structured it made it difficult to accept. The basic salary was okay but I had to chase rainbows to make the bonuses. The incentives they offered were massive but to obtain them I would have needed to be Superman. One of the bonuses required me to score 30 goals for each of the next three seasons and in return I could have pocketed tens of thousands of pounds.

They wanted 90 goals off me in three seasons and wouldn't take an average for the period. So if I had scored 31 goals one season and then 29 the next then I wouldn't have got a penny. It also didn't take into account for injuries or perhaps the team's loss of form.

What annoyed me was Grimsby went public with their offer and made it appear that all the bonus money was guaranteed. It looked like they had pushed the boat out. Maybe if they had offered me the money guaranteed then I would have thought about re-signing but it was all part of their spin to make me out to be the bad guy. I was portrayed as Mr Greedy, holding the club to ransom. I was the player who was turning his back on his local town for a few pieces of silver. I know a lot of Grimsby fans still believe that to be the case but I can assure them it wasn't. I didn't desert them. The reality is that Grimsby didn't really make a genuine attempt to keep me. The directors, including the chairman Dudley Ramsden, were just trying to keep themselves onside with the fans. The reality was borne out when Grimsby's contract offer was presented at the tribunal.

Grimsby thought they would be okay because they had turned down decent offers over the years. The bids had been as high as £300,000 from the likes of Middlesbrough, Leeds and Manchester City. They thought they would get at least that and just laughed at Norwich when they bid £140,000. I knew my deal could still collapse if the tribunal priced me out of things and that was a real concern. It made for a long and nervous summer because I had agreed terms with Norwich even though the tribunal wasn't due to sit until late-July.

The one thing I certainly didn't expect to see was Norwich crashing out of the top flight but a bizarre sequence of results saw precisely that. The circumstances of Norwich's fall from grace were pretty spectacular. Coventry had hardly won a game all season but a bizarre fixture pile-up left Norwich's rivals with four games to play after the Canaries had signed off. Amazingly Coventry won three games of those final games to condemn Norwich to Division Two.

The fixture scheduling just didn't seem fair especially when Coventry were asked to play Luton in their second last game. The

Hatters had just returned from an end of season booze-up to play the fixture and there was very little chance of a slip-up there. Coventry met an Everton reserve side in their final game and crushed them 4–1 to save themselves.

Ironically, my transfer tribunal was held at Highfield Road. The team sheets for that final game with Everton were still up on the board when I walked in. Everton's line-up wasn't anywhere close to the team they had used over the course of that season.

So here I was expecting my first crack at the English top flight and suddenly the reality was that I was back in the same league I had just tried to escape. It was a real blow and it wasn't to end there. It became a double whammy when my dream of playing in Europe also disappeared because of the Heysel disaster. I remember sitting watching that European Cup final between Liverpool and Juventus. I just couldn't get over what a tragedy it had been. I think everyone in football felt the same.

I didn't think for one moment it would have an effect on my own career but a few weeks later it did, when English clubs were banned from Europe for five years. I hadn't even kicked a ball or signed for Norwich and suddenly the big attractions had disappeared.

To be fair to Norwich they still tried to seal the deal and I was in Ken's office when he phoned Dave Booth to make one final take it or leave it £165,000 offer. I know Booth wanted to accept it but it had to be agreed by the Grimsby board. Unfortunately for Dave and me, they turned it down.

I still hadn't been back to Grimsby and had done pre-season, including a trip to Sweden, with Norwich. It had been hard for me, and especially Andrea because we had bought a new house and we were just praying the deal wasn't going to collapse.

Eventually judgement day arrived. Grimsby had their say and Norwich put their case forward. I went outside and started to talk to the Grimsby secretary Bernard Fleming and to Booth. They said they had left space in the car because they believed I would be going back to Grimsby with them.

We had a wee laugh and a joke about things. Bernard and I decided to put a £5 bet on the transfer fee. We both put our money into an envelope and wrote our guesses on the back, with the closest getting the money. He, like the rest of the Grimsby board, were confident the tribunal would price Norwich out of the market. I took a punt on £100,000 and Bernard put something like £300,000 down.

We were all called back in and the committee asked me how I saw the situation. I explained I had given good service to Grimsby and they had been reluctant to let me further my career. I also thought Norwich had made a fair offer. They asked about the contract I had been offered at Grimsby. Once I explained that and the bonuses, I think that made their decision for them.

It was announced Norwich had to make a one-off payment of £105,000 with no add-ons or sell-ons, which saw Grimsby lose £60,000. The Norwich side were jumping for joy while Grimsby were left feeling like they had been robbed.

Booth was good enough to come over and shake my hand. He wished me all the best and admitted he wouldn't be able to replace me with the money they were to receive. I took that as a compliment because it showed that whatever went on behind the scenes my former manager appreciated the job I had done.

I went back to Norwich knowing I was a Canary finally set to fly. Just before I kicked off my career at Carrow Road I had one final piece of unfinished business. I went back to Blundell Park to pick up my £5 winnings from Bernard.

He still couldn't believe what had happened. He felt the club had been done and what happened only exasperated people's views that I had sold my soul for a couple of shillings. Now the tribunal had ruled against them, it was my fault that Grimsby had been stung even though the tribunal had judged the case on its own merits. It had nothing to do with anything I said or did but 25 years later there are still Grimsby fans, maybe only a small minority, who still haven't forgiven me. They forget the nine years I gave the club and the hundred and odd goals I scored for them.

That was shown when I returned that following season and I was booed by a section of the home support. That was disappointing but what happened will never change my feelings for the club. They were my team as a boy and I was privileged to come through the ranks and to play for them alongside my best pals. It was a boyhood dream and Grimsby are the first result I look for. I was also greatly honoured when I was short-listed for the greatest ever Grimsby Town player back in 2007. For a local lad that was something special and the club will always have a special place in my heart. That is why it hurts me so much to have seen Grimsby slip out of the senior ranks. I just hope the tide turns and the Mariners can get back into the Football League and can get back to the glory days once again.

7

THE ON-SONG CANARIES
ARE TOP-FLIGHT BOUND

THE first day I went to training, Mel Machin, Ken Brown's assistant, welcomed me to the club. As I walked past him he asked if I smoked. I said yes and told him I'd just had a cigarette in the car. I wasn't about to lie on my first day. He turned and told me I was the only one at the football club who smoked. I was a bit taken aback.

It was different to Grimsby; there were six or seven of us sitting in the dressing room after the game having a smoke. Now I was left feeling a little awkward knowing I was the only smoker at the club, although it later transpired there were one or two others who liked the occasional, sly puff.

Ironically, Machin himself liked a cigar on the way home from away matches. I had a laugh about that later, especially as he had been the one who had initially dug me up.

The Norwich boys did all they could to make me feel part of things from the start. There was a good buzz about the place and the fact Brown had made four other signings that summer also helped me to settle. He brought in Mike Phelan, Dave Williams, who went on to play for and manage Wales, Garry Brooke and the goalkeeper Graham Benstead. I don't know about Dave, who was more experienced, but for the rest of us it was our first big move.

We knew we were going into an excellent team even though Norwich had been relegated. They may have been looking at a season in Division Two but, for me, they were still an English top-flight side in all but name. They had a good mix of international players, like Chris Woods and Dave Watson, and a backbone of home-grown youngsters, like Mark Barham, who had just come back from a cruciate injury but had also claimed full England honours. There were also the younger boys in the background, such as Louie Donowa and Dale 'Disco' Gordon, who were beginning to push through. There was a real good mixture and chemistry in that dressing room.

It was such a welcoming place and the players enjoyed being at Norwich. 'Woodsie' and Watson could have quite easily chapped on the door and demanded to leave but they didn't seem to be in any rush to move. Maybe they felt they had been part of the club's demise and didn't want to be seen leaving the club in the lurch or maybe there was an agreement in place that they could leave if they got us back up. I don't know.

Funnily enough, Woodsie was a player I longed to emulate at the start of my career. I remember him when he was a teenager breaking through at Nottingham Forest, where he played in the League Cup final. I was at Grimsby and we were down playing one of the London clubs that weekend and we decided to stay down for the final.

Woodsie was a good young keeper but was only playing for Forest because Peter Shilton was cup-tied. I watched this 18-year-old keeper from the stand and was green with envy. I thought to myself it must be amazing to play at Wembley so early in your career. I was only 17 and thought that was the stuff dreams were made of. Woodsie didn't let his side down. He kept a clean sheet in the final and again in the replay, before John Robertson eventually scored the goal which sunk Liverpool and gave Forest the trophy.

Now here I was set to play in the same team as Woodsie some years later at Norwich. Here was an international-class goalkeeper playing in the Second Division. That showed the quality we had at Carrow Road.

We also had other experienced professionals like John Deehan and Steve Bruce at the club. We were a good, good team, so I knew I would have to work hard and up my game if I wanted to make my mark.

I was desperate to show I was good enough to be in Ken's side. There was added pressure on the club to bounce back, after the double whammy of relegation and the European ban. We thought the only way was up but there was to be one final blow before we could get back on the straight and narrow. That summer the main stand, which contained the dressing rooms at Carrow Road, was destroyed by fire. It was a case of everything that could go wrong did go wrong!

The good thing was that, despite all the set-backs, the club managed to remain vibrant. Norwich continued to develop on and off the park. That is the reality of football. You have to look forward. You can't afford to sit around and wallow in the past or you will soon be left behind. Nobody at Carrow Road wanted us to be seen as a club on the slide.

We knew we had a team that was good enough to be in the top half of Division One and we were determined to prove it.

I wasn't exactly overjoyed at the time when I found out Norwich had been relegated. It had been a burning ambition to play in the English top flight and suddenly it had been snatched away from me through no fault of my own.

Looking back with hindsight, though, it actually turned out to be a blessing in disguise. It allowed me to find my feet in a less pressurised environment, away from the intense spotlight of the top flight. I was also part of a top team that was good enough to go out and win the league. At Grimsby, without being disrespectful, we had a good side, who could hold our own, but we never had enough strength in depth to sustain a championship charge. This time I believed things would be different and I fully expected Norwich to be pushing all the way.

My luck started to change when the tribunal ruled in Norwich's favour. It allowed me to finally get my Carrow Road career up and running. The uncertainty was over and it was now up to me.

My competitive debut in green and yellow came at home against Oldham Athletic. It was a very strange atmosphere because we only had three stands and were forced to change in Portakabins, which took a bit of getting used to.

All the new boys knew it would take time for us all to gel but it took a bit longer than we expected. We did, though, get off to winning ways when we beat Oldham 1–0 thanks to a goal from my new neighbour Peter Mendham.

When Andrea and I were looking for a house we found this lovely area of East Anglia, around Eaton and Cringleford. There was a house for sale and as we drove past I noticed Peter in the garden a couple of doors up. I said to Andrea, 'I think that is one of my Norwich team mates' but I wasn't 100 per cent sure.

We stopped and had a chat with Peter and his wife, Gabrielle, and ended up buying the house beside them. Moving away from Grimsby for the first time was a real experience. I'm sure the professionals of today have all their removals sorted for them, but, for me, it was a case of loading up a couple of vans and pulling in some favours from my pals John 'Killer' Croft and Alan Marley to help us with our big move.

One added advantage was that Alan was a carpet fitter and worked through the night to get our new home ready. We were in there, ready and settled before that first game against Oldham because I was determined homesickness wasn't going to be my downfall.

We became very friendly with Peter and Gabby and another couple, Bob and Jill Gibson, over those early months. It helped with Bob and Peter introducing me to their local pub The Red Lion – which over the next three years became my home from home.

Peter was a good guy even though he has had a few problems since he quit the game. I had a lot of time for Peter although he could also be a little strange at times. We used to take turns to drive to training and there were times when I would go and chap on his door and Gabby would say he had disappeared off fishing in the middle of the night. He would head off with his fishing rod and torch and when you arrived at Carrow Road he would be sitting there with his wellies and all his gear beside him. Peter was a bit of a night owl and on the pitch he was also a predator.

Peter was a great box-to-box midfielder. Through that first year he did really well although by the end of it he started to struggle with pelvic problems. That eventually cost him his career when he had to retire in his mid-twenties.

After that Oldham win we quickly realised it wasn't going to be plain sailing.

We lost 2–1 at Blackburn and that was followed by another nightmare journey to Millwall. We went down to The Den and got done 4–2.

I was really struggling for goals and confidence. I remember Ken stopped the bus on the way back and brought on the usual carry-out, a crate of beers for the boys and a bottle of gin for himself. He saw I was feeling a bit low and went into his top pocket and threw me a packet of Benson and Hedges. He told me to cheer up and to keep my head up because things would come good. That was Ken. He was always trying to keep everybody happy.

Ken might not have been the greatest on the training pitch but he didn't need to be because his right-hand man Machin was a top coach. Ken's strength was in the dressing room, motivating and boosting morale. His other main forte was spotting a player.

Ken could definitely see potential. That was shown with the number of players he picked up and sold on for massive fees. You only have to look at 'Brucey'. The big man was rejected by Newcastle United but Ken saw something in him to take a gamble and sign him from Gillingham. Brucey was a strong character and was very vocal within the dressing room. Watson, who was the captain, was less vocal but just as important. He was another Brown signing who he had taken from Liverpool's reserves. Dave always led by example on the pitch. He wouldn't go about shouting at people but would make tackles, blocks and headers that would inspire others around him.

Ken also picked up 'Woodsie' from QPR, where he wasn't exactly setting the heather alight, and suddenly at Carrow Road he blossomed into an England international. Further down the line the club continued to profit from Ken's ability to unearth those unpolished gems – with the sales of Phelan, Robert Fleck and myself – long after the manager had gone. It is fair to say he left a half-decent legacy at Carrow Road. He made the club millions thanks to his wheeling and dealing.

Yet in those early weeks of my Norwich career, Ken's job was more about keeping the confidence and spirits up. We might have been the pre-season tips for the league but suddenly we had crashed down to 15th. Throughout that period Ken always kept on at us to keep the faith.

The pressure was starting to grow and things weren't helped when our away-day blues continued at Portsmouth. We lost 2–0 and that was where the situation finally came to a head. The disappointment and frustration of everything just boiled over. Things got so bad that Ken actually ordered the coach driver to pull over at the nearest pub. Everyone was really down after the game and the atmosphere was just horrendous amongst the boys. We were all wondering where it was all going to end. I was the same, wondering if I would every score another goal. I hadn't missed any sitters but the ball just wasn't dropping anywhere near the six yard box. I wasn't getting many chances but I still felt a sense of guilt over our dismal start.

Ken decided we couldn't shy away from things any longer and it was best for us all if we confronted it head on. I think that was a good move on Ken's part. We all trooped off the bus and into this country pub. He asked us what we wanted to drink. We all told him we wanted a Coke or a lemonade but he told us we would be having a drink and that was the end of it. Ken then had his say and left the floor open for us all to chip in.

Like Ken, we knew we had good players but we just didn't seem to be getting the breaks. We hadn't gelled. We didn't have an understanding or the cohesion. Things, for whatever reason, just weren't clicking. I don't think anybody pointed any fingers although we were all equally frustrated.

Maybe for the boys that had been there before there had been a hangover from the relegation. Also Woodsie and big Watson were still in the England squad and our lowly league position didn't reflect too well on them either. We all knew we had to play our part.

The meeting was good because it showed all the staff and players were all thinking along the same lines. Ken gave us confidence by saying he was in no doubt we were a good team. He also reiterated he had made the right signings and things would come good. There was a corner to be turned and we would go and turn it together. Ken's message was along the lines of 'trust me and if you continue to work hard then we will climb up the table'.

I think everybody was pleased that Ken had addressed things and shown real leadership. We all stepped back on the coach with a quiet determination to prove our critics wrong.

We did precisely that as we thrashed Sheffield United at home the next week. Brucey set us on our way before I finally broke my duck with a double. Paul Haylock capped off a brilliant performance by wrapping up the scoring.

I don't know what it was about Sheffield United but they always seemed to be a lucky team for me. I always seemed to score against them when I was at Grimsby and I had opened my account against them for Norwich. The Blades had tried to buy me in the past but the deal had never come off and I just seemed to come back and haunt them.

Suddenly on the back of that one result the whole mood swung. We drew at Middlesbrough although we should have won. We left disappointed after we had surrendered a first-half lead. I did get a goal to make it three goals in two games. I was beginning to wonder what all the fuss about my lack of goals was about. Mind you, there was nobody flapping more than myself.

We at least knew we were on the right road. We managed to come out on top in a seven-goal thriller against Crystal Palace at Carrow Road. Watson, Barham, Phelan and myself all got on the scoresheet, as we continued our surge up the table, although we still weren't hitting top gear on our travels. We registered another stalemate in a goalless draw at Huddersfield. Carrow Road, though, despite our lack of a main stand, had turned into something of a fortress, as Robert Rosario and Mendham did the damage against Hull City.

We were now riding high on the crest of a wave. We put together a five-match unbeaten run that took us back to eighth. Unfortunately, we were brought crashing back to earth with a bang as we lost to our promotion rivals Wimbledon. I got on the scoresheet but we went down 2–1 at Plough Lane. That was a sore one to take.

I found it hard to swallow because Wimbledon were the total opposite of ourselves. We liked to get the ball down and play good football but Wimbledon simply lived up to their 'Crazy Gang' nickname.

They were just bully boys who tried to kick and intimidate the opposition, they weren't interested in the beautiful game. Their unique style certainly worked because it got them through the leagues but their 'route one' approach was a feeble excuse for football.

Gary Lineker once famously said the best way to watch Wimbledon was on Ceefax. He was spot on.

They had the likes of Vinny Jones, John Fashanu and Dennis Wise. They were all in your face, trying every dirty trick in the book to intimidate. Their rough-house tactics certainly didn't frighten me but there were other players and teams who did buckle.

Wimbledon would start their antics in the tunnel, by threatening to injure you and would then take it on to the field. Most of the time it was just hot air. Fashanu was more often than not at the centre of their madness. After I had scored my goal he turned around and said, 'The Fash is creating a war zone' – pointing to a specific area of the field. He would then followed that up by saying, 'Whoever dares to come in better be ready for war.'

Wimbledon used to do that a lot, they brought it into their game whenever they wanted to noise up the opposition or to gee themselves up.

Vinny was normally in the thick of things although I don't think he would have been as brave if he didn't have 'Fash' by his side.

Fashanu, himself, always seemed to have an issue with me. He would always make it his mission to mark me at corners and free kicks. He would try every underhand tactic he could to try and put me off my game. He would punch or kick me, whenever he could, but was sly enough to make sure it was out of the referee's sight. There was one incident at a corner where he punched me in the kidneys. He winded me but I just looked at him because there was no way I was going to go down. He wasn't going to get one over on me. My skipper Watson, who had played with Fashanu previously at Norwich, stormed across and had a right go at him. Fashanu stared back at him like this crazed psychopath. I just stuck to my game and let my football do the talking. I always tried to do that throughout my career. I didn't see the point of taking the bait and getting myself sent off. I knew I could do more damage on the field.

I think Fashanu had an issue with me because he had kicked off his career at Norwich and had been released a couple of years before I arrived. He had been a budding centre forward but had only made a handful of appearances before he was shipped out. He had a couple of loan spells before he was eventually let go. He moved on to Lincoln and ended up at Wimbledon. I think Fashanu was jealous because I had come in as the big-money centre forward and taken the place he thought should have been his.

Losing that game at Carrow Road was a setback, but, to be honest, it also turned out to be the best thing that could have happened to us. We never looked back.

We headed to struggling Carlisle and thrashed them 4–0. Rosario, Phelan, Brooks and myself did the damage. It was also an away trip with a difference. The club paid for a flight rather than forcing us to make the day-long trip to Cumbria and back on a coach.

We actually flew over Grimsby and the Dock Tower. I remember we were flying that low that I tried to look down to see my dad down on the docks. Normally away trips were a couple of days out of our lives but that day I was back in the local at 6.30pm. I always preferred to return there rather than hit the high spots in the city centre. I was more a spit and sawdust guy than a man about town.

The flight was great but it was also strange because our away-day coach trips were a major part in the team's togetherness. There were only a couple of A roads out of Norwich at that time so it took more than two hours to get to a motorway. Right away we got into the routine and for every away game we had to stay overnight.

That helped build up the camaraderie amongst the squad. We would arrive at training on the Friday, with our match-day kit, train, have a bite to eat and head off on the coach. We were basically living in each other's pockets and so we all became close friends.

We actually had one of those team coaches where there were stairs at the back of the bus with a television and seats. We had an Irish defender called John Devine, who had played for Arsenal and Watford.

He played the guitar and on some of the longer trips brought it onto the bus. The players would all get involved in a giant sing-along. It makes me laugh now, guys like Brucey and Watson killing classics from the likes of the Eagles and Dire Straits.

Thankfully I wasn't hitting too many bum notes on the pitch. My goalscoring run continued when I netted in a 3–1 win against Shrewsbury and then we beat Sunderland 2–0, thanks to Williams and Mendham. That took us up to fifth and suddenly, after being in crisis, we were pushing for a top-flight return.

We remained in the top six despite three consecutive draws, away to Brighton and Stoke, where I netted again, and at home against Bradford.

That was also the point where our Milk Cup adventure turned sour. We had beaten Preston over two legs and Luton but lost to Oxford United, who had a decent side at that time.

They had hardened pros like Gary Briggs, who I had played against in the juvenile ranks when he was at Middlesbrough, Malcolm Shotton and Billy Whitehurst. They were as tough as they come.

They weren't as vocal as Wimbledon but they were certainly a lot more intimidating. Their players didn't make threats; they just went on to the pitch and did whatever was needed to win the game. I would never say I have been scared on a football pitch in my life but that was one game where I was always grateful to be able to walk off the pitch at the final whistle.

Don't get me wrong, around that time, Oxford United had a decent side as well, who could also play a bit. They had quality players like John Aldridge and Ray Houghton who were really top drawer and complemented the likes of Shotton and Briggs.

With our cup adventure over it allowed us to move into a class of our own in the league as we beat Grimsby, Leeds United, Blackburn Rovers and Oldham Athletic. I kept my good run going by scoring in a couple of those games in the middle of December. Those goals were pleasing but the most important thing for us all was the fact we were now top of the table.

Things were perfect on the pitch and we were coining it in off it. The likes of Phelan, Williams and myself had all signed contracts with bonuses that were based on the club being in the top flight. It was a boost to the rest of our team mates because the club had to pay them the same even though their contracts stated they had to take a drop if Norwich were relegated.

I was earning £450-a-week but our bonuses were paid on a roll-on basis. We were on £100-a-win and that continued up to a maximum of £500-a-win. If we drew then it would rollover to the next game and so on that run we ended up walking away with £950-a-week, which was a tremendous wage for most top-flight clubs, never mind a team in Division 2.

We sent out a chilling warning to our rivals that we weren't to be moved, as we hit Millwall for six. We finished off the year with a Boxing Day win at Charlton. I got a brace and Deehan got the other.

I was bought to partner John but it didn't really work out like that. He was unlucky with injuries and couldn't get a run going. As you would imagine he got very little sympathy from the rest of the dressing room. It was a bit of a shame because people started to think he was a bit of a hypochondriac. John became absolutely paranoid about things. His situation was made worse when he would get pain in his ankle but by the time he saw the physio or the doctor it had disappeared. They would ask him where it had been sore and he would be left feeling stupid because he couldn't pinpoint the problem area. He got so worked up about things one day he actually came into training looking like a tactics board. When he took his socks and shoes off there were arrows up and down his leg and foot. He had done it so he could show the doctor where he was getting the pain. It was funny and I am sure John, looking back, would now agree, even though he didn't at the time.

I was really disappointed that I never got the chance to play with John as often as I would have liked because he was a big influence on me. He helped take my game to another level. I learned a lot from him. He made me feel a lot more comfortable accepting the ball. Everything was so simple for him and he made others round him feel more confident.

He was much the same as Trevor Whymark. They both helped me take my game on. I always tried to listen and learn from the more experienced pros.

John's tips must have helped because by the end of December I had netted 13 goals for Norwich, which I was pleased about after a sluggish start. We went on first footing to Fulham and I managed to get the only goal to ensure it was a Happy New Year.

The only blip on our report card was our FA Cup campaign. We were drawn against the mighty Liverpool. We went there full of confidence but that was soon thrashed out of us. We got absolutely humiliated 5–0 at Anfield.

Kevin MacDonald, Paul Walsh, Steve McMahon, Ronnie Whelan and John Wark all scored as Liverpool handed us a footballing lesson.

It was bad enough we got hammered but we then had to face another seven or eight hours on a bus to get back home to Norwich. Happy days. That return journey left us in dire straits – and I'm not talking about the karaoke!

Ken tried to lift the spirits once again but a forklift truck would have struggled to pick us up that afternoon. We drowned our sorrows with our carry-out but we knew we couldn't let the hang-over carry on into the league.

We beat Middlesbrough and Portsmouth, where I got in on the act, and then again at Crystal Palace. That took us to 10 straight wins before we drew at Barnsley and beat Shrewsbury, where I grabbed another couple of goals. We frustratingly fell to our old foes Wimbledon again. It gave them something to celebrate but we knew come the end of the season we would have the last laugh. We beat Huddersfield Town and Carlisle and I kept things going against my lucky team, Sheffield United, in a 5–2 victory. We claimed maximum points against Fulham before we tripped up against Charlton.

We were already well clear at the top of the table and strength-ened our position by beating Brighton. I grabbed another goal in that game before we drew with Sunderland. The title clincher was against Bradford City at their temporary home, the Odsal Stadium. I set us on our way while Wayne Biggins grabbed the second to seal that famous win. The title was ours. We saw it out with a home draw against Stoke and lost to Grimsby, which was a hard one for me to stomach. I had headed back home with the cham-pions and thought we would take the points but we ended up losing 1–0. It was a sore one for me because I took a lot of stick from the Grimsby fans because they weren't aware of the full story of my departure – being labelled a money-grabber and a Judas was hard to take. That night hurt me but it was a lot worse for my mum, dad and brothers, who witnessed the abuse at first hand. They were furious but only because they knew the truth. We signed off the season in style with a 4–0 win at home to Leeds. Nearly 18,000 packed into Carrow Road to see us finish the season on a high. I also took my grand total to 23 league goals for the season.

Barham finished our second top scorer with 10 goals but claimed his tally was actually 33. He said my goals were actually his because his delivery had been that good that they had just hit off me on the way in. My take is slightly different and it was enough for me to win the divisional golden boot award. That was great but the big thing for me was the title. Despite wasting those end of season games with Grimsby and Hull we still finished seven points ahead of Charlton and a further point ahead of Wimbledon. Thankfully justice had been done and we proved that football was the winner.

Celebrating the title was another great evening. Norwich used to be full of market stalls but they were all cleared away that night. There were fans all over the city centre, as we took our bow in front of the town hall.

We didn't need a second invite to celebrate.

Personally, I thought the season couldn't have got any better but it did. I was named as the club's player of the year. I was presented with my Colman's player of the year award by the legendary English cricketer Fred Trueman. Here was me at the start of the season worrying that I was on a sticky wicket and by the end of it I had helped Norwich hit the rest of Division 2 for six. I was honoured to be named as Norwich's top performer and also to receive my award from a sporting great like Trueman. It also showed a season can be a long time in football.

Our domestic campaign might have been over but we still had one outstanding fixture to see out. It was the second leg of our ScreenSport Super Cup semi-final. With English teams banned from Europe, the Football Association decided to organise this tournament as an alternative. The top clubs lost fortunes from the suspension and they thought this all-English showcase could help boost the coffers. Champions Everton, FA Cup winners Manchester United, Liverpool, Tottenham, Southampton and ourselves were to grace the new competition, as the six teams who would have played in Europe if it hadn't been for the ban.

The competition was split into two groups of three with each team playing each other home and away. The group section started in September and ran to the January. We were drawn with Everton and Manchester United.

We lost at Everton to a goal from Gary Lineker but managed to gain our revenge at Carrow Road when Mendham hit the winner in a 1–0 win. That put us back into contention. We then drew home and away with United to finish second behind Everton.

We met Liverpool, who had won the other section. They travelled to Carrow Road at the start of February and we held them to a draw. I managed to get a goal but Kenny Dalglish also got on the scoresheet for the Reds.

We had a month to prepare for the return at Anfield but they had too much for us again, although they didn't beat us by five goals this time. Kevin MacDonald, a Jan Molby penalty and another from Craig Johnston gave Liverpool an easy victory. We were disappointed to lose but we had put on a decent showing and sent out a warning to the top flight that we weren't coming back up to be cannon fodder.

As a Second Division side we had done reasonably well in the Super Cup but the concept never really took off. It failed to generate the interest or sponsorship the FA had hoped for. In fact ScreenSport only stepped in to sponsor the final because our conquerors Liverpool were set to meet their Merseyside rivals Everton.

The competition's standing was hit again when the final had to be delayed until the summer because of fixture congestion. For the record, Liverpool won it with a 7–2 aggregate win over their neighbours. That proved to be the end of the ScreenSport Super Cup. It was the competition's one and only airing before it disappeared into the history books.

8

HELPING OSSIE AND NORWICH
TO MAKE THEIR MARK

THE new season was something we were all looking forward to. For me it was massive. I was finally going to get my chance to play in the English top flight – a year later than I had expected!

I knew there were still question marks over me. I might have finished top scorer in the Second Division but people wanted to see if I could cut it at the highest level. I was desperate to make my mark. My manager, Ken Brown, certainly believed I would make the grade.

Ken, as I've said, was a great man-manager and a guy who had a major influence on my career. He was first class and that was nothing to do with his nickname 'the Postman'. That was down to the fact he used to come into the dressing room every morning to hand out the players' mail. He would have all these letters in his hands and say, 'Here is some fan mail for Steve Bruce and a couple for Chris Woods' and then slaughter myself or any other player who hadn't received any mail that day.

It became a standing joke that delivering the players' mail was Ken's main job because he seemed to leave most of the training ground stuff to Mel Machin. He would take some of the drills but the majority of the routines were left to his assistant. Mel was a top coach and definitely helped me to develop my game. He made me a better all-round player and become more tactically aware.

Mel went on to become a boss in his own right, managing Manchester City and Barnsley. It was hardly a surprise because he had played a major part in Norwich City's success.

I decided to go and see Ken during the summer because I felt it was time the club gave me a new contract. I had stamped my mark on the team and was worthy of a wage rise. Ken had promised me when I signed he would look at my contract if I helped get Norwich back into the top flight. We did precisely that so I went off and chapped on Ken's door.

There was no way I was earning the same money as Woods, Brucey or Dave Watson. I knew that. I had only arrived the year before and had to earn that sort of contract over the longer term. I knew if I could produce in the top flight then that would propel me into that bracket.

Ken stayed true to his word and put my case to the board. Next time I saw him he pulled me in and said, 'I have sorted everything for you. The board have recognised the job you have done and are prepared to give you a £25-a-week rise.' It wasn't anything like I had hoped for, but I thanked him anyway and walked off. After all it wasn't all about the money because I was enjoying my football and looking forward to playing in the top flight.

I was confident we could make an impression but then we lost two of our biggest stars. Woods was sold to Rangers and Watson got his big-money switch to Everton. They were major losses because they were English internationals but they were ambitious and wanted to further their careers. They had shown loyalty by staying to help the club back up and now felt it was time to move on.

We were disappointed, as a squad, to lose players of that quality but we were delighted for them as individuals. Watson came from Liverpool and it gave him the chance to prove a few people wrong by heading back for the blue side of Merseyside. It was also a decent move for Woodsie because he was moving to Scotland to play under Graeme Souness at Rangers.

But it left two major voids at Carrow Road and they had to be filled. We already had Graham Benstead to replace Woodsie but the manager also decided to bring another goalkeeper called Bryan Gunn. He had been back-up to Jim Leighton at Aberdeen. I remember the first time he trained with us because he scared us all to death. He hardly caught a thing and the ball seemed to be like a bar of soap every time he went near it. He looked exactly what he was – inexperienced. We all thought, 'What has Ken done here?', but over time he proved to be another inspirational signing and a wonderful servant to Norwich City.

I have to say I am surprised at just how well Bryan did because he spent most of those early days digging his shorts out of his backside than he did saving shots. For whatever reasons, Bryan used to always wear shorts that were too small and so he was always pulling them out from his backside. Even our own fans would wind him up over his antics.

Bryan had to bide his time but he dislodged Benstead and quickly established himself after a rather bumpy introduction. Every mistake Bryan made or goal he conceded in those early days was magnified and the fans would always say: 'Woodsie would have saved that!' That was the big thing because Woodsie had been such a big player for Norwich and it was going to be hard for whoever was going to replace him.

Bryan proved he was up for the challenge and went on to become a pillar of Norwich City Football Club. He has held just about every position at the club and even went on to have a spell as manager. Bryan remains a firm favourite with the fans even though his spell in the dugout didn't go the way he had hoped.

Maybe looking back he regrets stepping into the firing line and taking over the hot seat at such a difficult time. I suppose nobody could blame him for taking the job because it was a real once in a lifetime opportunity.

In those early days he was still adapting to life in East Anglia, like our fellow summer signings. We signed Shaun Elliott as a replacement for Watson. I played against him a few times when he was at Sunderland. He had been their captain and was another good player. Another of Elliott's former team mates Dave Hodgson came in to add more competition to the front line. We also signed a few guys from the capital who quickly became known as the 'London crew'. Ian Crook, a midfielder, arrived from Tottenham while Trevor Putney made the switch from our rivals Ipswich Town. Defender Ian Butterworth came in on-loan from Nottingham Forest before the club eventually signed him on a permanent basis.

There were also departures, including our colourful Dutchman Dennis Van Wyk. He was so laid-back he was almost horizontal. Dennis came across and helped the team to win the Milk Cup but was never one to look to the long term. He would only ever sign one-year deals because he didn't know what he was going to do the following season.

Dennis was a funny guy and he used to take a lot of stick amongst the lads. He always went out with clothes that didn't match and no matter what he wore he always seemed to look like a scruffy tramp. He was a good player but he decided to chuck Norwich because he didn't fancy playing in the English top tier again. Here I was champing at the bit and he was walking away from it. I just couldn't fathom his decision but it takes all sorts of people to make the world go round.

Tony Spearing arrived to ably fill the gap at left back. He was another bubbly Southerner who came through the ranks and deserved his chance.

Our reward for getting promotion was a pre-season trip to Los Angeles. We stayed in one of those big hotels off Sunset Strip. Dave Williams was my room mate during that pre-season. He was the complete opposite to me. He didn't smoke and hardly touched alcohol. He was the ultimate professional and a student of the game. Dave was a late developer; it wasn't until he was in his 30s that he finally broke into the Welsh international team.

We all went down for breakfast one morning before Dave made his late entry. He came down wearing matching corduroy shorts and slippers. We all took the mickey and it earned him the nickname

'Pop' because he always seemed old beyond his years. Dave took it well. He was also a great player and I would liken him to Ray Wilkins. He was a great set-piece taker and was just as dangerous with either foot.

That pre-season trip set us up nicely for the real thing. We were going back into the top flight looking to consolidate first and foremost. We made a solid start with a goalless draw at Chelsea. We returned to Carrow Road for the first time since our title win and it was as if I had never been away. I scored after just six minutes, to claim my first top-flight goal. Williams swung in a cross and I slammed a left-foot volley low past England and Southampton's No. 1 Peter Shilton. It was a moment that will live with me forever. The match turned into something of a goal avalanche. Dale Gordon, Williams and Brucey all scored as we won 4–3. It was Crook's Carrow Road debut and he was given a present to forget after the game: Southampton's notorious hardman Mick Dennis motioned to shake his hand and then punched him. Not surprisingly, he was sent off for his moment of madness.

We kept our unbeaten run going with a 2–2 draw at Maine Road and headed to The Valley where I scored the opener against Charlton Athletic. I was beginning to think the English top flight wasn't the massive step I feared it was going to be. Charlton equalised before Williams grabbed the points for us with a second-half winner. We were four games unbeaten and up to sixth in the table. I think we surprised a lot of people with the flying start we made.

Around that time the English League were due to play a game against an Irish League Select. Our Norwich boss, Brown, was named as the manager for the English League team. Ken was allowed to take his pick from the Football League, which, at that time, also encompassed the English top flight.

The game was to be played on 8 September at Windsor Park. Some of the Norwich boys felt we had a chance of getting into that squad. We were playing well on our return to League One and also had the added advantage that our boss was involved in picking the squad.

Williams, Brucey and myself were all delighted to get the shout. He also went for some big-name players, including Newcastle United's Brazilian striker Mirandinha, Ossie Ardiles and Johnny Metgod from Tottenham and Liverpool's Bruce Grobbelaar.

There was also Mel Sterland, who was at Sheffield Wednesday, Nigel Winterburn of Arsenal, Watford's John McClelland, Colin Gibson at Manchester United and Wayne Fereday of QPR.

We had some team and we were up against players from Linfield, Glentoran and Crusaders. Guys like George Dunlop, Bill Caskey and Gerry Mullan, who were good players at that level but shouldn't have been a match for our team.

It was a great honour to be picked. I travelled up to Manchester with the manager, Dave and Brucey. We flew up from Ipswich airport and it was one of the worst flights I have ever been on in my life. It was on one of those small 12-seater propeller planes and we just seemed to get battered about the sky. We would have been as well sitting out on the wing. Brucey was in a terrible state although I wasn't too far behind. We wondered if we would ever see land again never mind another football field.

We eventually got to Manchester, surprisingly in one piece, and met up with the squad to get our connecting flight to Belfast. It was at a time when Northern Ireland's troubles were at their height.

We landed on the runway and were met by armed soldiers to escort us to the coach. Then we had umpteen motorcycle outriders flanking us as we were escorted to our hotel. When we looked outside of our hotel room windows the roofs and shrubbery were crawling with British soldiers. I roomed with Brucey and we both asked, 'What are we doing here?'

Even going to the game, the road to the ground was flanked by soldiers on both sides. The fact that it was an English League select side meant the authorities were keen the game was going to pass without incident.

I started that game alongside Mirandinha and I remember Kerry Dixon's face was absolutely tripping him because he didn't get the nod. He was the top striker at Chelsea and was also in the

England squad and expected to be the main man and was unhappy he had been left out.

Looking back he was probably safer sitting on the bench. I remember during the game a number of gunshots went off in the background. It was something the Irish boys were used to but we were all turning around and ready to run for cover. It was certainly a different shooting practice from what I had been used to!

The game itself ended 2–2. Gibson had put us in front before goals from Sid Burrows and Caskey put the Irish ahead. We eventually pulled ourselves level with 12 minutes to go through Mirandinha. The Brazilian was a decent player who was never short of confidence. One of his first games for Newcastle was against Norwich. I gave away a foul midway inside their half and one of the central defenders ended up rolling the ball on to the halfway line to take the free kick. As soon as Mirandinha saw that he ran back and pushed his team mate out the way. We thought he was going to chip it into the box but he put the ball down and then attempted to shoot. We couldn't believe it.

He was a South American and had scored a few free kicks in his time but his woeful effort didn't even reach our 18-yard box. Mirandinha was always willing to try something out of the ordinary.

Our clash with the Irish select wasn't exactly a classic but I always remember Ardiles that night. He might have been the captain but he took an absolute roasting from the Irish fans because it was only a few years after the Falklands War. So that made the little Argentinian Public Enemy No. 1. There was an Irish midfielder called Roy McCreadie, who played for Portadown. He shadowed Ossie all over the pitch, wherever he went. We thought he was going to follow him into our dressing room at half-time. We were on the verge of applying for a restraining order, things were getting that bad.

Whenever Ardiles got near the ball McCreadie just clobbered him. After the first tackle Ossie got up shaking his head and said, 'It is only a friendly.' The Irishman just snarled at him.

Ten minutes later the same thing happened. Ossie was furious and got up again and said: 'I thought it was only a friendly.'

By that time Ardiles knew he was getting nowhere being a diplomat. So the next time the ball broke McCreadie was clearly going to win the ball. It was 80/20 in his favour. Suddenly Ossie dived into a challenge, knee high and took the boy right out of it. McCreadie ended up needing a stretcher and as he was carried off, Ardiles said: 'Sorry, it is only a friendly. Don't f*** with me.'

After the game Ardiles was the last one on to the bus. We were all sitting waiting for him when he walked on with this black rain-coat on. It was buttoned right up and he had the collar turned up. He was like an Italian gangster from the Godfather. He said: 'Nobody f**** with me.' It gave all the boys a good laugh.

Then it was straight back to the airport and back to Manchester, where all the boys had a drinking session, which ended as a bit of a blur.

Once the hangover had disappeared it was back to Carrow Road to get back to our bread and butter. We had started well but none of us were getting carried away. It was just as well because we ended up being stung at home by the Hornets of Watford. Williams gave us a first-half lead but a second-half collapse saw us crash 3–1.

It was a warning sign that we couldn't afford to take anything for granted. It did get us refocused and we came out fighting with a 2–1 win at home to Leicester City.

Barham scored our first before Biggins grabbed the clincher. We made it a Midlands double three days later when we outclassed Aston Villa. Phelan and Biggins scored before Gordon and Brucey completed our 4–1 Villa Park massacre.

That result catapulted us up to second place and suddenly everybody was sitting up and taking notice of the high-flying Canaries. It was predicted that we would buckle under the pressure but we showed no immediate signs of that.

I netted a brace in a 2–0 win over Newcastle and 'Disco' Gordon's only goal against QPR made it four wins on the spin. Not surprisingly there was a real buzz about the place.

We headed to Luton looking to go top of the table. The problem was the Hatters were a decent side back then and Kenilworth Road was never the easiest venues to visit, especially with that dreadful plastic pitch they had.

You would have been as well playing in their front car park because their pitch was so hard and unnatural. I hear modern players complaining about the current artificial pitches but they are light years ahead of those pioneering Luton and QPR surfaces.

We failed to match the heights of our previous performances on the plastic and had to make do with a goalless draw. We were a bit disappointed when we walked off the park but that was soon washed away when we heard we had gone top. The date was 11 October 1986 and Norwich City were sitting proudly at the top of Division One, ahead of the big guns like Liverpool, Everton, Arsenal and Tottenham Hotspur. The feat was even more remarkable as 12 months earlier we had been in the Second Division.

More than 22,000 fans packed into Carrow Road to see the league leaders take on West Ham United in our next game. I grabbed a goal but unfortunately we had to settle for a point after a 1–1 draw. It saw us drop back down to second spot. Maybe subconsciously the pressure did get to us.

We lost our next two games and they were crushing defeats. We slumped to Wimbledon and were hit for six by defending champions Liverpool. Phelan and Hodgson did get on the scoresheet but they were nothing but face-savers.

Sandwiched in between those games we managed to see off Millwall in the Milk Cup. We had already beaten Peterborough over two games in the previous round and were looking to progress against our latest lower league opponents. We did that and I got on the scoresheet in a 4–1 win. I actually scored from the penalty spot. As the main striker at Grimsby and Norwich I had never really taken the penalties. That was down to the fact we always seem to have a spot-kick specialist. I was more than happy to leave it to them but sometimes, I wonder if I had been more selfish and taken them then I could have added another four or five goals-a-season to my goal tally.

We managed to stop the rot in the league when Tottenham were the latest big scalp to fall foul of Norwich. Ex-Tottenham midfielder Crook and Elliott were the men who did the damage in our 2–1 win.

That kept us in the top four but our failure to break Manchester United's stiff resistance saw us drop a point in a goalless draw at Carrow Road. It was the start of a short frustrating period.

Our Milk Cup adventure came to an abrupt end in the fourth round against Everton, while we lost 2–1 away to Coventry. Disco and myself managed to steady the ship as we beat Oxford 2–1.

We were steam-rollered again, this time in the league, by Everton, although we got a morale-lifting point away to Arsenal. It was around that time that Rosario really made his mark in the team. He had become my regular strike partner. He was a decent big striker, who had come through the ranks after being spotted playing non-league football with Harrow and Hillingdon Borough. He helped us get a 1–1 draw against Arsenal, where I managed to get the goal at Highbury. I think that performance and point gave us the belief we were good enough to go out and compete with the best. That proved to be the catalyst for a seven-game unbeaten run in the league. We drew at Watford and beat Nottingham Forest 2–1 on our own patch.

My good goalscoring run continued when I scored the only goal in our 1–0 win over Manchester United. A low cross was swung into the near post and I powered a diving header into the net. It was enough to give Norwich their first ever win at Old Trafford. The Theatre of Dreams was always a great place to play your football, although back then United were struggling but more than 44,000 fans were still there to witness my goal. Norwich City records were falling thick and fast at that point. That win also took us back up to fourth. Who said the bubble had burst?

We kept our run going but had to settle for three draws. I scored the goal in a 1–1 draw against Sheffield Wednesday at Hillsborough.

We then dropped points at home in a 1–1 draw with Charlton before I scored again as we shared four goals with Chelsea.

I claimed another glorious double when our second daughter, Charlotte, arrived on 9 November 1986. Once again I was down the pub when I got the call. By that time the midwife had arrived and when it was time she called for an ambulance to take us to the hospital. This time Andrea was in and Charlotte had arrived within 45 minutes. I thought 90 minutes were tiring but my hat comes off to Andrea for that and for giving us two lovely and beautiful girls.

Around that time we drew Huddersfield in the FA Cup. I scored in the first game but Duncan Shearer squared things up and forced a replay. Fortunately we had too much for them as we went on to win 4–2.

We were going well in the league and fancied our chances of a half-decent cup run but that was quickly hit on the head when we lost 1–0 at Wigan. We were quite literally caught cold. When we arrived in Lancashire the pitch was frozen and at the last minute we had to rush off into the town centre to buy trainers because the Springfield Park pitch wouldn't take a stud.

We did, however, have a half-decent run in the Full Members Cup. It was set up, like the ScreenSport Super Cup, to generate more funds for banned English clubs but it is fair to say this competition was far more successful. It allowed all the clubs in the top two divisions to battle it out for silverware. We kicked off by beating Coventry 2–1 at home thanks to a double from myself. We then headed to The Dell where we saw off Southampton, 2–1, after extra time. We continued our impressive form when we smashed Portsmouth 3–1 at home.

That set-up a last four clash with Charlton Athletic but they managed to sneak through by the odd goal in three. I was devastated because the final was at Wembley, and that was to be the closest I came to playing at the national stadium. It was a real blow having to watch the final thinking about what could have been. Charlton eventually lost 1–0 to Blackburn Rovers but it still didn't help us make up for our own disappointment.

It did, however, allow us to concentrate on the league. We headed to Southampton. Phelan scored before I grabbed our all-important second in a 2–1 win. That was the game where Kenny Brown, the manager's son, finally got a run after Ian Culverhouse's injury.

Kenny was a decent prospect but his big problem was the fact his dad was the manager. He never seemed to get a fair crack at things because of that and the fans were always too quick to judge him. He played the rest of that season and did well but you always got the feeling that people only thought he was in the team because of his old man. I think Ken senior knew that and that was the reason why he eventually allowed his son to move on to West Ham United. He played a good few games for them and showed he was good enough to carve out a career for himself in the English top flight. The last I heard he was playing in the lower leagues in Spain and had got himself a management job out there. If he is half as good as his dad then he should make a real name for himself.

There were a couple of youngsters who were also given a taste of the first-team action during that period. They were Ruel Fox and Jeremy Goss, who in time would go on to make real names for themselves at Carrow Road.

I spoke to Jeremy a few times because the club wanted him to go out on loan to Cambridge United but I told him to stick in and he would get his chance. The boys were both good prospects and were given a taste of things but they weren't quite ready at that stage to go in every week. It was left to the more experienced campaigners to keep things going.

We kept our unbeaten run with a draw with Manchester City, a win at Leicester City and draws with Aston Villa and Wimbledon.

I got back amongst the goals when I scored in our win over West Ham United. That took us back up to sixth place. We drew 0–0 with Luton and dropped another point as I scored away in the 1–1 stalemate with QPR.

That took our league run to an amazing 15 games unbeaten but that record disappeared with a 3–0 hiding at White Hart Lane.

That knocked the confidence and my strike at St James' Park was nothing more than a counter in our 4–1 thrashing by Newcastle in our next game.

We had lost two on the bounce and it certainly didn't help that the champions Liverpool were up next. The omens weren't good. They had thumped us in the cup the previous season and thrashed us 6–2 at Anfield a few months earlier. We had also played them in the ScreenSport Super Cup but that was hardly seen as competitive. Kenny Dalglish and his side would hardly have been losing any sleep over their trip to East Anglia. Their confidence was also bolstered further in the game when their legendary goal getter Ian Rush put them ahead. It was a fact that every time the Welshman scored Liverpool had never lost in the league. We, though, had other ideas. Trevor Putney equalised and with a couple of minutes to go I claimed my own piece of footballing history. I picked the ball up, played a one-two with Rosario, before I charged into the box and from the tightest of angles slammed a fierce shot past Grobbelaar. It sealed a famous win for Norwich and also made us a pub quiz favourite as who were the first team to beat Liverpool in a league match after a certain Mr Rush had scored? It was a nice bit of nostalgia but more importantly, as a team, it showed how much we had grown. I remember Kenny Dalglish locked his team in the away dressing room for more than 40 minutes after that game but we didn't really notice because we were too busy celebrating another famous scalp.

Putney scored for the second consecutive week with the only goal in a 1–0 home win over Sheffield Wednesday. Trevor Putney was a good player but was a guy I just didn't really get on with. Off the pitch we were chalk and cheese. He was from the outskirts of London but put on this charade as if he was a born and bred Cockney. Everything was bigger and better and he just seemed to rub me up the wrong way but out on the pitch, as a professional footballer, I had the utmost respect for him. His hard work and contribution certainly added a lot to our Norwich side.

We were still in the fight for the European spots, if the ban was going to be lifted. The English clubs were certainly lobbying hard for that. We bolstered our hopes with a Disco-inspired win at Oxford but lost at home to Everton before our final day win at Highbury saw us finish the season in fifth spot. Crook and Putney got the goals in another famous win.

I finished the season top scorer and player of the year for the second consecutive season. The good thing from a personal point of view was that the majority of my goals had been important to the team. Most of my strikes were in matches where we won or at least took a point. I also only claimed the one double, so the other 16 I scored in the league were all really important. I grabbed another three in the Littlewoods and FA Cups, so it wasn't a bad return for my first season in the top flight. I was proud to say I had played in every Division One match for Norwich that season. I never liked to miss a game and would always play through the pain barrier if I had to. I also lay proud claim to the fact our phys-iotherapist, Tim Sheppard, never had to come on to the pitch to give me treatment. I wouldn't let him. I just used to dust myself down and get on with things.

I felt I had now shown I could play at the highest level and my move to Norwich hadn't shown a lack of ambition. The only disappointment was the English teams failed to get the European ban lifted and for the second, consecutive season I was left disap-pointed.

9

WHY WOULD I WANT TO LEAVE
FOR MANCHESTER UNITED?

IT WAS at the end of that first season in the top flight when Ken Brown pulled me into his office. He said, 'Before I start I want to make it clear that you are a massive part of my plans and I don't want you to go anywhere.' I didn't have a clue what he was on about. He said, 'I want you to stay because you are one of our top players and you are an integral part of my future plans.' Ken was a bit on edge and then he dropped the bombshell that Alex Ferguson, who wasn't a knight of the realm at that point, had come in for me. I think Ken was worried that I was ready to pick up my boots and jump straight in the car for Old Trafford. It was a career-changing moment but what bowled me over more than anything was Ken's determination to keep me. He was adamant he didn't want me to go.

He had also told Ferguson that I wasn't for sale and not to waste his time coming back in because he wasn't interested in his money. His big concern was that I would want to go and might rock the boat to get to United.

It was a difficult one because Ferguson had taken over at Old Trafford the previous November. It was his first pre-season and he was trying to rebuild and stamp his own mark on the perennial under-achievers. There was no questioning their potential but for so long they had lived in the shadows of the Merseyside and

London clubs. Ferguson had split the Rangers and Celtic cartel with Aberdeen in Scotland and was keen to do the same on the other side of the border.

Mark Hughes, their main striker, had been sold to Barcelona and Ferguson was still searching for a long-term replacement. He had seen me as player who could fill the void left by the talented Welshman.

United were a club with a great history and tradition but they were still very much in the doldrums. They were nothing like the club they are today. Old Trafford was half-empty and the crowds of 76,000 they get now had looked nothing more than a pipe dream.

They still had some great players like Bryan Robson, Jesper Olsen, Viv Anderson and Gordon Strachan but they weren't a great team yet. That first season Ferguson replaced Ron Atkinson, they finished 11th in the top flight. Norwich had just finished fifth in the league, six places above United and I honestly felt, weighing everything up, we had a much better team than United at that time. I was also settled at Norwich and the club had improved my contract so I didn't really feel the urge or need to jump ship. I could have earned a bit more money but football-wise I felt Norwich was the better option.

I didn't even have to think twice about it because I loved working under Ken and felt we could go on to achieve even more under him. Loyalty was also a big thing for me. Norwich and Ken had stood by me and taken a chance on me at the tribunal and if I had wanted to walk out, which I didn't, it wouldn't have been right.

I was flattered Ferguson had tried to sign me but it just wasn't for me and Norwich City weren't standing still either. We were a club who were constantly evolving.

The fans might not have liked it but we were still a selling club. Norwich always picked up untapped talent and then sold them on for huge profits. They had done it with Chris Woods and Dave Watson. The shock departure of that summer wasn't from the playing pool but from the coaching staff.

Our assistant, Mel Machin decided to end his successful managerial partnership with Ken. He was handed the chance to become the main man at Manchester City. Nobody could blame Mel for leaving because he was a top coach and it was a big job with a club who had massive potential.

When Mel went it left Ken with a major problem. He had to find a top coach with the same tactical know-how as Machin. Ken decided to promote from within and moved Dave Stringer up from his post as youth coach. Dave had been a former Norwich player. He had worn the yellow and green jersey with distinction and had returned to coach the youngsters. He had a degree of success at that level and led the young Canaries to the 1984 FA Youth Cup.

It was an appointment which wasn't going to rock the boat or affect the confidence or mood within the dressing room. The switch didn't seem to change things on the training pitch or tactically but for whatever reason we were unable to replicate our impressive form of the previous campaign.

We hadn't really been active in the transfer market either. Our main addition had been the Welsh international left back Mark Bowen from Tottenham. I think Ken paid something like £90,000 for him and he was the latest arrival from White Hart Lane. Ken might not have got the benefit over the longer term but Mark proved to be a real bargain and went on to become a stalwart in the Welsh national team.

Apart from that it was pretty much the same squad who had finished fifth. We were confident we could repeat that feat but we all seemed to misjudge the importance of the Machin factor.

We made a desperate start as we lost 1–0 to Everton and Southampton. We thought the corner had been turned when I netted a double in a 3–1 win over Coventry but that was to be nothing more than a false dawn. We crashed at West Ham, drew at home to Newcastle and scrambled past Watford thanks to a Steve Bruce goal.

We had dropped as low as 16th but that win took us back up

another five places, in a season which turned out to be a game of snakes rather than ladders. We lost to Derby County, Chelsea, Nottingham Forest and Oxford. That left us toiling and down in 19th position, which was one of the relegation positions. We also crashed out of the Littlewoods Cup to Burnley, which was another major blow. The pressure began to build on the manager.

We bounced back with a 2–1 win over Tottenham, with Wayne Biggins and myself getting the goals, but we still had a long way to go. The fans were beginning to feel uneasy and the board had started to make rumbling noises. All was not well but every one of the players believed that, together, we could turn it around. Ken had done it before in the Second Division. We had made a terrible start but still ended up with the title. Why couldn't we do it again? I mean have a successful season rather than being crowned the champions of England. Surely Ken deserved time? Also if the club were going to sack him then surely they would have done it the summer I arrived after the club had been relegated.

The manager wasn't helped as we lost again away to Manchester United and Sheffield Wednesday. We picked up a point at home to QPR but we couldn't get away from the drop zone. The board were getting twitchy. Our next match was away at Charlton Athletic. They weren't the most ambitious of clubs and we were confident we could beat them. Their sole aim was top-flight survival.

We lost 2–0 and I didn't help the manager's cause when I missed a penalty. I went to place it and sent their keeper, Bob Bolder, the wrong way but he was still able to block it with his feet. I felt really guilty because if I had scored then the final outcome may have been different.

Ken was his usual upbeat self after the game and on the way back from London he once again stopped the bus off at a pub to lift our spirits. This time there was to be no solace.

It was the end of the road for Brown's Norwich reign. We arrived at training on the Monday and Ken came into the dressing room to tell us he had been sacked. We couldn't believe it. Surely after everything he had done for the club he had deserved more loyalty? There was a lot of anger amongst the senior pros when Ken told us what had happened. Ken had been the reason why many of us had come to Norwich and the board had dropped him like a stone when the going had got tough.

Ken was the main reason why I had turned down Manchester United. If I had known Ken was going to be sacked then I would have gone to Old Trafford. Ken had shown faith and loyalty in me but just a few months later he was on the managerial scrapheap.

I felt angry but at the same time I also felt a sense of guilt. I kept thinking about my penalty miss. If I had scored would Ken still have been in a job? Also, I had scored goals for fun in the previous two seasons but in 15 league games we had only won three – the same amount of goals that I had netted in the campaign. I think everybody was left wondering, what if?

It was a sad, sad way for Ken's tenure at Norwich to come to an end. It was wrong and I still believe the chairman Robert Chase had been too hasty in pulling the trigger. He was more interested in the financial side of things and, for me, he wasn't really a football man at heart.

Looking back it was hard to put our finger on why things hadn't gone as well for us. Maybe it was simply a case of second-year syndrome. We had come up from Division Two and surpassed all expectations by finishing fifth.

That for a club like Norwich was a massive achievement and also heightened the expectations. There was a far bigger media spotlight and maybe subconsciously we were unable to handle it all. We were also constantly selling our best players and maybe in the end that also took its toll.

Days later Stringer was named as Ken's replacement. It was an easy appointment and at least he was a man who knew the players and the club. He was also a really nice guy and had Norwich City at heart.

The players were unhappy with Brown's sacking but we were

still under contract to Norwich and they were paying our wages. It all came down to professional pride but I know for guys like Brucey and myself things at Norwich were never going to be the same again.

Stringer did his best but he inherited a team which was low in confidence and struggling. I scored a brace against Arsenal but it wasn't enough as we lost 4–2. We were now bang in the middle of a relegation dogfight. Our performance against the Gunners at least gave the new manager hope. We then held Liverpool to a goalless draw at Anfield, but lost to Portsmouth before we headed away to Luton at the start of December.

I was rooming with Brucey at that stage. We were good friends and we also had the same agent, John Mac. We had just settled down in our room on the Friday evening when the phone went. I picked it up and it was John. We exchanged pleasantries and then he asked to speak to Brucey.

He went on the phone and didn't give much away but enough for me to know something was in the offing. Brucey came off the phone and told me Manchester United were in for him. Norwich had turned down their initial offer but United were ready to go in again if he wanted the move. It had been similar to the approach they had made for me. Brucey knew about that and asked me my thoughts on his situation. I asked him what he was going to do. For him it was a no-brainer. He was going to Manchester United and God help anyone who tried to stand in his way. Brucey, like myself, was still annoyed by the sacking of Ken. I think if Ken had still been in charge he might have stayed. The fact that the man who turned his career around had been bulleted meant he felt very little loyalty to Norwich. It was easier for him to cut his ties and walk away. He played the next day at Luton, which we won 2–1, thanks to Ian Crook and Dale Gordon. That proved to be Brucey's last appearance in a Norwich City shirt.

As soon as he got off the bus back at Carrow Road he jumped into his car and headed straight out to the chairman's house, near Yarmouth. The story goes he chapped on Robert Chase's door and told him to get a deal done because he was going to Manchester United whether he liked it or not. It was reported he refused to play for Norwich again. I don't know if that was the case or not but in the end he got his wish and his career went from strength to strength.

Brucey went on to be a real stalwart for United and I agree with a lot of people who think he was one of the best defenders never to win an England cap. He was just unlucky he was around when the country had some top defenders like Tony Adams, Watson, Martin Keown, Terry Butcher and Garry Pallister.

It was his resilience and will to win which was a big part of his make-up and the reason why he was such a successful player. Those were also major factors in Brucey breaking into management.

He got his big chance at Sheffield United although he struggled there and again at Huddersfield. That was perhaps when he got lucky because many other managers might not have got another chance when Wigan gave him a job. Since then his managerial career has never looked back. He is seen, quite rightly, as one of the top English managers in the game today, after his spells at Crystal Palace, Birmingham, Wigan again and now Sunderland.

Brucey's move to Old Trafford also showed what Ferguson thought about our Norwich team. He had tried to sign me, landed Brucey and a couple of years later he bought Mike Phelan as well.

Mike arrived at the same time as me and went on to make a real name for himself at Carrow Road. He could play in midfield or in either full back position and was a great player to have in your team. He might not have been one of the glamour players but he was always a '7 or 8 out of 10' man every week. Mike was a great tackler, good passer and always put in a real shift. He was a player's player rather than a crowd pleaser.

Phelan was another example of Brown's eye for a player. He had signed Phelan from Burnley, who had just been relegated to England's bottom tier. Yet Ken saw something in him, like he had with Brucey and myself, that could benefit his team.

I got on really well with Mike. He was top guy and a typical Lancashire lad and even now he has never lost his distinctive accent. The one thing about Mike was his professionalism. He was also a student of the game.

A lot of the young players today could learn a thing or two from Mike. It was that commitment and desire that eventually got him his move to United and also saw him win his England cap. Having played alongside him I don't think anyone could begrudge Mike the success he had.

It wasn't exactly a surprise that Mike also moved into coaching and like Brucey he has had to take some knocks along the way. He returned to Carrow Road as assistant to Gary Megson. That partnership didn't work although Phelan followed Megson to Blackpool and Stockport.

Phelan then started with the youth academy at Manchester United and has now worked his way up to one of the top jobs in English football, as Sir Alex's No. 2. It is funny when you see him after games on a Saturday night on *Match of the Day*, but, as I have said, it is all credit to Mike and the dedication he showed to his football.

Back to Brucey's initial departure which left a big, gaping hole in our defence and dressing room. We signed the Northern Irish World Cup star John O'Neill as his replacement. He had played for Leicester and QPR and was a very good central defender. We all thought he was a great signing but unfortunately his Norwich career only lasted 34 minutes. He made his debut against our old adversaries, Wimbledon, at Plough Lane. He made a good solid start until disaster struck. As he went to clear the ball John Fashanu charged in to close him down and made a poor challenge after the ball had gone, knocking John to the ground. I think everyone in the ground knew as soon as O'Neill hit the turf that he was in trouble. We were shocked, however, to later find out that the injury was so serious it would force John to retire.

O'Neill had to rely on the use of a leg calliper to get about his day-to-day life. John ended up taking legal action against Fashanu and eventually agreed on an out-of-court settlement. It was a shame for O'Neill because he was left facing up to life outside of football. He has since bounced back and made a name for himself commentating on Northern Ireland's international games. It is good to see him still involved in the game.

Another player who made his league debut for Norwich against Wimbledon that day was my new strike partner Robert Fleck. The club had signed him for a then record fee of £500,000.

I didn't know much about him apart from the fact we had paid a lot of money to buy him from Rangers. He was a typical bubbly Scottish guy who come in and fitted in right away. He was a good player with plenty of energy and I think his arrival also gave us all a bit of a lift. The transfer had been agreed by Ken but it was Stringer who became the main beneficiary.

Fleck went on to be a big player for Norwich and was another who was sold on for big money – more than £2 million when he made his move to Chelsea.

The gutsy Scot helped us rally at the end of that year. He scored in our win at Derby County, while I netted in our 3–0 win over Chelsea.

My personality clash with Putney never seemed to be far away from the fore and it boiled over again at our Christmas night out.

Putney insisted that it was to be fancy dress although that was never really my bag. The players all went and hired suits and costumes from the local joke shops for the night. I was unsure what I was going to wear. In the end, I decided to wear a suit, put on a dickie bow and took my snooker cue to do my best Steve Davis impression. I turned up and everybody was dressed up in these far-out guises. What I would say is most of my team mates had a lot more bottle than me to hit the streets in the shape they did. Disco Gordon deserves a special mention. He went out dressed as a giant Tampax. He was unbelievable. He wore a white doctor's jacket and painted all his body white. He then wore a red hat, had a string up his back and had all these red tampons all over his outfit. He had put a lot of thought and effort into his attire.

Putney decided to get the local bar staff to judge our fancy dress competition. To Putney's disgust I ended up getting the vote because the bar staff thought my outfit was the most authentic and original. I didn't even have to bribe them!

Back on the park I scored another in a 4–1 home win against West Ham on New Year's Day. That took us up to the dizzy heights of 15th. We were back on the rise.

10

CHASE-D OUT AND EL TEL
TURNS INTO EL HELL

I WAS confident 1988 was going to see us bring a bit of stability back to the club, after a difficult end to the previous year. We were settling down under Dave Stringer and had started to play like we had under Ken Brown. The manager had also moved to appoint Dave Williams as his assistant, which was a good appointment because 'Pop' was well respected in the dressing room.

I was quite happy to stay but then I was hit with the bombshell news that left my Norwich City career at rock-bottom. Stringer pulled me in and told me the club were considering an offer for me from Tottenham. I was left totally shocked and stunned. I had shown loyalty by knocking back Manchester United and now they seemed ready to push me out the door.

Stringer didn't want to sell me but told me the board were seriously considering Spurs' £500,000 offer. That totally broke my trust and faith in the club and, in particular, chairman Robert Chase.

I looked to be latest big-name Chase wanted to cash in on. Now I had to consider my future and what was best for my family and career. I felt I could no longer play for a man like Chase. He should have shown more loyalty to Ken after the job he had done and now here he was trying to push his top scorer out the door. The way he treated me still angers me. If Brown had still been in charge there would have been no way Chase would have been allowed to sell me.

Times, though, had changed and so had Norwich. It wasn't the same club it had been in the previous two seasons. The results weren't as good on the pitch. It wasn't down to a lack of effort or commitment but for whatever reason we couldn't replicate our previous successes and would blow hot and cold.

Chase felt he needed to make changes and to do that he needed to generate funds. As the top scorer I was the prime candidate. If he had come to me and said he needed the money then I would have shook his hand and said fair enough but he didn't even have the bottle to come and tell me to my face. I knew the end was near and it was a case of where rather than when.

There was no shortage of takers but Terry Venables at Spurs was the man who showed the most desire to get me. The go-between for Venables and myself was my old boss Brown. They were both friendly. I was never officially given permission to speak to Tottenham but there was a point where I was getting really frustrated with the way the whole thing was dragging on. Ken decided to phone Venables and I was told to sit tight because he really wanted me and would do everything in his power to get me. He had some top players like Paul Gascoigne and Chris Waddle and was keen to help Tottenham break the Liverpool, Everton and Arsenal domination of that period.

Everything went pretty well, even to the stage where I began house hunting in Chigwell and Epping. Andrea and I decided to grab the bull by the horns and to look at houses in the capital because we thought it was nailed on I would be going to Tottenham.

Chase had made it clear my Norwich days were numbered – whether I liked it or not! It was a big decision but Tottenham were a top club. I felt it was the next natural step for my career. Norwich had more than matched Spurs in the previous season but Tottenham also had the tradition, history and potentially massive fan base. In saying that, leaving the fans at Norwich was also going to be a massive wrench because they were magnificent towards me and I had built up a great rapport with them.

I thought the Tottenham deal was going to happen when they agreed to meet Norwich's £500,000 asking price but then Chase got cold feet. He felt Spurs had been too quick to agree a deal. He thought he had undervalued me and feared he would face a backlash from the fans unless he got top dollar. Chase then had the cheek to go back to Spurs and demand £600,000.

Ken was still keeping me up to speed with Venables' thoughts. I was told to sit tight because Spurs still wanted me. He was true to his word and Spurs again matched Norwich's asking price but Chase then moved the goalposts for a second time. He thought he could hold Tottenham to ransom and push my value up again. This time the price went to £750,000 and Chase's greed got too much for Tottenham. Their chairman, Irving Scholar, refused to be held to ransom and told Chase to forget it and he would never do business with him again. That left me raging because Chase had said he wanted to sell me, and then when a club had matched his valuation, twice, he tried to extract even more. By this time I felt like a piece of meat that was going to be sold to the highest bidder – regardless of where I wanted to go.

Chase had broken my trust and just used me. He was also looking to stall in the hope it started an auction because West Ham and QPR, amongst others, were also interested.

Tottenham didn't hang about and went out and bought Paul Walsh from Liverpool. I thought that was the end of things but I was assured Venables still wanted me and would come back in.

Spurs then went out and signed Paul Stewart from Manchester City for £2 million. I thought that was definitely the end of my Tottenham dream but Terry once again insisted I was the striker he wanted. He planned to play me up front with Stewart, with Walsh in the hole behind us. That gave me a bit of a lift and the Tottenham speculation in the newspapers never seemed to be too far away. John Lyall also went public on his bid to take me to West Ham United. Queen's Park Rangers were interested but that wasn't a move I fancied, while Billy McNeill was also linked with signing me during his spells at Manchester City, Aston Villa and Celtic.

I was annoyed the Tottenham deal had been pulled and I was being forced to return to play for Norwich. They were still paying my wages so I was obliged to go out and give it my best for the fans – if not for the chairman!

We lost to Everton but stabilised again with draws against Southampton and Watford. We then beat Newcastle, where I scored but was outshone by Fleck's double.

We drew with Coventry and then went on a three-game run, which went a long way to securing our top-flight status. We beat Manchester United, I netted in our 3–1 win at Tottenham and again in a 4–2 win Oxford United. That lifted us up to 13th and gave us enough breathing space to get away from the drop zone.

It was funny because I was still being linked with Tottenham after I had scored at White Hart Lane. That only heightened the speculation further. It got that bad that 'Gazza' and Waddle came up to me in the players' lounge and asked when I was joining them. It was unsettling but I knew I had to concentrate on my football. Scoring goals was the only way I was going to get the move I craved and I certainly didn't want to be seen to be jumping ship with Norwich being relegated. I wanted to do everything to ensure Norwich remained a Division One club.

There was cause for concern again when we lost to QPR and Sheffield Wednesday. We were still winning at home and I got another goal in a 2–0 win over Charlton. That was to be my final win as a Norwich City player.

After that we lost to Arsenal and churned out draws against Liverpool, Portsmouth, Luton and Nottingham Forest. I scored our opening goal against Luton and that was to be my last goal for Norwich. It came on 30 April at Carrow Road. It was the final time the old scoreboard above the stand displayed the words GOAL DRINKELL.

I brought the curtain down on my Norwich career against

Wimbledon. Once again the 'Crazy Gang' came back to haunt us as Wimbledon won 1–0.

It was a disappointing way for my time at Norwich to end, even though, at that time, I still didn't know where I was going. I'd had a half-decent season, scoring 12 goals for a team who had struggled. We had finished 14th, which for a club like Norwich wasn't the worst of positions. Norwich's main priority had to be to retain their top-flight status and anything above that was always going to be a bonus. They didn't have the same financial muscles as the bigger clubs, who often came in and cherry-picked their best players.

That is the way the club has continued, selling the likes of Ruel Fox, Craig Bellamy and Chris Sutton in recent seasons for big money. It is a way of life in football and unfortunately it eventually took its toll and Norwich were unable to maintain their top-flight status.

As for my own future, at that time, it was all going to come down to money. There were a few bids but nobody would match Norwich's escalating value. I made it clear to the club I wanted to go and there was no turning back. I went to see Chase and he had the cheek to tell me: 'If we don't get the money we want then you will just need to get your head down and get on with it.'

I told him to forget it. I politely reminded him that he had instigated the move to sell me and had no intention of staying just because he couldn't get the over-inflated fee he had been holding out for. I told him to go out and get the best deal for the club because I no longer wanted to play for him. Too much had happened for me just to say, 'Okay, I will stay'.

So I headed off for my holidays not knowing what the future held. I felt I had given my all to Norwich and had shown loyalty but in the end that had been one way. I think the fans appreciated my three seasons at Norwich. The club were also going to turn over a profit on the modest fee they paid to Grimsby just three seasons earlier, so all in all my time at Norwich had worked out well for the club and myself.

I still get a good reception when I return to Norwich and they are still a club who I hold close to my heart. That was why I was so humbled to be inducted into the club's Hall of Fame in 2002. It is a great honour to be named amongst some of the club's greatest ever players. I had some of my best career moments at Carrow Road and it is a period of my life, apart from the last few months, I will remember with great fondness.

The only thing that saddens me now is seeing Norwich slump out of the Premier League, and then out of the Championship and into League One.

A club the size of Norwich should be an established Premier League side , at worst a top Championship side, and it just disappoints me to see them under-achieving the way they have in recent seasons.

The good news is that they are now back in the Championship and hopefully they will eventually get back to the Premier League again, where they belong, because the fans and people of East Anglia certainly deserve a club of that standing.

11

THERE IS NO WAY I'M GOING
TO RANGERS!

I WOULD love to say I was over the moon about my switch to
Rangers from the off but that wasn't exactly the case. It had nothing
to do with any personal misgivings about moving to Scotland or
playing for Rangers. It was more down to a simple misunder-
standing between my agent and me.

I was visiting Andrea's parents in Grimsby when I took the call
from John Mac. It came after Tottenham, West Ham and QPR had
all failed to meet Norwich's demands.

QPR were an established top-flight side but I have to be honest
and say it wasn't a move that appealed to me. I felt swapping
Norwich for Loftus Road would have been a step back and wasn't
something I was prepared to do. So you can imagine my shock
and horror when I took the call from John and he said: 'That is
it, I have agreed a deal that will take you to Rangers.' My initial
thoughts were Queen's Park Rangers and I let John have it with
both barrels. I snapped and ranted something along the lines of:
'Look, John, I don't know what you are up to but there is absolutely
no chance of me going to QPR. I don't even know why you have
bothered to string them along.' He let me get things off my chest,
laughed and then said: 'No, you idiot, not Queen's Park Rangers
– it's Glasgow Rangers!'

Now that was a slightly different proposition. I knew a fair bit about Rangers because I had stayed in touch with Chris Woods, after he had made the same move from Norwich a couple of seasons earlier.

The Glasgow giants had grabbed a lot of attention and head-lines south of the border by appointing Graeme Souness as their player-manager. They had followed that up by signing some of England's top stars, like Terry Butcher, Ray Wilkins and 'Woodsie'.

There had been a bit of speculation the previous Christmas that Rangers had wanted to sign me as well but nothing had come of it. It had been mooted as part of a swap deal for Robert Fleck but only one half of that transfer came to fruition when Norwich took the Rangers striker to Carrow Road.

Souness later confirmed he had tried to get me earlier but Norwich had priced me out of the market. They had been holding out for £1 million.

Now Norwich knew I wanted out and if they sold me to Rangers then I wouldn't come back to haunt them. That might not have been the case if I had gone to Tottenham, West Ham United or even QPR.

John told me I had permission to talk to Rangers and I needed to get to Heathrow Airport as quickly as I could. I said: 'That's okay, John, but there is one slight problem – I'm in Grimsby not Norwich.'

I came off the phone and explained to Andrea what had happened. I told her I was going down to listen to what Rangers had to say but I had no intention of jumping into anything. I would be back later that night to discuss things with her – or so she thought!

When I finally arrived at the hotel I was introduced to Walter Smith, who was No. 2 to Souness, and Phil Boersma, who was his first-team coach.

I sat and had a chat with them. They told me how desperately Graeme wanted to sign me and how they felt moving to Rangers would benefit my career.

They put up a strong case and without agreeing terms, my mind was pretty much made up. I was impressed with their ambitions and the way they had sold the club. Rangers were massive and I also knew I was at the end of the road at Norwich.

It was a big decision moving to Scotland because I had never set foot north of the border, but everything just seemed right. There might be a bit of snobbery from the English Premier League towards the SPL today but back then that wasn't the case. It was more of a level playing field and Rangers, arguably, had more financial muscle than a lot of their English counterparts.

Woodsie and Terry had moved up there and done well and it hadn't affected their international careers. Terry was still the England captain in Bryan Robson's absence.

Rangers were also playing in Europe, unlike the English clubs who were still banned. There were a lot of positives and pull for top English players. I was also being asked to join a team which could already boast Butcher, Woods, Ray Wilkins and Mark Walters. Walter and Phil also told me they were on the verge of signing the England international full back Gary Stevens from Everton. These were guys who were amongst the top names in British football. If I had been the first Englishman to join Rangers then I might have had second thoughts but it was a well-trodden path.

I was still chatting with Walter and Phil when Robert Chase pitched up at the hotel. I knew then the deal was pretty close. Chase had played silly games with Tottenham, West Ham and QPR but this time the Norwich chairman didn't have the same power. I was sitting with Rangers officials and he knew I wanted to make the move. I also only had a year left on my Norwich contract, although that was before the days of Bosman and the swing towards player power.

Chase went into a separate room for the negotiations which seemed to go on forever. At one point I was ready to burst into the room but fortunately I was calmed down and a late night compromise was eventually reached – leaving everybody happy. The teams had agreed on a fee of around £580,000.

Walter immediately welcomed me to Rangers. I then went up

to Chase and shook his hand – albeit very coldly. He had messed me about and I wasn't happy with the way he had soured my time at Norwich but it was time to move on. It was sad, looking back, because it left a bitter taste about Norwich but I was only upset with one man: the same guy who had just sanctioned my move to Rangers.

The Norwich chapter of my career was at a close and now it was all about the future and Rangers. Andrea and the kids were still in Grimsby and I had to get them out of their beds to tell them we would be moving to Scotland.

I flew up to Glasgow the next morning but before I could do that I had to do a bit of airport shopping. I didn't even have a toothbrush never mind a change of clothes. Remember I was only going to Heathrow for a brief chat – nothing more, or so Andrea thought!

When I arrived in Glasgow I have to admit I started to get cold feet and it wasn't just down to the weather. It was wet and miserable and everywhere I looked seemed so grey and industrial. Even when we took the junction for Ibrox we were met with those massive downtrodden skyscrapers and tenements, which the local authorities are currently in the process of redeveloping. I remember thinking, 'Is this really the right move for me? Do I really want to leave sleepy, picturesque Norwich for this?'

I was having serious doubts until we turned the corner and I saw the façade of Ibrox. Just the sheer size and grandeur of the ground immediately lifted my spirits and changed my negative mindset. I immediately got a feel for the club and its great tradition.

I was taken straight to the manager's office, where Souness was waiting. He welcomed me on-board and predicted I would be a big success at Rangers.

I went for my medical, signed and before I knew it my whirlwind day saw me back on a flight to Heathrow. By that time I had no doubts. Everything was perfect and I wanted to be a Rangers player. I headed south to put the 'For Sale' sign up and get the Drinkell family ready for another adventure.

Financially, I was going to be a lot better off because Rangers were all but doubling my basic wage. From that point of view it was a no-brainer and it was now up to me to make things happen on the pitch.

Bonding with my new team mates was never going to hold the same concerns. I was already friendly with Woodsie and had also got to know Gary Stevens because we were both staying at the Holiday Inn. I also knew a couple of other faces and Phil and Walter were there to help break the ice. Wilkins came across and wished me all the best, while Walter introduced me to Ally McCoist for the first time. Walter said to me: 'Don't be too concerned but you are his 23rd strike partner in the last four or five years. He is just as deadly finding the net as he is at seeing off his fellow strikers.' I took that to be a joke but it would later ring true.

The one thing about 'Coisty' is he always liked a laugh and a joke but he was a very determined character, who had a real competitive streak. That is why I am not surprised he has gone into management. Many people see Ally as the court jester but when it comes to football there is nobody more serious or dedicated – if you overlook his poor time keeping! Working under Walter Smith will also have helped prepare him for management in his own right. He has been lined up as a future Rangers manager and I wouldn't be surprised if that were to happen. He is a big favourite at Ibrox and would certainly have the backing of the Rangers support.

When I arrived he was an Ibrox idol. He was the top striker at the club and that wasn't a title he was prepared to surrender without a fight and he quite clearly saw me as direct competition.

I took a seat next to the legendary Davie Cooper when the dressing room door burst open and in rushed a fresh-faced youngster, who went by the name of Ian Durrant. His shirt was all over the place and his tie was outside his collar. He looked like he had been dragged through a hedge backwards. That was a major achievement because Souness made it a club rule that everybody had to look smart and that meant wearing a shirt and tie, even to training.

Durrant looked around the dressing room and somebody shouted, 'This is Gary Stevens,' and then he saw me out of the corner of his eye. Quick as a flash, he cheekily shouted: 'F*** me, we've signed Chi-Chi the Panda!' It was a reference to my characteristic black eyes. My black bags had been made worse by my lack of sleep and the upheaval of the move.

'Durranty' still hadn't even said hello when he turned his sights on some other unsuspecting victim. This time it was Wilkins and he said: 'How are you, hairy back?' That is Durrant. He was your typical cheeky chap.

That nickname has stuck with me ever since. Whenever I speak to Ian McCall, Neale Cooper, Nicky Walker or Durranty they still greet me as Chi-Chi rather than 'Kev' or 'Drinks'.

I also have Mr Durrant to thank for obliterating my music collection in those early weeks. Ian wasn't driving. Let's just say he had a slight altercation with a roundabout and the police!

Unsuspectingly, I gave him a lift into the city centre after training. The next I knew he was opening the glove compartment and raking through my cassettes. Then the window opened and he launched one of the tapes out of it.

He said: 'I am not having that. You're not allowed to listen to U2.' I just shook my head as I looked through my rear-view mirror to see the tape smash into a thousand bits. Needless to say I never took any of my U2 albums in for the dressing-room ghetto blaster!

I thought I had found my heaven when I signed for Rangers but when it came to pre-season it was more like hell. We were flogged around nearby Bellahouston Park and then taken back to Ibrox for lung-bursting terracing runs. I thought they were trying to finish me off! It was absolute torture being asked to run up and down the stands, trying to catch flying machines like Richard Gough and John Brown. They could run all day without breaking sweat while I was more accustomed to 20 cigarettes a day. I would often be off hiding or out a back door having a quick puff. Fortunately, it was never a problem as long as I produced on the pitch.

My mood perked up when I heard we were heading to Italy to continue our pre-season preparations, but I quickly found out that our Il Ciocco base, near Pisa, was to be anything but a holiday camp.

Souness and Walter were determined to crack the whip and get the team into shape because they had just lost the title to Celtic, who had won the double in their centenary season. That had stolen a lot of the limelight away from what Souness had been trying to achieve at Ibrox. So, for him, it was vital Rangers won the title back.

The gaffer knew what he wanted and had a steely determination to achieve precisely that. So if any of us grumbled or complained about the training he would turn around and snap: 'We have to be ready, we can't let Celtic do us again.'

The training was more intense than anything I had previously experienced but we needed to hit the ground running. Il Ciocco was the perfect place for that. Our hotel was halfway up a mountain and it was fair to say it was an uphill struggle in every way for me.

SPL side Kilmarnock have used Il Ciocco as their summer base in recent years and some of the players I represent there tell me it hasn't changed since my Rangers days.

It was like boot camp. We were up at 7.30am and after some intense training we would go for lunch and a sleep. That was only to avoid the midday sun.

We would be back out again at 4pm for another session and after that it was dinner at 7pm and lights off! Who said a footballer's life is all glitz and glamour?

I think we did that for something like six or seven days before I fell ill with a viral infection and believe me it was genuine! I had a sore throat but the medical staff checked me out and told me I had picked up a virus.

It was bad news and I had to stay in bed for the rest of the trip. I felt so bad I would rather have been sweating it out on the training pitch than under my duvet. That is how bad it was.

Nicky Walker came to visit me and revealed he had been floored by the same virus. He had ended being rushed to hospital and kept on a drip for a week. That made me feel so much better!

There was very little improvement in my condition by the time we were ready to fly home. I was in such a state on the return flight from Italy that the gaffer agreed to let me get off in London and drive to Norwich rather than take the connecting flight to Glasgow.

That virus caused me to miss the first few games of the pre-season and left me playing catch-up, although I was determined to be fit for Davie Cooper's testimonial match. It was against the French giants Bordeaux, who boasted top stars like Jean Tigana and Clive Allen.

That was my first experience of playing at Ibrox, in front of more than 40,000 fans. The stadium was packed and as soon as I took to the field I knew it was going to be an amazing arena to play my football in. I managed to score and although it didn't count for much it at least showed the Rangers fans what I was capable of.

The day, though, wasn't about me. It was about the legendary Davie Cooper. I was still getting to know him but everybody at Rangers couldn't speak more highly about him or his footballing abilities. Amongst the fans he was a true great. I know that phrase is sometimes over-used but for 'Coops' it fitted almost as perfectly as his legendary left boot.

By the time I arrived he was entering the veteran stage and there were some doubts whether he could still cut it at the top level. He went on to prove those doubters wrong by going to Motherwell and helping them to lift the Scottish Cup and getting himself back into the Scotland squad. Maybe Rangers were too hasty in letting him go but Coops wanted to play and later I could see where he was coming from.

Coops, the man, was a very funny guy. He always came across as this dour, grumpy individual, but that was just an act. He certainly revelled in his Albert Tatlock nickname.

100

When he stepped on to the field he was in his element. What he could do with a ball was just mesmerising. The joke was he only used his right foot for standing on. That was 100 per cent true!

On the topic of Ibrox legends I also have to mention Willie Waddell and Willie Thornton. When I first arrived at Rangers I often stayed longer in the afternoons to try and avoid the four walls of my hotel room. Waddell and Thornton were club ambassadors and they would give the fans and visitors daily trips around Ibrox.

They were real gentlemen, really down-to-earth guys, despite everything they had achieved in the game. Thornton had been stationed near Grimsby during the war and he knew all about my hometown. We used to talk for hours on end about Grimsby but what captivated me more than anything were their stories from their own playing careers. What they achieved I could only dream of. These true Ibrox greats should be an inspiration to everybody who pulls on the light blue jersey.

I just hoped to try and make some kind of impact at Rangers. After all the glitz and glamour of my Ibrox introduction, my Scottish Premier League debut felt like a million miles away when we made the trip to Douglas Park. I am pleased to say Hamilton now have a new, custom-built stadium because back then their ground was a dump. It was so bad that it must have been a health hazard!

It was the first match of the new season and everybody saw it as a chance to start afresh. It gave us an opportunity to put down an early marker and show we were the team to beat.

The manager's view was pretty much the same: 'Let's go and topple Celtic. If you play well you will win the title.' That was how simple the manager's philosophy was.

We made a positive start with a 2–0 win at Hamilton but it was our other summer arrival, Stevens, who stole my thunder. I arrived as the big-money centre forward but it was our right back who got in on the scoring act, with the aid of a slight deflection.

I broke my duck in the Skol Cup when I netted the opener in

a 3–0 win over Clyde at Firhill. It may only have been the third round but for me it could have been the World Cup final because it was just such a relief to get off the mark.

I kept my goal-a-game ratio going in the Skol Cup when I scored in the next tie in a six-goal thrashing of the now-defunct Clydebank. I was really starting to enjoy my football and beginning to make an impact in my new surroundings.

12

THE OLD FIRM WITH A BANG!

I KNEW the Old Firm rivalry was intense but I didn't realise how full on it was until I was thrown into the lion's den. It was unbelievable. It really is one of the most passionate games in world football.

I have sampled a few local derbies in my time but Norwich versus Ipswich or Grimsby against Hull or Lincoln was never going to hold a candle to their Glasgow counterpart. Derbies are important to all fans, but the Old Firm game was something else.

Things were cranked up even more because Celtic were the champions and we were under real pressure to get that first big win of the season.

It was the one and only topic of discussion in Glasgow and the build-up started weeks before the game. It was also my first Rangers game where the team stayed in a hotel the night before a home game. It was a wise ploy because it got us away from the goldfish bowl and let us focus on the game.

I started to get a wee tingle of nerves as I stepped off the coach and made my way into the stadium. By the time I got into the dressing room I thought I had walked into one of the Queen's private rooms at Buckingham Palace or Balmoral!

We always had a portrait of the Queen up in the dressing room but that day there were seven or eight pictures of her plastered across all four walls. They ranged from photographs to pictures simply torn out of magazines. She was everywhere.

I knew religion played a big part in the Old Firm fixture but I didn't realise how much until that afternoon. I asked a few of my Scottish team mates what it was all about and they explained it in pretty simplistic terms. They said: 'Look Kev, at the end of the day we are all loyalists and this club fully supports Queen and country. A lot of the Celtic supporters don't have the same beliefs. They don't recognise the Queen as our head of state and some of their more radical followers have even threatened to blow her up.'

Thankfully, massive steps have been taken by both Rangers and Celtic since those dark days to stamp out bigotry. It may never be erased but both clubs deserve to be applauded for tackling the issue head on. I would now like to think the focus amongst the Old Firm fans is more on the football than any other social or political issues.

I was taken aback by it all but the rest of the guys said: 'Kev, that is the way it is!' I have always tried to stay away from reli-gious issues throughout my life. I was, though, a staunch loyalist. I grew up respecting our monarchy and being told I was playing for Queen and Country was all the motivation I needed.

As I said, religion didn't really bother me. I was brought up through the Church of England but I always saw it as a place for weddings and funerals rather than somewhere for regular worship.

I calmed my pre-match nerves and filled in time, the usual way, by having a quick cigarette in the toilet.

I never did warm-ups and so I didn't go out until just before kick-off. When I did finally enter the field it was like somebody had flicked a switch. The noise was cranked right up thanks to more than 45,000 fanatical fans – on both sides. The segregation was nowhere near as strict as it is today and that added to the atmosphere. I think they had about 6,000 fanatical punters who were determined to make themselves heard.

It was just as frantic on the pitch. Celtic players went flying into challenges. After one early challenge Peter Grant was up and in my face screaming: 'Get it up you, you Proddie b******!' That was me labelled and I knew which side I was on.

The mood of our own supporters was hardly helped in that game when Celtic scored within two minutes, through Frank McAvennie. He was always the Ibrox villain after his part in the Terry Butcher, Graham Roberts and Chris Woods court case. To them he had been the main culprit although the Celtic fans and McAvennie take a slightly different view.

I still remember his goal to this day. The ball hit the net and a stunned realisation swept round the ground and was followed by a deathly silence.

I went to take the kick-off and all we could hear were disgruntled voices from the home support, aimed at certain individuals. I looked to the bench and Graeme and Walter just stared back at us all, shaking their heads before they screamed in unison: 'Get it sorted.'

Thankfully we managed to do just that. We turned the game on its head. Ally McCoist got a double and another from Ray Wilkins put us 3–1 up.

I then grabbed my moment of glory, when I netted the fourth. I think Mark Walters only managed five step-overs on the right before he dropped his shoulder and landed a perfect cross on the penalty spot. I came on to ball and met it perfectly with a diving header. I knew as soon as I made contact the ball was going to fly high past the Celtic keeper, Ian Andrews.

People always ask me how I felt at that moment and I always tell them it was more relief than anything else. When I kicked off my career, scoring goals was always a joy but by the end of your career they become more of a relief. You build up a reputation and kudos as a goalscorer and that is then what you are expected to do. You have to deal with that pressure and when you move to another club you have to prove yourself over again. There was no better way for me to do that than to score my first SPL goal in an Old Firm game. That goal would prove important in my fight to win over the Rangers fans.

Walters wrapped up a marvellous result and day with the fifth goal – although, it is fair to say, not everybody in the Rangers camp was happy with the final outcome.

Coisty was left absolutely livid the final goal had been allowed to stand. He felt we should have had a penalty. He had been hauled down inside the box before Walters followed up and tapped the ball into the empty net. Coisty wanted the spot kick for the chance to claim his hat-trick and was even arguing with the referee to disallow the goal. Try telling me Coisty doesn't take his football seriously!

A bit of acrimony even spilled into our dressing room after the match – even though we had just stuffed our greatest rivals, and the champions, 5–1. It had been our biggest win over Celtic in 29 years but the Scottish-born players had wanted to go on and heap further embarrassment on our big rivals. But by then most of the players had taken their foot off the gas because the points were already in the bag.

The experience of that first Old Firm game was a day I will never forget. The only downside was the fact I was still living in the hotel and my family weren't there to share the day with me.

A few of the lads came round to the hotel and we ended up in the town. It was a bit of a drunken affair but it was a great night and I don't think any of us had to put our hands into our pockets.

Rangers fans were buying us drink wherever we went while most of the Celtic punters had gone off into hiding. It ended up being a messy affair – even though I had an 8am flight back to Norwich the next morning.

Thankfully my hangover wasn't too long-lasting and after a few days with the family I was ready to kick on from our Old Firm heroics. I got back on the score sheet netting the opener in a 2–0 win at Motherwell. That whetted my appetite for my long-awaited European debut.

It had been three years in the waiting, but, if I am being honest, being drawn against the Polish side Katowice in the UEFA Cup was hardly the fixture I had been hoping for. They weren't exactly a world-renowned name but it didn't stop more than 40,000 fans packing into Ibrox for the first leg. The supporters helped turn it into a real occasion even though we struggled on the park. We were by far the better team but the Poles came to Glasgow to defend and limit the damage.

We eventually broke their resistance midway through the second half, when Walters put us in front. We went looking for a second but they parked every one of their players and the team bus inside their 18-yard box and we couldn't find another goal.

The Katowice players were delighted to get away with a 1–0 defeat and celebrated like they had just won the tournament. We were still in the driving seat but we knew we had to see the job out on our travels.

On that note, I was still living out of a suitcase. I was almost beginning to feel like a member of staff as I had been staying in the Holiday Inn that long. The problem was that I just couldn't find a house I liked anywhere.

It got that bad Souness said: 'Have you not found anywhere yet?' I replied: 'No, but I had seen this shell of a new build in Stirling I quite fancy trying to finish – but I don't know how to!' He thought I was joking but when he realised I was being serious he told me to go and see the chairman, David Holmes. He knew he would be able to help me out with his background in the construction industry.

I think the manager was also concerned that my hotel bill was getting out of control. Not only did he have my accommodation to pay for but he also had a weekly drinks and food bill for half of the Rangers first team.

Coisty, Derek Ferguson and Durranty were all regulars at the Holiday Inn. They would make it their meeting place for nights out because they could get a few drinks and then leave it on my tab or Gary Stevens', knowing the club would foot the bill.

Others like Ian McCall were just as bad. Instead of turning up at the start of the night he would chap my door in the early hours of the morning.

I would normally be sound asleep when Ian would pitch up uninvited at my door. It was normally after he had been out for a drink or two and had been unable to get food. He knew he could get 24-hour room service and would regularly take advantage of it.

I would open the door and let him in. He would order himself a steak or burger and chips and a beer or a coffee. I used to go back to my bed and leave him to it and when I woke up again in the morning all that was left was an empty tray.

So it was understandable why Souness was keen to get me into my own house. I explained the situation to Mr Holmes. I told him the house had no floor or roof, never mind heating or electricity.

The chairman just looked at me as if I was mad but he knew I had set my heart on it. He knew people at Forth Electrical Services, a local company in Stirling, and arranged for them to visit the site with us to see what could be done.

Souness also tagged along but I think that was more down to curiosity than a genuine concern for my living arrangements.

The chairman introduced me to the FES guys, Duncan Fletcher, his brother Hunter and their operations manager, Alan Beaton. Since that day I have gone on to become close friends with all three of them.

They agreed to put a plan together and I was proud as punch I had found my dream home. Then just as I was about to walk away from the site Souness completely stole my thunder. He turned to the estate agent, who had come out with us, and said: 'Is there anything else around here suitable for me?' He was looking to move but needed something with at least 10 acres for his children's horses.

Just like all those years ago, when I was on holiday with Andrea in Mallorca, Graeme had unwittingly upstaged me. We actually went on and looked at a property for him, which was reasonably close by, but he never firmed up his interest in it. Maybe he was just on the wind-up?

I was just delighted with my own purchase and it meant I could focus on my football knowing I had found a place that Andrea, the kids and I could call home.

Things were coming together off the pitch when disaster struck on it. It was down to a Souness switch that backfired big-time. Most footballers tend to be superstitious and I can understand why after my Tynecastle nightmare.

We were about to take on Hearts when the manager changed my long-running pre-match ritual. That meant no rub and definitely no cigarette. Souness, who had named himself as a substitute, told me to join in the warm-up. I laughed and told him: 'You know I don't get involved in all that.' I explained how I didn't feel right going out at 2.20pm and then coming back in at 2.45pm to sit in the dressing room to get cold all over again.

The manager was having none of it and told me to go out and warm up with him. We went out and did a bit of jogging and started passing the ball to each other.

I felt great but when I went back into the dressing room, of course, my temperature dropped and I started to get cold. My worst fears were realised when minutes into the game I pulled my hamstring. A ball was launched over the top and as I went for it I felt a twinge.

I tried to play on but knew it wasn't right and I had to go off. I dejectedly trooped off and sat on the advertising boards at the side of the dugout. Souness apologetically turned his head and said: 'I think we should just leave you to your own preparations in future.'

I was left absolutely devastated because it meant I missed the Skol Cup semi-final with Hearts. I had never played at Hampden and I was gutted at missing that game. I was left as a frustrated spectator, as the team strolled to an easy 3–0 win. Walters scored two goals and put on one of the best solo performances I have ever seen. It was a great night for the lads and at least I had the consolation of knowing that I might get my chance to play at Hampden in the final.

I came back in and opened the scoring in a 2–0 home win over Dundee. It was another trademark header. I later cracked in a shot when a Dundee defender caught me full on the shin with his studs. There was nothing malicious in the challenge but it left me in total agony. I never thought any more about it until 15 minutes to go when the manager took me off. It was more of a precaution because it was my first game back and we were due to head to Poland for the second leg of our UEFA Cup tie.

I wasn't too despondent when I took my seat in the dugout because I had got my goal. I also thought I had done well and was looking forward to my first European trip.

But as I sat down I rolled my sock down and my shinpad was split in two. I looked down at my leg and it was like a scene out of *Casualty*. There was a gaping two-inch hole. It looked horrendous with blood everywhere.

I knew I was in trouble because it had been similar to the injury I had suffered all those years ago at Charlton, albeit on the opposite shin. I used a couple of expletives and threw what was left of my shinpad onto the track.

Souness thought I was annoyed at being substituted and shouted: 'I am just saving you for the European game.' I showed him my shin and he winced when he saw the depth of the wound.

I was lucky because the Rangers surgeon was at the game. He came down and cleaned the wound and inserted seven or eight stitches into my leg. He then hit me with the hammer blow that there was no chance of making the trip to Poland.

I was devastated but thankfully the team eased through with a 4–2 win in Katowice. Hopefully I would get a chance of a trip in the next round.

I worked over-time back at Ibrox because I desperate to be fit for our next game at Aberdeen.

They were a decent team and had been breathing down our necks in the title race. The manager came up to me on the coach on the way to Pittodrie and asked if there was any chance I would play for him?

I didn't need to be asked twice. I knew it was a massive game and my reply was: 'Gaffer, I am desperate to play.' I stuffed something like half a ton of cotton wool down the back of my shinpad and went out and played.

There was a real rivalry between both sets of fans but I didn't quite realise the extent of the hatred until that afternoon. I would go as far as saying that some Aberdeen fans dislike Rangers more than many Celtic supporters.

That was probably down to the fact Aberdeen had been a top team in their own right over the previous decade and Rangers were starting to wrestle that superiority away from them. It was something the Aberdeen fans weren't going to readily accept, especially as their own team was still full of top international stars, like Alex McLeish and Willie Miller.

I played against big McLeish that day. It was a real physical affair. Coisty had to go off with a head wound after a second-half tussle with the big defender. I felt McLeish had been overly aggressive and so I took matters into my own hands. It didn't take me long to catch him and he had to get stitches above his eye. I wouldn't like to say it was a deliberate elbow. It was more of an outstretched arm.

Unfortunately worse was to follow with the infamous Ian Durrant tackle.

I was five yards away and the challenge was one of the worst I have ever seen. What made it even more damning for Neil Simpson was the photographs showing the expression on his face as he made the challenge. I saw that in the flesh and that is what makes it even more harrowing. I couldn't believe a professional footballer could go out and injure a fellow player like that. You just wonder what went through Neil's mind when he lunged in.

He seemed to lose the plot and the red mist descended. We all saw the pain Durranty was in on the ground and Neil quickly realised the seriousness of his crime.

I don't think anyone can make excuses for what Neil did but I am sure the atmosphere amongst the rival fans that day had something to do with it. I didn't know Neil personally before that game but he certainly didn't have a reputation for being a dirty player, although that tackle was to hover over him. The whole Durrant affair would eventually have a damaging affect on him as a player and a person. Neil was never the same player again. He probably ended up pulling out of more challenges than he went into. Maybe his confidence took a dent and that same aggression and wholehearted approach disappeared from his play.

For Durranty it was a sickening blow. With Ian being so young and vulnerable the more senior pros like Ray Wilkins, Butcher and myself really felt for him.

It is easy to make excuses but after everything that had happened the match become an afterthought. Our minds were elsewhere. We were all genuinely too concerned and shaken about Ian. We lost to a goal from Charlie Nicholas and a penalty from Jim Bett.

What I found absolutely galling was that tackle seemed to galvanise the Aberdeen support and pump them up for the remainder of the game. I found it sickening that the Aberdeen fans cheered Neil every time he touched the ball.

It just shows how deep the hatred of Rangers is for some of these so-called Aberdeen fans. It may only be a small minority but it doesn't look like they will ever let things lie. These are the same sick and twisted individuals who still sing and taunt the Rangers fans about the Ibrox disaster and the Durrant challenge. It is something historical and deep and I just find it really sad and depressing. It is so petty and small-minded and it has nothing to do with football.

Butcher chased after the referee after the game and ended up kicking his dressing-room door in. The same patched-up door still hangs in Pittodrie today, like some sort of trophy of the day Aberdeen took care of Rangers.

If we had beaten them we would have gone clear in the league. The result and the circumstances of the Aberdeen trip meant it was going to be a far tighter title race. Thrown into that we had lost one of our bright, young stars for the season – if not longer.

It was a long trip home, with Durrant in pieces on the back seat. We all wondered if he was ever going to play again. It was at a time when cruciate injuries were pretty much career-threatening. It was going to be a long and hard road back to fitness for one of Scotland's brightest talents.

13

SILVERWARE FOR
BILLY DRINKELL

WE MANAGED get back on the rails against Hibs. I played my part, heading a long Terry Butcher ball down for Ally McCoist to net the only goal. That was the perfect pick-me-up for the team ahead of the Skol Cup final. It was amazing: just three months into my Rangers career I was looking forward to a cup final. Both finals in England were played in the second half of the season and so this was a new experience for me.

It was a big thing because it was my first taste of the national stadium and there was a bit of added edge because our cup final opponents were Aberdeen. It was our first game against the Dons since the Ian Durrant mayhem.

It is fair to say we didn't need much motivating. I remember Graeme Souness's team talk. He went to great lengths to ensure none of us went out looking for revenge. He made it clear he didn't want any grudges being held and lifting the Skol Cup would be the best pick-me-up we could give Durranty.

The match itself provided end-to-end entertainment. We took the lead through a penalty. The Aberdeen defender David Robertson tried to throw the ball back to Theo Snelders but was short and it allowed me to nip in. I enticed the Dutchman out of his box and then I charged into the area. As I went round him he tried to claw the ball back and brought me down. Some people thought I was a little bit over enthusiastic with my fall but it was a definite penalty, although I had suckered the Aberdeen keeper into the challenge.

Coisty stuck it away but Davie Dodds levelled before Ian Ferguson put us back in front. We couldn't hold our lead and again Dodds was the Aberdeen hero. We had been the better team but suddenly found ourselves on the ropes. Jim Bett had a great chance to win it for the Dons but fired agonisingly wide.

We managed to regroup and bounce back as Coisty grabbed the winner, although it should never have stood.

A corner came in and Coisty miscued a shot. It was on target but was about to be blocked by Willie Miller. I saw the Aberdeen captain going to block it so I flew into him. He tried to make a last-ditch challenge but was off-balance and Ally's effort managed to sneak past him and Snelders. Willie got up, in his usual manner, hands in the air, shouting at the referee, looking for the goal to be disallowed.

By that time, Coisty was already in amongst the crowd celebrating because the referee had signalled for the goal. Even I was surprised Aberdeen hadn't been given the free kick for my challenge. The only thing I can say in defence of the referee was that the box was crowded and there were a lot of bodies jostling for the ball. I didn't care and neither did the 40,000 or so Rangers fans celebrating inside the stadium.

That goal came two minutes from the end and allowed us to sneak the win and the first trophy of my Rangers career. It topped off a brilliant day. It had been a great game, the atmosphere had been top drawer and I walked away with a winner's medal.

I was 28 going on 29 and lifting that cup was massive for me. Another big thing for us all was the fact that we had done it for Durranty. The club gave Ian a medal, which I felt was a great touch. It helped raise his spirits, as he continued along his rehabilitation. He might not have played but his presence was out there with us.

There wasn't too much time to celebrate because 48 hours later we were on our travels. Our reward for getting past Katowice was a tie against the crack Germans, Cologne. I was finally able to experience an away day in Europe. I was up against their big defender Jurgen Kohler, who went on to become a German international and a top star with Borussia Dortmund.

We played well, although our game plan was more about containment than anything else. Coisty had a couple of chances and we were holding our own until the game turned in the last 15 minutes. Cologne scored through Olaf Janssen and Ally got himself sent off. Kohler did him like a kipper. Coisty had gone for the ball but Kohler went down, making the most of the challenge. It gave the German crowd a massive lift and Thomas Allofs went on to net their killer second three minutes from time. It left us up against it going back to Ibrox.

Domestically, we were able to keep ourselves ahead of the competition. We drew with St Mirren, with a veteran Andy Gray getting his first goal for us. The other talking point from that match was the loss of Coisty with a torn hamstring.

He was out for a good few months and left me playing with umpteen different striker partners, from Mark Walters to Gray and even our central defender Scott Nisbet. If it wasn't one of them then I was playing up front on my own, so it was a case of make do.

We still managed to extend our unbeaten run. We beat Hearts at Ibrox and then I scored a last-minute winner against Motherwell. The 'Well game was a big day for me personally because it was the first time my dad had seen me play for Rangers. It was also an important one for the team. John 'Bomber' Brown had put us ahead before a brilliant, virtuoso effort from the former Rangers player Bobby Russell looked like salvaging Motherwell an unlikely point.

We kept pushing for the goal but Motherwell had 11 men behind the ball and tried to waste time at every opportunity. We were becoming more and more frustrated but our patience finally paid off in the final minute.

Bomber turned provider with the cross, which Ian Ferguson flicked on and I managed to get in at the back post to head home from close range.

The Rangers fans used to sing 'There's only one Billy Drinkell', and that chant went up as the ball hit the net. I couldn't have scripted things better and my dad had been there to see my moment of glory.

He had been up in the players' lounge and had been treated like royalty. He had a great day and I couldn't wait to see him. I went upstairs as proud as punch and asked him what he thought? I was fully expecting him to be really excited and say 'Well done, son' – but when I stepped into the players' lounge he was really subdued. I said: 'Did you not enjoy the game?' He replied: 'Yes, it was great, but you haven't made much of an impression up here. The Rangers fans don't even know your name yet. They kept singing for "Billy" Drinkell, not Kevin.' I had to explain to him that it was nothing personal but the Rangers fans didn't really take to the name Kevin because of its connections to Ireland. It was like Ted McMinn. Kevin was the name on his birth certificate but the Rangers fans always called him Ted.

My dad was clearly relieved when I explained the situation and headed back home happy that his son was making an impact at his new club even if he had been renamed. The win gave us a wee confidence booster ahead of our UEFA Cup return. We knew it was a major challenge as Cologne came looking to see out the tie.

The Germans were disciplined and kept it goalless until well into the second half before I eventually scored. It was a half-decent goal as I outjumped Kohler to power home a header. It gave us a real chance because we were on top in the game and there were still 15 minutes to go.

From then on though, time seemed to stand still. Cologne killed the game off. They had so many injuries and players needing treatment it was like a war zone. It got so ridiculous that at one stage they had three different players down and had three different guys from their bench on, giving what appeared to be the kiss of life.

We started to get frustrated. Nisbet picked up one of the medical bags and tried to hurl it away but its contents scattered all over the pitch and that caused another unwanted delay.

We went gung-ho trying to get the equaliser but Cologne hit us on break in the final minute when Janssen scored. That goal was completely irrelevant because we were going out anyway and the real killer was being unable to get the second goal.

It was very disappointing because over the two legs we felt we were as good as, if not better than, Cologne.

Unfortunately, European competition back then was not like it is today. It was a lot tougher to have success back in those days. If you got a tough draw in the early rounds you could be out quickly but these days if you get beaten there are still the group sections and parachutes into the Europa League.

Our European exit was compounded when we returned to the SPL and crashed to Celtic at Parkhead. They beat us fair and square 3–1. It left a far different feeling from the highs of my Old Firm debut at Ibrox.

I got back in on the scoring act as we beat Hamilton 3–1 and followed that up with a draw at Dundee.

I was finally able to say my farewells to the Holiday Inn. The house, after some hard work and toil, was ready and the Drinkell family could finally be reunited.

I was also left a lovely house-warming present by some mischievous Celtic fans who, quite literally, left me F-ing and C-ing. I came back from training and everything looked fine until I took a frantic phone call from the chairman David Holmes, who was in a real fluster.

He came on and said: 'Kevin, we have a problem.' He then explained the newspapers had got a hold of a story that the workmen laying my driveway had used the white chips within the mix to imprint CFC into the middle of my drive.

I raced outside and sure enough the initials of our great rivals

118

Part of the Grimsby School's select (I'm third from left in front row)

Getting my hands on some early silverware in a school five-a-side tournament (I'm holding the trophy)

Firing Grimsby Town youths to success

Making a splash as I celebrate with my Grimsby team mates in the bath

Taking a bow during our Civic Reception to celebrate our promotion from Division Four

My hat-trick goal which seals the Third Division title

Effortless control!

Challenging Charlton's Joe McLaughlin

England B cap

Playing in goals for
Falkirk, trying to
keep the ball out
of the net against
Motherwell, 1992

Falkirk celebrate their B&Q Cup success in
December 1993 at Fir Park after beating
St Mirren 3-0

Celebrating John Hughes'
B&Q Cup goal

The new Canary

Showing off the Canon League Two
championship trophy with John Deehan

Taking a well-earned championship lap of honour with Dave Watson,
Stevie Bruce and Chris Woods

Getting my Colmans
Player of the Year
award from the
legendary
Freddie Trueman

Launching another
air raid on the
Manchester
United defence

No room for
reputations as
Drinks muscles
in on Arsenal's
David O'Leary

Rangers v Aberdeen
Skol Cup final October
1988 (3-2) –
Theo Snelders takes
me down for a penalty

Scoring on my
Old Firm debut
in a 5-1 win over
Celtic at Ibrox
August 1988

Celebrating Skol Cup
Final success with
Rangers in 1988

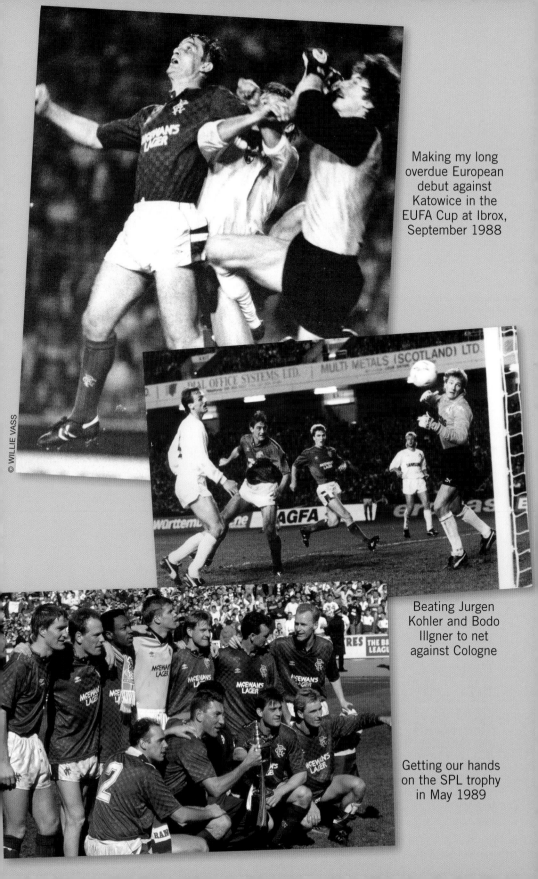

© WILLIE VASS

Making my long overdue European debut against Katowice in the EUFA Cup at Ibrox, September 1988

Beating Jurgen Kohler and Bodo Illgner to net against Cologne

Getting our hands on the SPL trophy in May 1989

The Stirling squad celebrate our Second Division title success

© WILLIE VASS

I am presented with my manager of the year award with Walter Smith, Jim Leishman and Allan McGraw

© DAILY EXPRESS

My girls – Charlotte, Andrea and Alexandra

Happy families at Norwich (Kevin, Andrea, Alexandra and Charlotte)

were emblazoned right across my freshly laid Tarmac. It wasn't blatantly obvious but if you looked closely enough you could make it out.

I couldn't understand why a story like that would be of interest to a national newspaper but the chairman was in a right state. He said we have to get it sorted and he sent some other workmen round at 7.30pm to start taking the offending white chips out with their hands. All this to avoid it getting into the national press! I thought it was madness but I still didn't quite realise how big Old Firm news was.

I just laughed it off and, ironically, I bumped into a guy a couple of years ago and he confessed he had been one of the workmen who had put the CFC chips down. I had a good laugh and a joke with him about it.

I know guys like Neil Lennon, Aiden McGeady and Allan McGregor all get a lot of hassle off the field but I was quite lucky on that front. I managed to slip under the Old Firm radar without too much bother.

There was one night, however, after we had beaten Celtic, where I did end up on the front line. A couple of bricks were thrown at the front door but that was the extent of it. There was the occasional shout of 'Proddie b******' when I walked down the street but nothing to write home about.

I think that was due to the fact that I didn't really go out of my way to noise up the Celtic support. I just got on with my game and hopefully because of that I got a bit more respect from them. On the park I would do all I could to help Rangers but after I stepped off it that was it, finished.

Living in Stirling also meant I was a bit away from the bright lights of Glasgow. Instead I was more than happy to follow my normal trend of heading to my local pub. I remember leaving the house one night and having a decision do I go left or right. Left would take me to the town centre and right to the sleepy village of Cambusbarron. I decided to go right, knowing there was a popular pub called The Foresters just a few minutes walk away.

I walked in and ordered a pint and took a seat in the corner. I could see there were a group of people sitting up at the bar. One of them was Hunter Fletcher, who I had known from finishing off my house. He had informed the others who I was and minutes later one of the guys came over and offered to buy me a drink. He introduced himself as 'Alex "Gypsy" Lafferty – a wee Fenian B******!' That broke the ice and I joined him, Hunter and Stuart McKenzie at the bar.

That was me sorted and all I had to worry about was Andrea and the kids. I didn't have to worry too long because a trip into the local village newsagent introduced me to the Kilmarnock legend Frank Beattie and his wife Betty. It turned out Betty was 'Mrs Cambusbarron'. She knew everybody and within weeks she had the social lives of Andrea and the kids all mapped out. That was a big help because Betty and her family took Andrea and the kids under their wings.

There was also Jack Ogilvie and his family – who are behind Ogilvie Homes – who helped ease us into local life and gave us our first taste of a Scottish Hogmanay.

Those friendships have since blossomed over the last 20 years and are major reasons why I now call Scotland my home.

In those early days, it also helped having Chris Woods and Terry Butcher living close by. We used to car-share on our way into training or to games. I knew Woodsie well from his time at Norwich and he is the best goalkeeper I have played with. I had the privilege of playing with him at two different clubs and for me he is right up there with the best. He won a few England caps but he should have picked up so many more. He was just unfortunate to break through when Peter Shilton and Ray Clemence were still fighting it out for England's No. 1 jersey.

The one thing about Chris was his professionalism. It was second to none. He worked so hard on the training pitch and always tried to make himself better. I think that came from working under Shilton when he was a youngster at Nottingham Forest. Shilton's good habits rubbed off on Woodsie.

Chris was just an all-round, top keeper. People go on about how Andy Goram has been Rangers greatest keeper of recent times but for me Woodsie eclipsed him. Goram was a great keeper, especially around the time of nine-in-a-row when he helped to break Celtic fans' hearts, but I still believe Chris was better.

Not long after our Skol Cup win Rangers were given a major boost in our quest for glory. It was a move which went some way to reshaping the club's history.

Millionaire businessman and steel magnate David Murray purchased the club from Lawrence Marlborough for something like £6 million. It was a massive deal and great for the club, although I was sad to see David Holmes step down. He was absolutely brilliant to me. He had looked after my every need and a lot of people have actually forgotten the work he did in laying the foundations for the nine-in-a-row campaign. He gave Murray the base from which to build his Ibrox dynasty. We already had a big-name manager and top players. Murray saw that and with some major investment felt he could take the club on again.

There had been some rumblings about a possible takeover in previous months because Marlborough had seen a big investment in the United States hit the skids and he needed to sell the club.

My first meeting with Sir David, as he became, is one that I am sure still makes John Brown cringe. Bomber was never one to shirk a challenge but that afternoon he jumped in with both feet. We were coming down the main stairs at Ibrox after a game and there was this well-dressed guy who was struggling down the steps with two sticks. We didn't know who the gentleman was but that didn't deter Bomber. He was never known for his patience and became increasingly frustrated at the length of time it was taking to get to the bottom.

So Bomber piped up: 'Come along mate, speed it up.' Then he joked: 'Stick your backside up here on the banister and we'll help you slide down. It'll be a lot quicker.'

Little did we know the guy he had just harangued was a multi-millionaire and about to become our new owner. The first we knew about it was when the manager came in and introduced us to our new chairman, Mr David Murray. It was quite funny because Murray then turned to Bomber and asked if he still wanted him to slide down the banister? Bomber was a little red-faced but laughed it off, although he had very little option.

Murray went on to change the whole outlook of Rangers and Scottish football. He poured millions into the club over the best part of two decades, seeing very little cash back in return. I just wonder how lowly Ayr United feel now after they knocked back Murray's initial move to buy into Somerset Park?

Murray's timely takeover gave us the springboard to produce one of the biggest results of the season when Richard Gough scored the only goal of the game against Aberdeen. It pulled us through a sticky patch after we had lost to Dundee United and Hearts. It was also Aberdeen's first SPL defeat of the season.

Things continued to look up as we beat Hibs, where Coisty made his top-team return. I was delighted to have him back alongside me. I had played with a number of makeshift partners and it had started to take its toll.

We beat Hamilton to end the year top of the table although we were being pushed by United, who were two points behind, and third-placed Aberdeen. The Accies win set things up nicely for our New Year Old Firm showdown. The game took a similar pattern to our first Ibrox meeting.

Celtic went ahead through an early goal from Chris Morris. Terry Butcher pulled us level before I won a penalty. There didn't look to be much danger until I saw Anton Rogan racing towards me. He was one of these wholly committed players and charged at me. Hs eyes were glazed over and the veins were popping out of his neck. I thought to myself: 'You are not going to be that silly, are you?' So I eased back a little to make him think he could get the ball and sure enough he came crashing in and wiped me out. It was a stonewall penalty and Mark Walters stepped up to stick it away.

Ian Ferguson and Walters scored again to give us a convincing

4–1 win. We felt it was payback after the Parkhead defeat but the main priority was staying top of the table.

We were brought crashing back down to earth the next week when we lost 2–1 to relegation-threatened Motherwell. I put us ahead but Fraser Wishart equalised before Gough put through his own net.

It was a bad result but the afternoon was compounded by the touchline antics of the Motherwell manager Tommy McLean. Walters had been taken out by a late challenge and as he got up he reacted furiously, lifting his hands. He had every reason to be angry because it had been a shocking challenge but the next thing we knew McLean was up off the bench trying to get Mark sent off. His reaction was a bit over the top, trying to get a fellow professional red-carded.

Things came to a head when we headed back up the tunnel at the interval. One or two of the players, including 'Goughie', were having a go at McLean over his unsporting behaviour.

Souness then stepped up, looking his usual million-dollar self and told us all to calm down and get back into our dressing room. I was one of the last players in when I turned to see Souness grab Wee Tommy by the neck and pin him up against the wall. He screamed at him: 'Just you worry about your own team and don't try to get any of my players sent off ever again.' That was the gist of the exchange although it was put across in a slightly more industrial manner.

Losing matches against so-called lesser teams was something of an Achilles heel for us. We would win the big games then throw away silly points to give the New Firm, Aberdeen and Dundee United, a glimmer of hope.

When it came down to the next top of the table clash at Pittodrie we again showed our class and ability to rise to the occasion when it really mattered. Derek Ferguson put on a real performance, scoring both goals in a 2–1 victory.

It was a big win, not only for the title but it was also the first time we had been back at Pittodrie since the whole Durrant affair.

The atmosphere was pretty hostile but Derek produced a bit of magic, which proved to be the difference on the day.

The quality within our midfield meant Derek was often overlooked. It must have been hard. He was unlucky that we had Ray Wilkins and Ian Ferguson, who were always first picks for the central spots, along with Durrant before his injury.

That 'Fergie'-inspired win kicked us on and this time we didn't take the foot off the accelerator. We beat Dundee, drew with Dundee United and then swept past St Mirren, Hamilton and Hibs.

I scored the only goal at Easter Road. Gary Stevens' cross was half-cleared by Gordon Hunter and that allowed me to blast a shot past Goram. I was just pleased to come away with the points as I always hated going to Leith because the stadium was so run down. It was a case of getting the head down and getting out with the points.

Our SPL form was good and it gave us confidence to kick off our Scottish Cup campaign – although we hardly started with all guns blazing.

After being held 1–1 at Starks Park we managed to see off Raith Rovers, after a replay. I grabbed one of the goals in our 3–0 win. There were no such difficulties in the next round when I netted a brace in the 8–0 hiding of lowly Stranraer, which set up a quarter-final tie with Dundee United.

I continued my goal-a-game Scottish Cup record by cancelling out Kevin Gallacher's opener. Coisty put us in front before Mixu Paatelainen equalised to force a replay at Tannadice. Fortunately, we managed to squeeze through again thanks to a second-half goal from Coisty.

In the league, April Fool's Day was another big afternoon where we managed to get the last laugh on Celtic. That Parkhead result killed off all hope of our rivals regaining their crown.

I scored the opener with a header and we sealed the win with a goal, which to this day, remains a total figment of Coisty's imagination.

Ally claimed the goal but got nowhere near it. Ian Ferguson

cracked in a thunderbolt free kick, which Pat Bonner parried, but the power in the shot saw the ball spin back towards the goal.

Bonner, a defender and Coisty all closed in but only succeeded in getting in each other's way, allowing the ball to bounce straight in. That didn't stop Coisty running off to claim the glory. Ally claims it was his goal but the television replays show it was definitely Fergie's.

We held on for a great win although we were made to sweat a bit at the end.

Andy Walker pulled one back for Celtic and then they were awarded a penalty when the ball bobbled up off Gough's hand. Substitute Joe Miller had the chance from the spot but Woodsie made the save to give us our first win at Parkhead in nine years.

That winning goal helped Fergie make his mark at Rangers. He came in as a £1 million signing from St Mirren and had to fight hard to win over the fans because they favoured the homegrown talents of Durrant and Derek Ferguson. Ian's application and his ability quickly shone through and he became an integral part of the nine-in-a-row sides.

We let ourselves down badly in the semi-finals of the Scottish Cup when we drew with First Division St Johnstone. If I am being honest we were lucky still to be in the competition.

That, not surprisingly, led to another one of those rare occasions where the gaffer lost the plot. He went absolutely berserk in the dressing room and demanded we report to the old Albion training ground for a Sunday-morning session.

The big, heavy doors were almost taken off their hinges when Souness stormed in. He stopped the training and called us all over. He went absolutely mental at us and told us we had let everybody down.

He signed off by saying: 'It will be the same team on Tuesday for the replay and if you are not good enough and don't sort this out I will sell every single one of you and bring in a whole new team!'

I knew he had the capability to go out and replace me, but he made the point of singling out some of our biggest names, like Butcher and Wilkins.

We certainly weren't brave enough to run the wrath of Souness again. We went out and thumped St Johnstone by four goals, with Walters, Gary Stevens, Coisty and myself all getting on the score sheet.

We knew the manager wasn't a man to be messed with. From my very first meeting with him it was clear he was a guy who didn't suffer fools gladly. He made it crystal clear he had brought me to Rangers to help him win the league. His philosophy to his players was simple. Sort it out or I will make changes and bring in people who can win me silverware. That was the big stick he would wield if players weren't performing to his lofty standards. Rangers had the financial muscle and status to attract top names.

They were a big club, who could pay top wages and, unlike the top English teams, could offer European football into the bargain. That was something most top players at the time were desperate to experience.

Souness, the manager, was never really big on tactics. He was more reliant on making top signings and bringing the right type of characters to the club. Butcher, Woodsie, Willkins and Stevens were all experienced guys who the gaffer knew he could put his mortgage on. He believed that if we went out and did what we were good at then we would be too good for the opposition, regardless of who it was.

Walter Smith, his loyal No. 2, was more of the day-to-day man on the training field. They were both very close and they would discuss everything, although Souness always had the final say. Walter would relay things to the team but it was Graeme who made the big decisions. If he wanted to find a new player then he would go and identify the targets – nobody else. Walter was better with the man management of the squad and trying to get five or ten per cent more out of the players. I had nothing but respect for them and they were a good team along with Phil Boersma.

The great thing about Souness was the way he backed and supported his players. If you did your bit for him then he would do everything in his power to look after you. A lot of what Graeme said and did came across as arrogance, or even as an ego trip, but it wasn't. Most things he did were to protect his players. He got himself into more trouble sticking up for us, fighting our causes against referees, other managers and the SFA than anything else. You needed to get past him if you wanted to have a go at his players.

14

CHAMPIONS BUT CAUGHT SHORT
IN SEARCH OF A TREBLE

BY THE end of April the championship was within touching distance. We kept up our relentless charge by beating St Mirren before our day of destiny arrived on 29 April. Hearts were the visitors to Ibrox.

There were no signs of nerves as we went out and thumped them by four goals. Mel Sterland scored twice, to give his famous airplane celebration an airing, before I netted a brace of my own in the second half.

My first came when I got on the end of Ally McCoist's header to smash a right-foot shot past Hearts keeper Henry Smith. The second was a bit easier when I sprung the offside trap, gave Smith the eyes and as he went to ground I knocked the ball over him.

We were winning but we also needed Aberdeen to drop points if we wanted to clinch the title. The Dons were playing Celtic at Pittodrie and we weren't expecting any favours from either of our big rivals. We all thought we would have to wait another week or two.

We were just looking to win our game. I remember running into the corner in the final minutes to kill time when Ibrox suddenly erupted. I looked around because I thought somebody had been punched or something had happened off the ball. Then the news filtered through that Aberdeen had slipped up and drawn against Celtic. The title was ours.

The final whistle went and the champagne bottles were cracked open. We had achieved the goal set out for us at the start of the season. All the blood, sweat and toil had ended in glory.

I had won the Skol Cup with Rangers and titles with Norwich and Grimsby but winning the SPL eclipsed all that. I had taken my career to another level and felt I had played a major part in helping Rangers win the league.

The one memory that has stayed with me from those celebrations was a wonderful gesture from Ray Wilkins. There must have been about 50 bottles of champagne in the dressing room when Ray walked out with two under his arm. Everybody thought he was keeping them for himself but he took them round to the staff in the kitchen who had looked after us all season. Ray had played at the highest level but always found time to think about the people behind the scenes who had played their part in our success.

The title meant everything to me but I think it meant just as much, if not more, to the manager. He had won it in his first season but losing to Celtic the following season had hit him hard.

Second best was alien to him and that was why he had rung the changes. The pleasing thing was he had turned to me, as one of his new signings, to help improve his team. I felt I had done well enough and had repaid the faith he had shown in me.

The title race was over but we still had a few outstanding fixtures to see out. I scored as we beat Dundee United but by this time the focus had turned towards the Scottish Cup final, although we still had the final game of the season and the trophy presentation against Aberdeen.

The success of going for a treble started to take its toll. It had been a long hard season. Wilkins had already paid the price because he had to go in for a hernia operation and a few others also had to bow out in the final weeks.

The final farewell to our SPL season proved to be a big letdown. We got thrashed 3–0 at Ibrox by the Dons. It was a game we couldn't wait to see the back of. We just wanted the final whistle to go so we could finally get our hands on the SPL trophy.

We could now concentrate on bringing the curtain down on our silver-lined season in style with the Scottish Cup. We got the feeling it wasn't going to be our trophy days before the game. We were already missing several key players when Richard Gough went down with a stomach bug the day before the final.

Even on the team bus on the way to Hampden we didn't know what sort of team we were going to be able to put out. The manager had to name himself on the bench because we were so short.

When we finally arrived at the national stadium Gough was there and declared himself fit, so that gave us a pre-match lift although our team still had 'makeshift' written all over it. Sterland and Stuart Munro were asked to abandon their full back positions to form the centre of our midfield. They put in a decent shift and couldn't be blamed for our defeat but we just weren't at the races.

It ended up being a poor game and Celtic struck it lucky with a scrappy goal. We should have been given a throw-in but Roy Aitken conned the officials and took it quickly. The ball was launched deep into our half, where Gary Stevens made what was probably his only mistake of the season. He didn't get enough on a back pass and wee Joe Miller ran in and knocked the winner past Chris Woods.

The goal should never have been given. It should have been our throw but we should also have reacted better in the build-up and cleared the ball. Salt was rubbed into the wound when we were denied what was a perfectly legitimate goal. Terry Butcher netted with a header but the linesman gave offside against Davie Cooper. Everything went against us that day and in the end it cost us the treble.

I am in no doubt that wrapping up the title so early also cost us the Scottish Cup. We coasted through those final games and were unable to up the gears again for the final. After the game, you would have thought we had finished the season empty-handed such was the devastation within our dressing room.

We were all sitting there absolutely shocked when Souness

stormed in. He walked into the centre of the room and threw his loser's medal into the bath. We all expected the customary explosion but the manager surprised us all. He said: 'You have done well this season, don't get too upset. Let them [Celtic] have their moment of glory because we will be the ones having the last laugh! I have something that will blow them right out of the water!'

We all sat there totally bewildered. None of us had a clue what he was talking about. We certainly didn't think it would end up being the most controversial signing in Scottish football history.

Just when I thought my cup final heartbreak couldn't get any worse, I was picked for the drugs test. I was stuck in the Hampden medical room totally humiliated and unable to pass water. I started off with a couple of cans of lager and then some water but still nothing happened.

Celtic's Rogan and Miller, who had been picked from their side for the testing, came down. As you can imagine they were cock-a-hoop as they were celebrating their win and here I was stuck in the middle having to listen to them gloating merrily. It got that bad the official Rangers party gave up the ghost and headed back to Ibrox without me. The party was planned as a celebration but was more like a wake.

I had been in the drug-testing room for more than an hour when the club doctor Donald Cruickshank came down to see what was causing the delay. He told me the team bus had left and he would arrange a taxi to get me back to Ibrox. I asked if I could go to the public toilets and sit in the cubicle because that might help me supply my sample. The testers reluctantly agreed but once again it proved fruitless. I was at the end of my tether and as I walked out of the toilet I saw a punter coming towards me. I asked him to do me a favour and fill my sample bottle. He unwittingly obliged and I took it back to the testing room. I handed it in and disappeared out the door as quickly as I could.

I took the taxi back to Ibrox where Andrea was far from happy after being stood up for more than two hours. The doctor then came up and asked how I had got on. I told him what I had done. Not surprisingly he went absolutely berserk.

He knew my stupidity could have been career-threatening if the sample came back positive. Also earlier in the season he had expressed concern over my addiction to tea. I used to drink something like 20 cups a day and such high caffeine levels could put me at risk when it came to drug testing.

Thankfully the rogue sample was clear. Looking back, what I did at Hampden was madness. I don't think anyone would have believed the truth if I had failed the test. Fortunately nothing untoward came from my stupidity and I was able to thank my lucky stars. It was a relief and there was no chance of me doing something that stupid again.

Our reward for winning the double was an end-of-season trip to Israel. The exotic location was down to the manager; he wanted somewhere out of the way, where we wouldn't be hassled by photographers, the press and fans. He thought Tel Aviv was the perfect place to go to relax and recharge the batteries after a long, hard season. We had quite a few characters in our dressing room and the trip was never going to pass without incident.

The main one involved Neale Cooper getting stabbed. We were in a restaurant in the main square where the whole team was sitting down enjoying a sociable meal when one of the locals suddenly jumped up and started to chase 'Tattie' with a bread knife.

I don't know what Neale had said to upset the man but it was like something out of a Benny Hill sketch although Neale didn't see the funny side at the time, especially when the knife-wielding Israeli stabbed him in the bum.

The knife sliced through his jeans and drew blood. Neale ended up spending the remainder of the night in a local hospital. I think something had been lost in translation and the guy had got a hold of the wrong end of the stick – or the knife on that occasion!

The other incident was more of a personal one. I was reflecting on my first season and had been pleased with how I had done.

The family had also settled into their new surroundings in Stirling. Everything in the Drinkell garden looked rosy.

I had finished the season as the top scorer in the Scottish top flight and had walked away with the Golden Boot. I had also played a major part in getting Rangers back on the rails.

The end of the season was once again full of tabloid speculations about possible big-summer transfer targets. That was something you had to get used to at a club like Rangers. We had just won the league and the guessing games had already begun as to who Souness would sign next. The names mentioned were like a 'Who's Who' of European football.

I remember I was sitting at the bar of our Tel Aviv hotel when Boersma came up and joined me for a beer. He began talking about all the speculation and said: 'At least you won't be affected. The way you have played this season there is no chance of another striker coming in and taking your place.'

That gave me a wee boost because Phil was a key member of the manager's staff and I headed into our summer break absolutely over the moon, looking to come back and build on my first season's success.

15

ENGLAND NOT TO B

I WAS happy with my lot at the end of my debut campaign with Rangers. I had played well and even felt I had an outside chance of an England call-up. That summer the Rous Cup, an old end-of-season international tournament, was to be played at Hampden and Wembley. England, Scotland and Chile were the teams in the competition and I thought there was a possibility of a call-up. Why not?

I was playing as well as ever. I also felt it was a case of now or never. I had finished top scorer in Scotland, picked up the Golden Boot and helped fire Rangers to a League and Skol Cup double. I had a decent case for inclusion, especially as a host of big names had pulled out.

I knew if Gary Lineker, Peter Beardsley and Alan Smith had been available then I probably wouldn't have got a sniff but they weren't and I thought the door could be forced open.

The problem was Sir Bobby Robson was national coach and he brought in the former Wimbledon coach Don Howe to assist him. That led to England calling up a number of Howe's old boys, like Dennis Wise and John Fashanu. On top of that, Steve Bull of Wolves also got the shout.

I couldn't believe guys like that were being named in the England squad and I wasn't even being quoted.

I felt that was my only chance to play for my country and it had been well and truly crushed. It was a big regret but I don't think I could have done any more. I also think the FA and Robson didn't want to pick too many players from Rangers because it was seen as a slight on the English game. There was still a bit of jealousy from the big English clubs because Rangers were able to buy their top players.

They already had Gary Stevens, Trevor Steven, Terry Butcher and Chris Woods and didn't want to upset the big English clubs by ignoring the home-based players.

The perfect example, for me, was Mark Walters. When he was at Rangers he was playing as well as anybody in British football but still couldn't even get into that Rous Cup squad.

Wise came in from the backwater of Wimbledon while Mark had been winning titles, lifting cups, playing in Europe and scoring goals in the Old Firm matches. It was a joke Wise got in ahead of Mark.

Personally, it was always a dream to play for England but I had to accept that it was something that was never going to happen.

In the end, the nearest I got to wearing the three lions was my call-up for the B squad when I was at Norwich. The match was against the full Malta team.

I was named in the squad along with a few of my Norwich team mates, Steve Bruce, who was the captain, and Ian Crooks. I think the FA felt compelled to give Norwich some recognition because we had been flying high in the top flight.

So I made the trip but my dream quickly turned into a nightmare. I went away really excited and returned wishing I had stayed in the house. It had been a complete waste of time.

I sat on the bench for the entire game. Graham Taylor was in charge for that trip and cheesed me right off. It was one of those friendly games where you could make as many changes as you liked, but he got a bit of a scare when Malta scored.

We eventually recovered and got ourselves back in front but Taylor wanted to keep things tight and didn't want to make too many changes in case we let Malta back in again.

Taylor was keen to get a result because he felt it would boost his own England managerial prospects. That proved to be the case a few years later when he did get the job.

That night he tried to shut up shop and there were four or five of us, including Terry Fenwick, who spent the entire night sitting picking splinters from our behinds on the bench.

It was such a waste of time. Would it have killed Taylor if he had put us all on for 60 seconds? I remember on the flight back I was so angry I could have swung at Taylor. He came back really smug, thinking he had achieved something with the win. Was it really a big thing to beat Malta?

16

THREE INTO TWO
IS A MO-GO!

I HAD a great summer. I took the family to Florida and recharged the batteries. I felt great and was looking forward to coming back and kicking on from my first season.

It was back out to Il Ciocco for pre-season again. This time I was determined to come back in one piece. The whole team gathered at 5am at one of the airport hotels for our early morning flight to Italy. It was then the story broke that Rangers had pulled off one of the most controversial signings of all time. Rangers had paid big money for their first high-profile Roman Catholic when they signed Maurice Johnston. That, of course, had been the big secret Graeme Souness had alluded to after the Scottish Cup final.

The signing was even more remarkable because it looked like Johnston had been heading back to Celtic. He had posed in a Celtic top and scarf just weeks before the cup final and here he was six or seven weeks later set to become a Rangers player.

The press conference was called for Ibrox later that day and that allowed us to fly out to Italy and get away from the media circus, which was about to spin into an almighty hurricane.

To most of us the signing was a complete shock, but I think some of Mo's Scotland team mates, like Ally McCoist, had known about it but they hadn't uttered a word to any of the rest of us.

Mo was viewed as another quality player who was being added to the squad. It was a typical Souness signing.

He had snared the likes of Terry Butcher and Richard Gough but the capture of Johnston was one of the biggest Scottish football stories of all time. Souness had previously tried to break the mould when he had attempted to sign the Republic of Ireland midfielder Ray Houghton, who was actually Glasgow-born. He would have been the first modern-day Catholic player to come to Rangers had he not had second thoughts and decided to join Liverpool.

Souness, though, was determined to bring the whole religious thing to a head and the signing of Johnston allowed him to do just that. The transfer also showed the financial muscle Rangers had, compared with their competitors north or south of the border. Souness had signed two proven internationalists in Mo and Trevor Steven while Celtic had, no disrespect, only managed to add Tommy Coyne and Mike Galloway. That showed the differing ambitions of Rangers and Celtic during that period. There had been a big gap in quality the previous season and now that was about to widen. That was the case and would set the trend for the next eight seasons as Rangers powered ahead of their Old Firm rivals.

I wasn't in the slightest bit interested or worried about the religious side of Johnston's signing; as I said before, religion was never a big thing for me. I was more interested in how it was going to affect my position at Rangers. I have to say I initially felt a little deflated when I heard the news. How will that affect me? Will it be McCoist and Johnston or will I get my chance? How will the manager fit us all in? These were questions that were spinning around my head.

There had even been suggestions that Souness might play all three of us because Ray Wilkins was still recovering from his end-of-season operation.

This went on for a few days but I knew the best thing I could do was to get my head down and show everybody that I was the man for the job. I had finished the season as top scorer and I felt I could do it again.

The manager stayed back in Scotland for the signing and a couple of days later he and Mo joined us in Italy. Not to be outdone the pair flew into our training camp by helicopter. That was Souness all over. He always did everything in style.

The gaffer held a team meeting that afternoon. Everybody was there apart from Mo. As far as he was concerned he had signed Mo because he was going to improve our squad and our own chances, as a team, of being more successful. Then the manager said: 'If anybody has a problem with us signing Mo then you can come and see me later.' Rumour has it that one of our more experienced players went to see Souness about it but nobody said anything within the dressing room.

None of us realised the madness the signing had caused back home. Looking back I still can't understand the furore that surrounded the move. Some of my friends were big Rangers fans and were upset by the signing but that was something I couldn't fathom because I thought there had been plenty of other Catholic players for Rangers in the past, although they hadn't been as high-profile as Mo.

I don't think any of the squad had a problem with the fact that Mo was a Catholic but he had certainly upset one or two with the way he had gone about his business in the past.

He had curried favour with Celtic by posing with the strip weeks before and suddenly we had come in and offered him a few more shillings and he had jumped the dyke without as much as a second look.

Remember when he had played for Celtic he was one of the first to kiss the badge in the Old Firm games and now suddenly he wanted to be on your side. He always wanted to be in the middle of things. You just had to accept that was the way Mo was.

The whole thing just spun out of all control and a lot of it was fanned by Mo himself. He always liked to court controversy and be the centre of attention.

Three months on when things started to die down a bit Mo was still pitching up at Ibrox with three bodyguards. It was all a bit over the top but that was Mo.

That signing changed everything, including the feel-good factor within the squad. It began to impact on everybody, and even affected our daily routines. It got that bad we weren't even allowed to park our cars on the street. Instead we had to drive them into the stadium and leave them trackside. Then before we could go home we had to have them checked by police and security to make sure there weren't any bombs or explosives attached.

Once we got the all-clear, the gates would open and we would have to speed out in some sort of well-synchronised army manoeuvre.

That initial period, though, after we came back from Il Ciocco was the worst. Fans were burning their scarves and throwing their season tickets at the front door.

There may also have been death threats directed at Souness and Mo although I don't think there was anything aimed at the rest of us. But there weren't any risks being taken and security was stepped up wherever we went.

We had police out-riders with the team bus and when we arrived we had more security than a teenage chart-topping band. It was so over the top.

Mo, to be fair, did take a lot of stick everywhere he went, but to his credit he took it all in his stride. Whether it was just arrogance or he was really thick skinned I don't know. Certainly nobody in Glasgow was going to hold the door open for him, apart from maybe his minders. It was going to be difficult for him. He knew he would get hassle wherever he went in the city. That was part of the reason why he decided to stay with Souness in Edinburgh, just to keep himself out of the firing line.

The 'be all and end all' for me was that Mo was a very good player although I was still anxious to find out if I was going to start alongside him or if it was going to be Mo and Ally. The first indication came in our final pre-season game against Tottenham.

Wilkins was fit again and Souness had to put his strongest team out ahead of the start of our SPL campaign. He started with Mo and Ally and I wondered where that would leave me.

I still felt I had done well in pre-season. I had nicked a couple of goals and had linked up well with Mo, while Coisty had played just behind us. I was the top scorer the previous season so there was no reason why I shouldn't have been given one of the starting jerseys.

We kicked things off in the Skol Cup with a convincing win against Arbroath, although I was left on the bench again. My case wasn't helped when Coisty grabbed a hat-trick.

Souness went with Mo and Ally for the next two SPL games against St Mirren and Hibs. We lost both so I was hoping I would finally get my chance. It came in the next round of the Skol Cup against Morton at Cappielow. I remember it was an awful night. It wasn't the greatest of games but we did enough to sneak through.

That trip was followed by a visit to Parkhead on the Saturday. I fully expected the manager to revert back to Johnston and Coisty but he stuck by me. All I remember was Coisty's lip dropping when he heard he wasn't starting.

The match was all about Mo and his return to Parkhead as a Rangers player. That was at the height of his troubles. It would have been easier to break into Buckingham Palace than get close to Mo that day. I was playing alongside him and I was waiting for a couple of security guards to stand between us before we took the kick-off. All joking aside, though, it must have been a really frightening experience for Mo knowing he was hated by the Celtic fans and despised by a large section of the Rangers support. There had been a lot of threats and you just don't know what some idiots out there are capable of. I certainly don't think I could ever have put my family or myself in that position.

We knew that the slightest thing on the pitch could spark trouble off it. We were also aware we had to set an example on the pitch because the Old Firm game was still very much in the public eye. It was only a couple of years after the Butcher, Chris Woods,

Graham Roberts and Frank McAvennie court case. We knew the police were waiting to step in if any of us stepped out of line and we were warned not to get involved or to provoke the Celtic fans in any way.

It was the usual warm-up of a cigarette in the toilet although I did feel under a bit more pressure that day, but it was still nowhere near as much as my strike partner. Personally, I knew I had to go out and do well because Ally was waiting in the wings.

Mo was your usual happy-go-lucky sort of guy but that day you could see he was really nervous. It was no wonder. It must have been really frightening and intimidating for him. He was walking into the lion's den.

Fortunately, when the whistle went we were able to focus on the football. We didn't play brilliantly but put on a workman-like performance and managed to come away with a point. Butcher got the goal.

It was a big result because it was our first point of the season and got us up and running. It was also a massive landmark that Mo was able to finally put behind him. He had now been back at Parkhead and faced all the ill-feeling and hatred that was going to come his way. The next time he knew it wouldn't be as bad. I was delighted with the work and effort I had put in but I was also aware I still hadn't scored.

I then found myself back at square one a couple of days later when I was left on the bench for the midweek Skol Cup visit to Hamilton. That game was, probably, the beginning of the end of my Rangers career.

It was the night I took the decision, for the one and only time in my professional career, to refuse to take to the field. It all stemmed from the fact Souness had reverted back to the Johnston and McCoist partnership. I was gutted because I felt I had led the line well at Parkhead and wanted the chance to play against Accies, who we were expected to put a few goals past. It was a real kick in the teeth.

Scotland were due to play a World Cup qualifier in Yugoslavia that weekend. I remember Souness and Mo talking discreetly on the team coach on the way to the Accies game. The conversation was along the lines of substituting Mo during the game so they could tell the Scottish Football Association that he wouldn't be fit enough for the up-coming international.

Hearing that was the straw that broke the camel's back. I was disappointed enough I wasn't playing but then I had to listen to the pair of them concocting this cover-up story. It left me furious. I felt used but I decided to bite my lip and take my place on the bench.

I still remember the match as if it was yesterday. Souness was up in the stands, serving a touchline ban, but he was in constant contact with Phil Boersma, via walkie-talkie.

We eased through the match thanks to a couple of goals from Mark Walters and another from Steven. We got to about the hour mark and I was sitting on the bench, at the side of the dugout, when I heard Souness telling Boersma to take Mo off.

I was told to go and warm up and so I went for a quick run, as Phil shouted to Mo: 'We are taking you off in five minutes.' Mo shouted back: 'I'm not ready yet,' and 'Just leave it for now.' He hadn't scored yet and wanted to stay on because he fancied his chances of grabbing a goal against an Accies team who were already well beaten.

I just shook my head in disbelief and sat down again. A couple of minutes later Souness was back on the walkie-talkie to Phil, asking him why he had not taken Mo off yet. Phil told me to get warmed up again but Mo refused to budge. He kept asking for another five minutes. This went on until we hit the last 10 minutes when I decided enough was enough.

For me, it was as if Mo was calling the shots because he knew Souness was banned from the dugout and he could maybe get a bit more leeway. I was surprised because the manager had always ruled things with an iron fist. I was left absolutely fuming. I wasn't prepared to sit there like a puppet and jump when Johnston decided. So I stood up, walked along the track and headed back into the dressing room.

I stood in there and contemplated what to do next. I was totally brassed off with what I had just witnessed. I toyed with the idea of getting changed but I knew that would have been wrong and I decided to return to the away dugout, although I did wait until seconds before the referee was due to blow his whistle. I would never have reacted like that if the result had been in doubt, but the result was never in question and I felt I had to make a stand.

When I returned Phil was standing there totally exasperated and snapped: 'Where the hell have you been? We needed you to go on.' I just looked at him and said: 'I couldn't go on because I had suddenly developed the runs and didn't feel right.' He gave me the eyes as if to say you are pulling a fast one. He wasn't far wrong!

After the game, Souness came into the changing room and also gave me one of those knowing looks. I think he knew where I was coming from. He must have understood my frustrations because he wasn't angry or annoyed. He didn't even say anything about it. I didn't want to do it because I loved pulling on the Rangers jersey but I felt I had to stand up for myself. I wasn't prepared to be walked all over.

In the end, my decision not to play didn't really make any difference because Rangers still pulled Mo out of that Scotland squad. The manager claimed Mo had picked up a knock and was unlikely to play for Scotland – and he didn't.

I started to get the feeling Souness was starting to lean towards Coisty and Johnston and I wasn't prepared to sit about and let that happen. I wasn't helped by a lot of the press around that period because Johnston and Coisty were the first-choice Scotland partnership and always seemed to be favoured. The fans, to their credit, were still as good as gold but the media definitely started to turn. It might have had something to do with Souness's reputation with some sections of the press, who were just queuing up to have a go at him.

They felt that by not playing Mo and Coisty every week – and whenever he chose to play me he broke up their partnership – he was somehow doing the Scotland team a disservice.

The problem was that Rangers were doing well and it was hard to knock Souness so they had to find other ways to have a pop at him.

After the international break I was back in the starting XI for the top-of-the-table clash with Aberdeen. I was upfront with Mo in a partnership which worked well and was rubber-stamped by the wee man scoring his first competitive goal for Rangers in our 1–0 victory. He was as happy as Larry because it was a big moment in a decisive game.

When he scored there was a massive cheer then things went quiet because the crowd suddenly realised it was Mo who had netted. It was quite muted after that but at least it was a first step towards Mo winning the Rangers support over. I, like Coisty, was suspended for our European Cup first-leg clash with Bayern Munich, as a result of our misdemeanours from the previous season.

It was frustrating because Bayern were a top team and I really wanted to test myself at that level. The manager had limited striking options so decided to tread carefully and went with Mo and a five-man midfield. He didn't want to open up and leave the tie stone dead because Bayern had the quality in their ranks to do some serious damage. Unfortunately that proved to be the case, as they thumped us 3–1. Mark Walters got our goal from the penalty spot but efforts from Ludwig Kögl, Olaf Thon and Klaus Augenthaler had left them in total command ahead of the return in Munich.

I felt confident I would keep my place in the SPL but Coisty came back in and scored three goals in our next two games against Dundee and Dunfermline. That put him back in pole position to partner Mo.

I'd played against the big teams and done well and then Coisty came in against the lesser teams and grabbed all the headlines. I was left thinking, 'How is the manager going to drop Ally now?' It was starting to weigh heavily on my mind and so I decided to go and see Souness about the situation. I chapped the door and went in and asked where I fitted into his plans.

He sat me down and assured me I still had a major part to play.

He told me he wanted to rotate all three of his strikers over the course of the season. That took me back because I had never come across the rotation system in all my time in football. I had always been the No. 9 for Grimsby, Norwich and Rangers and when I had been fit I played. But Souness brought in this pioneering, new approach which most top teams now operate. You are lucky to see a club who don't have at least four top strikers vying for one or two places.

Souness said: 'Kev, you still have a big part to play and you will be my main striker for the games against Celtic, Aberdeen, Dundee United and Hearts. I need your physical presence for those matches. I know you can handle yourself and rough them up.' He said for the other games Mo and Ally will play because it suits their games better.

It put me in an awkward situation because I just couldn't get my head around not playing every week. Looking back, it is now a big regret because it is now part and parcel of football. You don't see Fernando Torres or Wayne Rooney playing every game but that is the way the game has changed.

Souness deserves a lot of credit for introducing it, even though at the time I thought he was wrong. Looking back I know now I should have just sat tight, kept my mouth shut and played my part when called upon. I would probably have still been involved in 70 per cent of the games and still have played a major part in Rangers' future successes.

But I didn't quite see it that way. I left his office still wondering what was going to happen and felt even more uncertain about my future.

Souness had told me I would play in all the big games and so I expected to start in the European Cup return against Bayern Munich. Everybody in the squad expected me to play because I was back from suspension and all the press interviews had been about how I would be the perfect foil for Mo. We might have been 3–1 down but we were going out there to be positive and to save the tie. Or so I thought!

When Souness announced his team Mo was named as the sole striker. The likes of Richard Gough and Terry Butcher were absolutely livid with the manager's decision but there was no point in arguing or confronting Souness because there was only ever going to be one winner.

The only time I had seen somebody challenge the manager about his team selection was a few weeks earlier when Ray Wilkins tried to intervene on Lindsay Hamilton's behalf.

Big Lindsay was meant to be playing in the Skol Cup against Arbroath because Woods had been ruled out. So in the afternoon we went across to the Bellahouston Hotel for a light bite and an afternoon sleep.

It was Lindsay's big day. He had arranged tickets for all his family and friends but Souness ended up pulling a rabbit out the hat. When all the boys made their way back across from the hotel we saw Walter out on the pitch warming up this goalkeeper and it emerged it was the Israeli international, Bonni Ginzburg. He had flown in via London because he needed to get his work permit before he arrived. He was thrown right into the team, even though there was no real need because Lindsay could have quite easily covered for that game.

Lindsay was left absolutely crushed. He saw his chance to make a rare start snatched from his grasp. It was even more embarrassing for him because he had bought all these tickets for his family and friends because he thought he would be playing. They were turning up to see Ginzburg make his debut.

Ray saw Lindsay was absolutely devastated and went to see the manager to argue his case. He told Souness the team were unhappy with his decision to play Ginzburg and we all felt Lindsay should be given his chance.

Souness didn't even think twice about it. I think he told Ray to f*** off and that team selection had absolutely nothing to do with him or us.

So I knew that night in Munich there was no chance of Souness changing his mind, regardless of what my team mates said or did.

147

I just had to accept it. I did get off the bench for the last 20 minutes, as we tried to open up a bit, but the manager was still more concerned about trying to come away with a face-saving draw than trying to win the game. We needed to score three goals to go through but Souness never really went for it. All the players flew out to Germany looking to have a go but the manager appeared to have other ideas.

Souness knew I wasn't happy after the match. I also don't know if something was already in the offing with regards my own future. I flew home angry but I didn't bother saying anything that night. I eventually got back to the house about three am in the morning. I had a lot to sleep on.

17

SENT TO COVENTRY

THE next thing I knew the phone was ringing at 8.30am. I had hardly been in bed for five hours when Andrea came up the stairs and told me Graeme Souness was on the phone. I was still half asleep. I thought I was still having a bad dream when I picked up the receiver and heard what Souness had to say. He told me Coventry City had made an offer which was acceptable to the board and it was now up to me to decide. I was stunned and said: 'I will come and speak to you.' Souness said something along the lines of there is no need. 'Just get your agent and see what Coventry have to offer.'

I got John Mac on the case with Coventry and then headed to Ibrox to speak to Souness face to face. I was almost in his office as much as I was in his first team over those previous couple of weeks.

He explained Coventry had been trying to get me for weeks and he had even increased his valuation to try and scare them off but they had come back in and matched it.

It was a good offer on the table and it was also a chance for Rangers to claw some of the money back they had spent that summer on Mo Johnston and Trevor Steven. It was a good opportunity for them to balance the books.

The frustrating thing for me was that Aston Villa, Manchester City and Norwich were all keen to sign me but none of them, apart from Coventry, had matched Rangers' demands.

If it had been today, in the time of Bosman, then I would have been able to go and speak to them all and then taken the deal that suited me best. I couldn't speak to anyone unless I was given permission by Rangers and the only club they allowed me to talk to was Coventry.

I eventually went down to talk to the Sky Blues but I have to admit I headed down to the Midlands with some reluctance. Souness didn't say he didn't want me to go, but, at the same time, he had opened the door to my possible exit.

All he said was: 'Go off and speak to them and see if you can look after your family. You have done really well for us but they are keen to get you, so go and listen to what they have to say. It is not all about football. It is a short career and you have to look after yourself and your family.'

Souness revealed he had been in a similar situation when he was at Liverpool. He felt he was one of the best midfielders in the world after Liverpool had just lifted the European Cup when he got a phone call from his chairman to come in and have a chat with him.

He thought he was going in to get a big wage rise and a new five-year contract but when he walked in he was told Liverpool had accepted an offer from Sampdoria and he was being sold. Souness told me he couldn't believe it because he felt he was one of the best players in the world and didn't think Liverpool would be the same team without him.

He said: 'It happens in football. Just go and do what is best for you and your family.'

Looking back now, I think Souness had already set the ball in motion and had been looking to cash in on me. He had bolstered the squad by signing Mo and had also gone out and signed Davie Dodds. He was another experienced Scottish international who we didn't really need because we already had Mo, Ally and myself. The previous season we had basically won the league with just Coisty and myself. Maybe he needed somebody, like Dodds, who would come in and play the odd game without rocking the boat too much. He knew I wasn't going to accept that. I suppose Souness was only doing his best for Rangers. He had spent a fair bit of money and was trying to balance the books.

Souness also knew my stock was high after finishing that first season as top scorer, but on the down side I was nearing 30 and my value was likely to drop. So, from a Rangers point of view, it probably made sense for them to cash in on me. David Murray was now in charge of the purse strings and I am sure he would have seen this as a good deal.

There was certainly a lot more competition for the striking positions. I was surprised by the signing of Dodds, from our rivals Aberdeen. To be fair, the big man still gave me one of the biggest dressing room laughs of my time at Ibrox.

He pitched up at Ibrox in this grey porter's suit and everybody could see it was miles too short for him. The trousers were halfway up his legs. He just looked like a total state.

He left his stuff on his peg when he went for his medical. Ian Durrant grabbed his gear, cut it up and tied it into knots, so there was very little chance of big Davie wearing it ever again. To be fair, Ian had done him a favour.

The story eventually ended up in the press that the boys had laughed at the state of Davie's clothes when he had first arrived. It then came out that he had been at the hotel but had forgotten to take his suit. He only had the clothes he was wearing, jeans and casual clothes. Davie was then told about the Ibrox dress code and in a panic he had borrowed a suit from the hotel porter.

The funny thing was that it was me that got it in the neck over that story. I was in Littlewoods a week or so later and this woman came up to me and asked: 'Are you Kevin Drinkell?' She introduced herself as the porter's wife and then started giving me a very public dressing down for slaughtering her husband's clothes in the press. She insisted it had been an expensive suit and who were we (the Rangers players) to rubbish her man's clothes?

I told her I had nothing to do with the dressing-room prank or for leaking the story to the newspapers but she was having none of it. As far as she was concerned I was the main culprit and I

151

had to stand there in the middle of this high-street shop, red-faced, as 'Mrs Porter' let off some steam.

I eventually agreed to fly down to Birmingham airport to meet with the Coventry City manager John 'Snozz' Sillett and his assistant George Curtis. My agent had already spoken to them and I knew the rough ball-park figures that were on offer.

We sat down and had a chat. My agent and I had agreed beforehand to try and keep pushing up the financial side of things. Their initial offer was actually very good and better than I was on at Rangers but we weren't going to jump into anything. Sillett then upped his offer from a two-year deal to three-and-a-half and also pushed up the money. The overall package was just too good to turn down.

Coventry were an established English top-flight club and had won the FA Cup a couple of years before, so the potential was certainly there for the club to move forward. Sillett also sold Coventry to me on the fact he wanted to transform the club into one of the top six or eight clubs in the country.

He had signed David Speedie from Chelsea just after the cup win and had famously said: 'Coventry City have shopped at Woolworths for far too long, from now on we're shopping at Harrods.'

He was desperately trying to take the club to the next level and I was seen as another one of those marquee signings. The club had agreed to make me their record signing and, all in all, including the tax, I was told my transfer was just under the £1 million mark. They wanted me to get the goals and push them towards the European places.

I half agreed to the move. I had looked at Coventry's recent history and although they were an established side they hadn't had anyone who had scored 20 goals in a season for them for years. I felt I could be the missing piece in the jigsaw. It was only later I realised why nobody had hit double figures.

I had been top scorer at Grimsby, Norwich and Rangers and I felt I could go down to Highfield Road and keep the goals flying in. It was a chance to get back to England and to bring a bit of stability to the family. That contract would also see me out until I was 33. It made a lot of sense to take it and so I shook hands with Sillett and agreed the deal.

I remember going back to the airport in Sillett's car and he had one of those early hands-free phones. He said he had to ring Souness to tell him what was happening. I said, 'Before you speak to him can you give me a bit of time to see if I can squeeze a few more pounds out of Rangers before I come down?'

Souness came on to the phone and asked how the Coventry boss had got on? Sillett said: 'I don't think we are too far away but Kev has to come back and see you about a couple of things.'

Souness quick as a flash said: 'I know Kevin is in the car. You can tell him he isn't getting another penny out of Rangers. If he wants more money then it will need to come from Coventry.' We all had a wee giggle about it all and I ended up heading back to Glasgow for the Hearts game on the Saturday. I had to laugh when I picked up the paper that morning because there was a double-page spread with Souness telling the fans that I didn't have to go although it didn't exactly say he was ready to give me a new deal either.

Terry Butcher and Chris Woods ended up giving me a lift to Ibrox for the Hearts game. They both asked how I had got on and if I was going to Coventry. I told them the deal was just about done. They were surprised and both questioned my decision.

They thought I would be better staying with Rangers but when I told them that I would be doubling my salary and I was also being given the added security of a three-and-a-half year contract they were surprised. They knew it was too good an offer to turn down. They were taken aback and could understand my reasons for accepting Coventry's offer.

When I arrived at Ibrox for the final time, the fans were, once again, brilliant to me, as they have been throughout my time in Scotland.

I remember some of them coming up to me and asking me not to go because Rangers still needed me. Even at that point, I was still swaying whether or not Coventry was the right move for me.

I was having second thoughts and at the same time still trying to weigh everything up. The family were all settled and loved it in Scotland but I had to think about the long term.

I wasn't playing every week and I also had to look at the contractual side of things. I only had a year left on my Rangers deal and what would happen to me at the end of the season?

Coventry had offered me more money than I had been on at Rangers and were also offering the security of a three-and-a-half year contract, which I knew was going to be my final big pay-day.

I spoke to Andrea and I think in the end I convinced myself I was doing the right thing and was looking after my family into the bargain.

Souness asked me if I would go on the bench for the Hearts game but I didn't feel right. My head was all over the place. I didn't know whether I was coming or going. I went and had one final chat with Souness on the Monday and he tipped things in Coventry's favour when he agreed to give me a percentage of the profit they had made on me. I then took my boots and gear, said my farewells and brought down the curtain on my short but enjoyable Rangers career.

Looking back, I have to admit, with the aid of hindsight, I was far too hasty in leaving Rangers. I should have at least seen out that second season. I might not have played every week but at least I would have been part of another title-winning side. Who knows, I might have got another contract beyond that. But as people say, hindsight is a wonderful thing and at the end of the day you stand and fall by the decisions you make.

If there was a shortfall in my career I should have left Grimsby far earlier than I did. I waited until I was 25 to go to Norwich and that move should have happened when I was 22 or 23. If I had done that then I could have been at a big club like Rangers when I was 25 or 26 rather than making the move when I was touching 30. That is my one disappointment. I think if I had done that, it would have helped me force open the England door.

18

I GUESS THAT'S WHY THEY CALL IT THE SKY BLUES

I WOULD have loved to have started my Coventry City career on the right footing but I was toiling before I had even put pen to paper. For some reason my right hip had started to play up. I remember being sent on my own for my medical. I had to travel to this local GP's surgery to get the once over. I went in to see the doctor and he told me to lie on the bed. He checked my blood pressure and listened to my heart and chest. Everything was fine and then he pulled up my right leg, trying to get the circular movement of the joint, but there wasn't much flexibility at all. I wondered if that might scupper the deal or at the very least lead to a second opinion but the doctor, rather surprisingly, gave me the all-clear. I expected Coventry to cover every possible base to protect their near £1 million investment, but they didn't seem to be bothered in the slightest. That medical was nowhere near as stringent as top players have to go through today. I went back to the club, signed my contract and my potential hip problem was never mentioned again, never mind questioned.

After the formalities were out of the way I had to turn my attentions to a quickfire debut, which, rather bizarrely, was a midweek Littlewoods Cup encounter against Grimsby. It is strange how these things work. I was straight in against my hometown team. It also gave the Drinkell family, including my parents and my brothers, the chance to come and see my Coventry debut. I really appreciated that because Andrea and the kids were still up in Scotland. My mum and dad hadn't been able to see me play as often as they would have liked when I was at Rangers but now I was a bit closer to home.

It was a difficult one for my family because they were all born and bred Grimsby fans although they also wanted to see me do well. They had also been hurt when the Grimsby fans had booed me when I returned for that last game with Norwich. That really cut them to the core because they knew I loved Grimsby and gave everything every time I had pulled on their shirt.

The game itself wasn't exactly the one I would have picked to kick off my new career. Coventry might have been the English top-flight side but we weren't exactly favourites going into that second leg. Grimsby had won the first leg 3–1 at Blundell Park and so we were up against it going into the Highfield Road return. So there was no pressure on the new boy! I hadn't even kicked a ball and already, as the club's record signing, the expectations were being heaped on my shoulders.

Thankfully I didn't need to worry for too long. In fact I couldn't have wished for a better start. Early in the first half the ball dropped behind me, around the penalty spot. I just swung at it and produced an acrobatic, overhead kick to fire us into the lead. Who said my right hip lacked mobility? That settled the team down nicely and we went on to win the game 3–0. That was enough to avoid an upset and put us through 4–3 on aggregate. Everyone in the Drinkell family was delighted – even though Grimsby were out of the cup.

My league bow in Sky Blue came against one of my old admirers – Alex Ferguson's Manchester United. The game was at Highfield Road but United had far too much quality for us and thrashed us 4–1. The one ray of light for me was the fact I grabbed our goal.

The games were coming thick and fast and the following midweek we were back in Littlewoods Cup action. This time we were away to Queen's Park Rangers at Loftus Road. We managed to squeeze through by the odd goal in three with Greg Downs and myself getting on the scoresheet. I had scored three early goals and was delighted with the flying start I had made at Coventry.

We also started to show a bit more promise as a team. We beat Liverpool at Anfield, through a Cyrille Regis goal. That was a big win and boosted the early-season confidence. Things kept rolling for us when I grabbed the only goal on the counter in our home win against Southampton. It wasn't a classic but they all count.

That win took us up to seventh in the table but then we lost the Midlands derby at Aston Villa 4–1.

We continued to make good progress in the Littlewoods Cup, when big Cyrille netted the winner to help us beat Manchester City at Maine Road. That took us into the semi-final. Suddenly everybody in Sky Blue was dreaming of a Wembley return.

The cup run was an added bonus but for the manager, John Sillett, the priority was trying to make strides in the league. The return of another of my former employers saw Cyrille continue his hot run, as he shot down Norwich, to take us up to the dizzy heights of sixth.

It had been a couple of games since I had scored but the team were still heading in the right direction. I was pleased but I knew it was still early in the season and the team and I still had a lot of work to do.

Unfortunately that was where my fortunes, and those of the team, nose-dived.

Looking back, Cyrille's scoring run didn't help my situation. I was delighted for Cyrille because he was a great player and a top professional. I was also pleased the team were doing well. For me, my team's success always came before any personal gain.

Cyrille's flying start to the season, though, did leave the manager with a major predicament. Sillett had brought me in as Cyrille's replacement because he thought Cyrille's legs were beginning to go. That didn't go down well in the dressing room or on the terraces. That was understandable because Cyrille had been a great performer for Coventry and deserved his legendary status, but the manager felt his best days were behind him. He was adamant the team needed to move on and to do that they had to replace Cyrille.

Unfortunately for me, I was the man who had been brought in to succeed Regis. It could have been anybody including Gary Lineker, Alan Shearer or Wayne Rooney and I still think the fans would have given them a hard time, too. I wasn't bothered about it because I respected the loyalty and affection they showed towards big Cyrille but, at the same time, it wasn't going to deter me from doing my best for Coventry City. I still felt I could go out and get into double figures and help the team on to greater things. I had been a fans' favourite at Grimsby, Norwich and Rangers and felt confident I could win over the Coventry faithful as well.

I did, however, find it a little more difficult to integrate in the Highfield Road dressing room than I did at any of my previous clubs. Most dressing rooms are quite welcoming but there were some people, for whatever reason, who refused to give me a fair crack at things. Don't get me wrong; I don't want to tar everybody with the same brush because there were some top guys at Coventry who did everything they could to help me and my family to settle. I got on well with the likes of Steve Ogrizovic, Downs and Dave Smith, who lived near us. Dave was a young lad who I tried to give a helping hand to. He was a player with a promising future. That was shown when he got his England under-21 call-up.

These guys and a few others were great but it was apparent from the day I walked in the door that they were averse to change of any kind. The club had done brilliantly to win the FA Cup in 1987 and that team, quite rightly, will go down as one of the greatest in Coventry's history. Those players and the management team of Sillett and George Curtis have, quite rightly, guaranteed themselves legendary status.

I take my hat off to every single one of them because I wished I had achieved that sort of success in my time with the Sky Blues. I certainly hoped that would be the case but for a variety of reasons I was never going to hit those extraordinary heights.

For me, the main reason why we struggled to move on as team was because too many of the survivors from that FA Cup team were living on past glories. A lot of those guys were stuck in a bit of a time warp. Guys like Trevor Peake, Brian Borrows, Brian Kilcline and Regis had been together for five or six years and were keen to see the status quo maintained. I might have been a team mate but I never really felt part of things. I was the outsider and it was there for all to see, even down to small things like the seats for the coach journeys to away games. I would climb on and jump in a seat only to be told you can't sit there because that is so and so's. The manager didn't exactly help. He would be bang in the middle of things, arranging his card school with all his old boys. He had this briefcase he would carry with him everywhere; as soon as he got on the bus he would stick it on the table and go through the same old routine. He would take out his sandwiches and apple and they would be quickly followed by the playing cards. I would say it was pretty much a closed shop. I found it very difficult to integrate. I just didn't feel welcome.

I don't know if that was the way the Coventry squad were to everyone or if it was a deliberate ploy to try and freeze me out. I don't think I will ever know.

I thought things might improve when Andrea and the kids came down. This time I didn't have the same troubles I had in Scotland trying to find a new home. I had also been relatively lucky up the road because there had been a guy who had wanted to buy my house in Stirling before I had even thought about leaving Rangers. So getting my house sold was a case of one phone call and it was gone. It all happened really quickly and that quick sale probably came back to haunt me. A few months later, when I wasn't really settled, it might have given me a get-out if I still had the house in Stirling. I didn't have that escape route and within weeks everything was done and dusted and we had moved into our new home in the lovely town of Kenilworth.

I remember I picked Andrea and the girls up at Birmingham

Airport. As Andrea got in the car she said: 'There's something wrong, isn't there?'

I didn't say anything and tried to change the subject but she knew by my face that something wasn't right. I tried to fob her off by saying everything was fine because I didn't want to tell her and the girls I had made a massive mistake, just hours after I had asked them to leave a place they loved and were settled in. I didn't want them to start their new life on a downer. I maintained everything was fine but Andrea knew from that day I had made a mistake signing for Coventry.

It wasn't as if I had been a disaster because I had started pretty well at Highfield Road but I always felt like I was on the fringes. One or two of the guys like big 'Oggy' knew how I was feeling. He along with Downs invited Andrea and me out with their wives, to try and help us settle, but it seemed to me that some of the others would have preferred to see me pack my bags and move on. Even Andrea noticed it when she finally came to Highfield Road for an early game. The players' lounge was in a cellar under the main stand. As you walked in everybody looked at you as you came down the steps. She got the feeling we weren't wanted and it was that bad she never set foot in that lounge again.

I don't know if the players liked the way it had been and didn't want it to change or it was some form of jealousy. They had won the cup but I was a £1 million player and probably earning better wages than the rest of them. I just wonder if that was the issue or not.

I was disappointed because together I felt we had potential. There was no doubt Rangers had a far better quality of player but Coventry had their own strengths. They had big Kilcline at the back, who liked to play alongside Peake. Brian was the rugged centre half while Trevor was the sweeper who tidied up behind.

They had Brian Borrows at right back for about 10 years and he was a good player who would get up and down the pitch. They had this defensive group, with Oggy between the sticks, along with guys like Micky Gynn. This was their team and they wanted to be left alone to get on with it. They had a system that worked for them and it required a certain type of personnel. They needed Regis, not Kevin Drinkell.

There was also a lot of pressure on Sillett because he had paid so much money to bring me in. In one sense he wanted it to work but in another he probably wished Cyrille had been a couple of years younger and had been able to carry on. When I did get the nod ahead of Regis my team mates didn't like that and neither did some of the fans. I still got on really well with Cyrille and I would like to think we had a mutual respect for what we had both achieved in the game.

By that point the team didn't really expect too many goals from him. If Cyrille scored then it was seen as bonus. They wanted him to contribute in other ways, like using his power and strength. He was fantastic at holding off defenders; you were lucky to get the ball off him when he had it at his feet but I was looking for the ball to be moved a lot quicker and their style didn't really suit my strengths. I thrived on decent delivery into the box but the perfect foil for Cyrille would have been somebody with a bit of pace who could get in behind defences. Our partnership ended up being a bit of a mismatch through no fault of our own.

The problems started to mount and we hit the skids in the league, losing to Everton and Arsenal. Those results hardly made for a Merry Christmas. Not that I was in the mood to celebrate. Christmas is meant to be a time when you are around friends and family. That was never going to be the case for me at Highfield Road, with the exception of a few of my team mates, who had broken ranks from the rest of the dressing room.

My situation was summed up a week or so before Christmas. Instead of hampers or vouchers, our present from the club was a turkey. I walked into the physio's room and there were 30-odd turkeys laid out on a table. They varied in weight from 9lbs to 14Ibs. Every bird had a player's name on the side. I looked for my name and there was a 14 lb turkey but by the time I had gone back to pick it up it had mysteriously shrunk or, more likely, had been switched. I was left with this 9 lb turkey, which didn't really bother me because my two daughters were still young, but that wasn't really the point. If somebody had asked me I would have happily switched but somebody just went behind my back and swapped them around. I couldn't believe somebody could be that sad or petty. Maybe it was their way of telling me to get stuffed! I don't know.

On the park we struggled past Wimbledon and drew with QPR. We then finished the year falling to Derby and I was in the middle of another barren spell.

I was concerned about my lack of goals, as was the manager.

I thought 1990 might bring a change of fortunes but my luck, like my goals, also seemed to run dry. I played against Tottenham before we were left red-faced as we crashed out of the FA Cup to Northampton Town. That game was absolutely horrendous.

It was raining and the wind was howling. It was at Northampton's old County Ground. There was the main stand and at one side was a simple rope and 100 yards behind it was the cricket ground. The pitch was just a mudbath and it was a case of going out and trying to batter the ball as far up the park as we could.

A guy called Steve Berry ended up nicking a goal from one of our mistakes to give Northampton their goal. We huffed and puffed but we couldn't get back in the game. It was a massive disappointment because it was only three years after the club had gone all the way in the competition. It was a massive shock but Coventry hadn't exactly had the best of records since they had lifted the famous old trophy.

The previous season, before I had arrived, they had crashed out to non-league Sutton United and so this was another major embarrassment for the club.

My pain was to become physical as well as mental as I was sidelined with a back problem. I didn't know that at the time but it was connected to the lack of movement in my right hip.

I missed the win at Crystal Palace and the Littlewoods Cup

quarter-final first leg at Sunderland. The club had tried everything in their power to get me fit, and had even delayed my fitness test until the morning of the game, but I still ended up failing it.

We had stayed overnight up in the north-east and it is fair to say Sillett had a very different approach from Graeme Souness. Wherever we went with Souness, the waiters and staff would come round and fuss all over him but he would always tell them to look after the players first because we were the ones who had to go out and do the business on the pitch.

Sillett, though, went completely the other way. We were sitting at lunch and the waiters went to the players and asked us what we wanted. Big Sillett wasn't happy and shouted down, 'Don't serve them first. They are going for a pre-match sleep and we are in a hurry because we are off for a game of golf.' The manager wanted to be the centre of attention. I'm not saying that approach was wrong because this same routine had helped them win the FA Cup, but it was different from what I had been used to. Don't get me wrong, Sillett was a really bubbly, funny character. Technically, as a coach, he didn't really teach me anything new during my time at Coventry but he was still a decent guy, who worked hard. There was one occasion when he took me out on the training ground and tried to work on things to get me back amongst the goals. He knew he needed results from his major investment and was trying everything he could to try and make it work.

We had been out doing a bit of play around the box but I knew it just wasn't to be. He was more of a personality manager than a coach. To be fair to him he was always approachable and, to his credit, always tried to keep the atmosphere light by cracking a joke or two.

We used to have a weekly five-a-side game where he would play in goal for one team and Curtis would play between the sticks for the other. They would pick their teams and, surprise, surprise, I was always the last pick.

We would play the game and after the match we were all given a piece of paper where we would nominate our worst player of the week. We would put a player's squad number on our slips and they would all go in a hat. Sillett would then hold court and count them out. The person with the most votes then had to wear the yellow jersey in training the following week.

Over the period, and I don't know why, people started to add comments to their nominations. It would be things like 'Drinkell – what a waste of money', or Smith would get 'long-haired useless a***!' These things started to get quite personal and more often than not I was on the end of a lot of the jibes.

So I thought I will use it to get my own back. So I wrote 'Sillett' and then added 'fat, useless clown!' To be fair, he was as good as gold, he opened it up and read it out. He joked: 'Here's one for me,' and he obviously knew who the author was because he said 'there is no need to be so personal, Drinks.'

George Curtis was his assistant and was the polar opposite of Sillett. He was a tough guy – and some people thought he was a bit of a bully. His way of sorting you out was to grab you by the nose and pull you around the dressing room until your eyes started to water. He did that to try and prove a point, but his bully-boy methods were so outdated. George had been a good solid defender for the club and was well respected at Coventry. He held a lot of power but acted as a foil for Sillett in this particular double act.

I might have missed that Sunderland game but we still managed to get a 0–0 draw. It gave us the advantage going into the Highfield Road return.

The manager tried to get me fit again but my back still didn't respond and I, frustratingly, had to sit it out. It didn't really matter in the end because the team won pretty convincingly without me.

Young Stevie Livingstone, who had replaced me, scored four of our five goals. I was absolutely delighted for him and after the game I went down into the dressing room to congratulate him. Everything had gone well for him and I just said: 'Brilliant,' and 'Well done, son. I am really pleased for you.' I was genuine in my praise because he was a young guy coming through while I was an experienced pro at the other opposite end of my career. I always tried to encourage the youngsters coming through. I had been given a lot of help when I had come through the ranks at Grimsby and I thought it was only right to try and help the next generation.

The dressing room after the Sunderland game was absolutely jumping but I still got the feeling of 'What are you doing here?' It was like 'You have nothing to do with this win. We have Livingstone now and we don't need you any more.'

Things were bad enough but that welcome and not being able to play just added to my frustrations. It did, though, give me time to analyse and consider why things weren't working out for me. It always fell back to the same thing – Coventry's tactics. Our play was very contained and they continually used Cyrille as the main target man. I didn't have the legs to run on to his flick-ons, although most of his work was done around the halfway line. I would win my headers and the ball from goal kicks but most of my work would be done deep or with my back to goal.

I remember having one of those frequent discussions on the training ground with Sillett about my lack of goals. He asked me why things weren't really working out. It wasn't as if I was missing a lot of chances because I wasn't really getting any.

I pointed out to the training pitch, in front of us, and I said the reason I am not scoring goals is because I am hardly ever in there, and I pointed to the 18-yard box. I didn't want to use excuses but it was the truth.

I also had a chat with David Speedie about things. He echoed how he had also struggled for goals when he first arrived. That was one of the reasons why he decided to drop into the midfield. He had come from Chelsea, where he had scored goals for fun alongside Kerry Dixon, but he found it a lot harder at Coventry. He had also found it hard to play for Coventry as a forward. Silllett had even come to him and suggested he moved on but he was determined he wasn't going to leave as a flop. He dropped back and became a competitive midfielder. He did really well and was still capable of nicking seven or eight goals from the middle of the park. His form was so good he got his move to Liverpool off the back of it.

Sillett, to be fair, asked what he could do to help. He told me he was thinking about bringing in a winger to give us a bit more width. Sillett also felt it would help us create a few more chances. I agreed it was a good idea. He said he had been recommended a couple of wingers from Scotland and asked me for my opinions because I had known them from my time at Rangers. The players he was considering were Kevin Gallacher of Dundee United and John Colquhoun of Hearts. I said: 'They are both good players but out of the two I would much rather you sign Colquhoun.' John was a natural winger, who provided good delivery into the box, while Kevin had played a lot of his games at United as a second striker. In the end, the manager decided to plump for Gallacher and agreed a club record fee to bring him down from Dundee United.

He came at a time when I was still out injured and was pitched straight into the role of centre forward. He made a decent impact, as we beat Chelsea. That result gave the squad a boost ahead of the first leg of our Littlewoods Cup semi-final at the City Ground. It was yet another game where my back problem forced me to become a restless spectator. We were unlucky not to get something as Nottingham Forest beat us 2–1. A Nigel Clough penalty and another from Stuart Pearce was enough for Forest, despite Livingstone pulling one back.

I sat out the Millwall win in the league but I was fit enough to take my place on the bench for the second leg of the Littlewoods Cup semi-final. Cup fever really seemed to grip the city and it was like 1987 all over again, even though the League Cup is never really viewed in the same light as the FA Cup. There was a real buzz around this match. It was a sell-out and the gate receipts were the highest in the club's history at that point. Remember we were potentially 90 minutes away from Wembley.

I was desperate to get on the pitch because it was still goalless,

I felt I could nick the goals we needed to get us through. What I remember about the game was being fouled by Brian Clough and I wasn't even on the pitch.

I was walking down the track, still with my tracksuit on and Clough started to follow me. He shadowed me and then stuck his foot out and caught my heel. I stumbled and almost fell. He just walked past and had a wee giggle to himself. I just looked at him and smirked. You couldn't do anything else because 'Cloughie' had a real aura about him. He was a true great in the game – even if he was slightly madcap in those later years.

I knew he was an admirer and had failed in a bid to sign me when I was at Norwich. I remember we were playing Forest when I was still at Norwich. I was fouled by one of their players but the referee never gave me the decision. So I chased after the official, shouting at him, when suddenly there was a shout from the touchline. This voice kept screaming: 'No. 8, No. 8!' I turned around and saw it was Clough but I was thinking to myself, 'What is he up to? He isn't my manager and has got nothing to do with me.'

He kept shouting until I turned around and looked at him again. He said: 'Yes, No. 8, you. You are a bloody good player. If you shut your mouth and get on with your football you'd be an even better player.' His methods were different but when a legend like that speaks you have no choice but to listen and as usual it was good advice.

Getting back to the semi-final, we didn't have many chances. I eventually got on but we still couldn't get the goals and crashed out 2–1 on aggregate. It was a real disappointment because we knew how close we had come to Wembley. We all knew we had potentially blown a massive opportunity.

I was still on the bench for the Midlands derby with Aston Villa. I came on to score with my first touch to help us win 2–0. It was a massive win, especially with the rivalry between the two sets of fans. Villa also held the upper hand over Coventry around that time so it finally gave the long-suffering Sky Blues fans something to shout about. Maybe now we were on the way back up? I was also praying it would be a turning point in my Coventry career and help me finally win over the City fans.

The arrival of Gallacher seemed to have had an initial impact on my own game because I scored in our next two games, a defeat at Luton and a home win over Forest. That run took us back up to sixth. I was quite happy around that time.

But no matter what I did on the pitch I always got the feeling I was never really going to be wholly accepted within the inner sanctum of our dressing room. I know it was a two-way street and there were probably little things I did that annoyed some of my team mates, like the time I refused to wear their official club blazer and continued to wear the one I had kept from my Rangers days.

My decision wasn't down to snobbery but due to the fact our tailor had got his measurements completely wrong. So I just stuck a Coventry badge on my old blazer and got on with it.

Some of my colleagues thought I was a big-time Charlie but it was down to the fact my Coventry jacket was simply too tight and short on the arms. From a distance you wouldn't see any difference but that seemed to upset Sillett and the old guard. They would mock me by saying things like: 'What is wrong with our blazer?' Then Sillett would pass it on to the players and say things like: 'Our stuff isn't good enough for Kev. Who does he think he is?' That hardly helped my position and standing within the dressing room.

On the pitch, we kept in sixth place for a couple of weeks before we began to slide again. It was around that time the goals stopped again. We drew a blank at Norwich while successive defeats to Sheffield Wednesday, Charlton and Manchester United ended all hope of us claiming a European spot. I was then bombed as we won at Derby, lost to Tottenham and drew with QPR. We had to resign ourselves to another season of mid-table mediocrity. We were 10th in the table when I came back in for the final three games of the season.

Very little changed as we struggled and hardly created a chance.

We drew 0–0 at Wimbledon, lost 2–0 to Southampton and finished off with a 6–1 thrashing at Liverpool. Very little else seemed to be going right for me or Coventry. We finished the season in 12th position, which was a big disappointment to me because I had expected us to do a lot better.

Sillett had also made it clear he had wanted us to kick on but we hadn't.

Personally, I was disappointed with my first season at Highfield Road. I still wasn't happy. I wasn't settled, I didn't feel part of the team and I certainly wasn't getting much in the way of chances. I ended up with a pitiful seven goals, which I felt was a poor return. Now I could see why no Coventry players had hit double figures for some time.

All in all I was just glad to see the back of the season. I could have quite easily cut my losses and said I wanted to move but I still felt l could turn things around. I was just looking for a fresh start in the next season. I tried to remain positive. I knew my team mates and they knew me a lot better now and hopefully that would help us all kick on to become a better team.

19

THE BUTCHER'S CHOP

WE RETURNED for action and our pre-season went well but we couldn't have asked for a tougher start. We were up against Manchester United and ended up crashing 2–0 at Old Trafford. We did, though, manage to register a win in our first home game, as we beat Everton 3–1. That, though, was the only high point in what was to be a desperate start to our campaign. We drew with Nottingham Forest and Wimbledon and lost the derby with Aston Villa and then at Luton.

I knew after the goalless draw with Wimbledon that things weren't going to happen for me – no matter what I tried. I remember a ball dropped in the box and I turned and curled it into the top corner. I ran off to celebrate but by the time I had turned round the linesman had put his flag up against Cyrille Regis. We really needed the win and I needed the goal but we got neither.

We crashed to fourth bottom and I had failed to score in our opening six matches. It was hardly surprising because we were short of confidence and had hardly created a chance. I spent most of my time tracking back and trying to win balls on the halfway line. It went back to the old argument I had with Sillett the previous season – I wasn't going to score unless I got the ball in the box.

After the Luton game I found myself dropped. I was in a similar position to Kevin MacDonald, who I had played with briefly at Rangers. One minute he had been in the Coventry first team and the next he was deemed surplus to requirements. We played together a lot in the reserves and I think all in he made something like seven first-team starts that season. We built up a close friendship because we were both in the same boat, like two outcasts together.

Sillett obviously thought I could still offer the team something but didn't necessarily see me as the main striker. In a David Speedie-like move, Sillett asked me if I fancied playing in midfield. He wanted to switch things around and make the most of a bad mix.

I told him that I was a centre forward and if I got the right service then I would get him goals. I didn't really fancy playing in midfield although I told him I would do it if he felt it would benefit the team. It might have worked for Speedie but I was a slightly different player. David was more of an all-action player compared with me. It was an act of desperation from a man who was up against it.

It was around that time both sides realised that it just wasn't going to work. Coventry were now willing to sell me although they wanted to recoup most of the money they had paid to Rangers.

The problem was Coventry had paid big money for a 29-year-old. Now I was 30 going on 31 and they were still looking for the same fee to let me go. It didn't make sense. There was no way any manager or chairman in their right mind would pay that sort of money for a player who had scored just seven goals the previous season and was entering the twilight of his career.

I went to see the chairman John Poynton about my situation. I was costing the team a lot of money. I wasn't in the team and I asked if there was any chance he would lower his demands and let me move on.

There were a lot of rumours around that time that Norwich wanted to take me back. I think they were willing to bid between £300,000 and £400,000 for me but that was a fraction of what Coventry wanted. It left an uneasy stand-off that left everybody frustrated. The Highfield Road board and Poynton, though, had more pressing matters than my position. The team were hovering around the relegation zone and there was an increasing concern the club could lose its top-flight status.

My omission from the team didn't seem to help the team too much as they continued to struggle. A lack of goals continued to be the theme. They won two out of our next six games before 'Snozz's' love affair with Coventry City was brought to a rather brutal and bloody end.

I honestly didn't think Coventry would sack Sillett after all he had done for the club. I thought they might move him upstairs or give him another position within the club. I didn't think, for one moment, they would cut all ties. But football, as I have found, is a rather ruthless game and Sillett was pulled in and told his services were no longer required. The FA Cup success was nothing more than a distant memory. I was genuinely disappointed to see Sillett get the boot. He had shown faith and paid a lot of money for me but it hadn't really worked out for either of us. There were reasons. I have stated my view why it didn't click but it certainly wasn't down to a lack of effort on my behalf. I never gave anything less than 100 per cent but at times you also need a bit of luck and willingness from others around you.

I wondered what the future would hold with a new manager coming in. Maybe the new man would come in and view things in a different light and put me back in the team?

We had no idea who the new manager was going to be but the board moved quickly to make their appointment. I remember I was in Warwick with Andrea when it came over on the car radio that we had appointed our new manager. To my total shock and surprise it was Terry Butcher.

Andrea looked at me and said 'That's brilliant!' I just looked at her and said, 'For me, that is the worst possible appointment.' I just knew there was no way the punters and some of my team mates would allow Terry to put me back in the team. I knew with Terry in charge I was unlikely to get a fair crack of the whip.

I know most people would have seen it as an old pals act from our Rangers days. It was clear the supporters didn't really want me back in the team. If it had been somebody else who didn't know me and hadn't worked with me then I might have had a chance, but this appointment was too close to home. If it had been somebody I didn't know then I could have shown them I was good enough to play without all the conspiracy theories that came from my friendship with Terry. The supporters and the board would have had to accept that my selection was down to merit but because it was Terry I knew they would be ready and waiting for me to flop.

What surprised me was that Terry had never cracked a light about the job. We still kept in touch after I left Rangers but he never mentioned it or gave any indication. After he was appointed he did come round to the house with his wife, Rita, for the evening.

He wanted to find out what it was like at Coventry and asked me my opinion on where things had gone wrong. I told him how the club was structured and gave him a bit of background to the players and their habits.

During those conversations he asked what was happening with my own situation. I told him to forget about me and just to concentrate on his own job. I explained my position was set in stone. They didn't want me and if I was being honest I didn't want to be there either. I told him there was no point in trying to resurrect things but he said: 'Leave it with me and I will have a look at things. If you are as good as the rest of my strikers then you will get your chance.' I told him he was wasting his time because things were beyond repair with the chairman. I told him to concentrate on himself and to watch his own back. I explained what I had faced and warned he had a major job on his hands because the dressing room was a closed shop. I explained it wasn't just me; guys like Speedie and MacDonald had found the same problems before me.

Terry had always faced things head on as a player and I expected him to do the same in management. I think Terry's first big mistake was appointing Mick Mills as his No. 2. He was an old team mate of Terry's from Ipswich and England. His pedigree as a top-class player couldn't be argued with but his reputation as a coach was a different matter. Mick's welcoming speech was a complete embarrassment. It made the rest of the players cringe, it was just so bad.

We were all sitting in the dressing room when Terry and Mick came in to introduce themselves. Mills, to everyone amazement, stood up and took centre stage. Pointing to Terry he said: 'See this man. This is the finest man you will ever meet in your life. He is a great player. He is a leader of men. A fantastic human being. A wonderful husband. A great father,' and so he went on. This went on for something like 10 minutes with Mick waxing lyrical about just how fantastic Terry was. He signed off by saying: 'We should be prepared to walk over hot coals for our new manager.'

I know Mills' motivational speech was meant to inspire us but it didn't. It had descended into farce and it came across more of a brown-nosing 'thank you for the job' speech than anything else.

And if anything, it worked against Terry in his efforts to get off on the right foot.

Terry and his entourage, although they didn't know it at the time, like myself, were viewed as outsiders coming into the club. 'El Tel' might have been the manager but the Coventry players still wanted to do things their own way. Just as they had done the previous five or six years – regardless of whether it had been successful or not. You would have thought the sacking of Sillett would have made them look at things in a different light but it didn't.

Terry's first game was against Liverpool and he decided to leave the team pretty much unchanged, although he did switch the system slightly by bringing himself in at the back. That changed things from a four- to a five-man back line, with four in midfield and one up front. We were down in 15th spot and Terry wanted to shore things up and make us hard to beat. Going with the one striker was hardly going to open the door for me, although the chairman would probably have made sure it was locked and bolted before I had even got near the handle.

We lost 1–0 to Liverpool but it wasn't the worst of results. At least the performance gave the rather fragile confidence a bit of a lift.

Terry played himself in the draw with Leeds and again at Crystal Palace but had to come off injured as we lost 2–1. He missed the next two to three games but handed me a recall against Everton.

The tin lid was put on things for me when it came to our FA Cup fourth-round clash with Southampton.

We drew 1–1 at Highfield Road and I had scored the goal. Brian Kilcline headed the ball down and I stood in front of Tim Flowers and managed to nick it past the big keeper.

I was pleased to be back amongst the goals. I almost won us the game when I cracked the crossbar late on but we ended up settling for a replay. It was still a decent result, but my joy was cut short by my own captain Trevor Peake, who hadn't even played, right after the game.

I came out the dressing room and Peake was holding court with the local journalists telling everybody that would listen that I hadn't touched the ball and it was Kilcline's goal. I couldn't believe it. Not only was it not true, but to make matters worse, those after-match interviews were also shown on a big screen in the players' lounge and the goal was eventually credited to Kilcline. The television replays later backed me up but it was a clear sign that a small minority of this Coventry squad still viewed me as an outsider.

I had spent most of the previous three months in the reserves. It had felt like the end of the earth going to the likes of Bradford and Doncaster on a cold, wet Wednesday night to play in front of a handful of hardcore fans. I still got on with it and I tried to help the young lads coming through the ranks as much as I could, but it was hard. I had played first-team football throughout my career and this new experience certainly wasn't a pleasant one.

I was, therefore, delighted to be back in the first-team fold and worked my socks off at Goodison Park, even though we lost 1–0. I kept my place for the 2–2 draw at Manchester United. I thought I had done well enough but found myself back on the bench when we lost at Chelsea.

I came on as a substitute as we overcame Norwich. That win,

which also saw Butcher make his return, was important but still couldn't lift us up the table. I forced my way back into the starting line-up for our game with Nottingham Forest but it proved to be a disaster. We lost 3–0 at the City Ground and another injury meant I missed the Midlands derby win over Aston Villa.

That proved to be Terry's last game for Coventry as a player. He decided to hang up his boots and concentrate on things from the dugout. I still don't know why Terry stopped there because he had brought a sense of stability to the team. His bad knee had left him in a lot of pain although he still got through the games, where he could organise while out on the pitch.

I know some of my team mates had voiced their discontent in the change of formation. They wanted to revert back to their tried and trusted flat back four, even though the switch suited the team.

They wanted Brian Borrows at right back, Brian Kilcline and Trevor Peake in the middle and Greg Downs or Lloyd McGrath on the left, with Steve Ogrizovic in goal. They didn't want to change and so they went and put their case to Terry. I thought, knowing Terry, the player, he would tell them where to go. He had never suffered fools gladly and I didn't expect him to change as a manager.

So I was absolutely stunned when he appeared to bow to their demands and took himself out of the team. It might well have been coincidence and Terry might have been ready to hang up his boots anyway but I don't think the timing of the decision helped or strengthened his position within the dressing room. Once again those same players, who had ruled the roost for so long, had got their way. It also showed signs that maybe the manager wasn't going to be the disciplinarian they had all feared.

I came back in for the Wimbledon and Sunderland games. We picked up one point from those matches. The Sunderland one was my final farewell for that season.

Around that time Poynton stepped down and was replaced by Derrick Robbins. He had just come back from South Africa and his dad had been a previous chairman of Coventry. I wondered if that might change my position.

I went to see him and he asked how we had all got into this situation and more importantly how were we going to get out of it? I was desperate to reach some sort of compromise to get out but Robbins was adamant he still wanted a substantial transfer fee and wouldn't consider paying me up or handing me a free. His inference was that I had been milking the club dry and that was something I wasn't prepared to accept. I had trained every day and always made myself available for the team. I wanted to play but it was the club's decision not to play me, not mine. Coventry had also been the team that had given me the contract so there was no way I was simply going to rip it up and walk out without a penny.

I was furious and told him that he had left me in an impossible situation by demanding a fee for me. I told him I knew there had been interest in me but the club had blocked all my possible escape routes by asking for far too much money.

I made two substitute appearances from February to the end of the season. The team had been struggling, we had hardly scored a goal and I still wasn't getting a game. I decided enough was enough and I went and chapped on Terry's door. I asked: 'Is there any chance of me getting back in the team?' The response was a simple: 'No.' For a bit of clarity I asked him if it was his decision or had it come from the powers above. I said: 'Are you telling me I am not good enough to be in your team?' He then stung me by saying: 'That is what I am saying, Kevin.'

Hurting, I snapped back: 'So do you think by putting me back in the team that it would make Coventry weaker?' He said: 'Yes' again. So I sniped back: 'That is a joke because your team, without me, has only won one of the last seven games. How much weaker can it get?' Our relationship was at an all-time low but things were to get far worse. Then to chastise me he hit me with another body blow: the chairman required me to hand back my club car. That was how petty things had got.

I just shrugged it off. I handed the keys back and went and bought myself a runaround of my own. I never spoke to the chairman again but there was still no escape route. I was still surplus to requirements and by the end of that season my value had plummeted. They were now willing to take the £400,000 that Norwich had offered earlier in the season but those bids were no longer on the table.

20

PINING FOR ANOTHER
ST ANDREWS

MY FINAL pre-season at Coventry saw me return to Scotland. We played games against Kilmarnock and Rangers. It was good to be back in familiar surroundings but unfortunately it was all too fleeting.

After we returned to the Midlands it was back to the reserves at Highfield Road. I was out in the cold and nowhere near the first team for our first six matches.

I hadn't started a competitive game for something like five months when out of the blue I was told I was starting away to Arsenal. Terry Butcher had found himself short of players and had pulled me out of the reserves to play at Highbury. It was always going to be a big ask but he wanted me to do him a turn. I wanted to play and Coventry were also paying my wages so there was also that sense of professional pride.

I was lacking match practice but I went out there and did my bit. I battered Steve Bould about and we won thanks to an own goal from Lee Dixon and another strike from Peter Ndlovu. It handed us a 2–1 victory and five minutes from time Terry took me off. I felt it was a job well done.

I got a pat on the back and a standing ovation from the Coventry fans as I took my place on the bench. Everything seemed great. Butcher told me I had worked hard and done a great job. Everyone was euphoric on the bus on the way back to the Midlands. Arsenal were one of the top teams at that point and it was a big result for Coventry. I was a bit stiff and sore but I thought maybe I had forced the first-team door open again.

I also took great pleasure from beating Arsenal because I always viewed Martin Keown as one of the toughest opponents I had played against. He was big, strong, athletic and you just couldn't rile him, no matter how hard you hit him. He would just bounce back for more, even when he was at Aston Villa.

Alan Hansen, Mark Lawrenson, Paul McGrath and David Watson might have been better footballers but as an out-and-out defender he took some shifting.

But after the game my hip tightened up again and I went to get treatment for a couple of days. I was back out on the training pitch by the Wednesday and raring to go. I went out and Mills was telling the players, as they came out to go 'over there with the gaffer'. It came to me and he said, 'You are over there with the reserves.'

I was hurt and really annoyed but I went away and did my bit. We finished and I waited for Butcher but he seemed keen to avoid confrontation. I decided enough was enough and I walked over and asked to speak to the gaffer. I asked what the story was and he told me I just wasn't in his plans for the weekend.

I looked him straight in the eye and said, 'Is that your choice?' Once again, he said it was.

It might have been the case. Maybe one of the other strikers was fit again and he didn't need me but I also knew there had been pressure from upstairs not to play me. Only Terry can tell if that was really behind his decision or not.

I felt really disappointed and let down by Terry. Even if I was not needed then surely he could have kept me around the first team. At least if he needed to call on me then he knew I would go out and do a job for him.

It really disappointed me the way Terry handled things. If he had been straightforward and up front then fine, but I don't think he was. I would certainly have had more respect for him if he had been.

I think that Chairman Robbins had a major influence on things and Terry didn't want to say that and end up looking like his puppet.

They both wanted shot of me. They tried to punt me to Swansea City on loan. They didn't even have the decency to tell me that they had given Swansea permission to talk to me.

I took a phone call from a guy called Doug Sharpe, who used to be the chairman of Swansea. He was a real character and came across as this really wide guy.

He came on the phone and said, 'I have been given permission to speak to you and I want you to come down and have a chat with us.' I told him I wasn't sure I should be speaking directly to him but he said: 'No, it's okay, Terry gave me your number.' That told me all I needed to know.

I went down to the game and it was the local derby with Cardiff. I had a chat with Frank Burrows, who was the manager. I watched the match and I have to admit it was some game. It was intense, the atmosphere was mental, and it was a full house. It was similar to the Old Firm game. I liked what I saw but it still wasn't for me, although Swansea were looking to progress.

The chairman pulled me after the game but I told him thanks for his interest but I wouldn't be coming to Wales. I had moved my family back down from Scotland and at 31 I don't think it would be right moving them again. The chairman had one final pop. He said: 'Have you thought about getting into management after your career is finished?' I told him I hadn't really thought about it at any great length but it was a consideration. He replied: 'Frank won't always be here. We would never sack him but he could, in time, be "moved upstairs".' He then added: 'I'm not saying you will get the job but you would come into the reckoning.' He tried to dangle that carrot but it just wasn't for me. I jumped back into the car and headed back to Coventry.

By that stage things couldn't get any lower for me at Highfield Road. I seemed to be staring up at rock bottom. I was playing for the reserves but if they could have stopped me playing there then they probably would have.

I was also starting to get more problems with my hamstrings. Up until that point they hadn't given me a day's bother but fitness-wise, a lack of activity was playing its part.

I remember one of Butcher's coaches came up to me and said the club were sending me to Lilleshall for rehabilitation. It was more a case of getting me out of sight and mind rather than trying to get me back to full fitness.

Terry had become fed up with me being in and around the dressing room. I was always in his face and a constant reminder to everyone that I was a big-money player they weren't prepared to play. I was always seen as this high-profile flop and it hurt me as much as anybody. I had scored goals and been a favourite at Grimsby, Norwich and Rangers and this was the first club where I hadn't made an impact. It was a blot on my own copybook and one I am still embarrassed about to this day. Yet it wasn't for the want of trying, because I wanted to succeed at Coventry. I did everything I could but it didn't matter because the damage had been done. My days were numbered. I would score for the reserves or play well but I always knew I was never going to get back into the first team.

When I did do well it put more pressure on Terry to play me and that was something he was determined wasn't going to happen. It got that bad he decided to send me away to Lilleshall to get me out of the way. That way he didn't have to look me in the eye day in and day out.

I agreed to go to Lilleshall but asked to stay at home and drive down daily for the sessions. It was only an hour away from the house so it would have been an easy commute. But Terry was adamant he wanted me to go down there and stay for the two weeks. I could have challenged him but I didn't bother because I knew it was more hassle than it was worth.

I went down to get the diagnosis on my injury and once again it showed my right hip wasn't giving me full movement. There were further complications because my hamstring was becoming over-stretched, as I tried to overcompensate for my hip. I basically stayed and got continuous treatment. I was starting to feel a bit better and thought after another week's treatment I would go back feeling a lot fitter and sharper.

Terry and Coventry had other ideas. On the Thursday I had a message telling me I had been given permission to open talks with Birmingham City.

They had phoned and asked to take me on a month's loan and Terry had once again agreed to their request.

I phoned the Birmingham manager Terry Cooper and explained to him my situation. I would have jumped at the chance of playing for Birmingham but I was still 10 days to a fortnight away from full fitness. He told me not to worry about it and to get myself across to St Andrews the next day so we could have a chat about things. I did my session at Lilleshall and then drove up to Birmingham.

I met Terry and he explained how the side had been stuttering in the league and he wanted to bring me in for my experience.

Birmingham were a massive club even though they were in Division 2, which is the current English League One. Terry said, 'We know you are not fully fit but we still want to sign you.' Birmingham were also keen to get the deal done that night because it was a five-game month and they had agreed to pay my wages for the month, so they were determined to get their money's worth.

Terry tried to talk me into it and said, 'We know you are struggling with your hip but will break you in gently. We will get you involved tomorrow against Stockport County but we will put you on the bench. You can watch the game and we will only throw you on if we need to.' So against my better judgement I agreed to his request. I was quite excited although I knew I was nowhere near fit.

The Saturday came and I drove up to St Andrews. I walked into the dressing room and the assistant manager, Ian Atkins, said; 'You are across there' and pointed me to my shirt.

He had a wee smirk on his face and when I walked over I could see why. He handed me the No. 9 shirt and told me I was starting. So much for breaking me in gently! Terry then came up and said, 'Just give us all you can and we will see how it goes.'

I didn't know many of the boys in the team although I did know Louie Donowa, who I had played alongside a few years earlier at Norwich. He had a few clubs in his time and he even pitched up in Scotland for a short time with Ayr United. He was a good player who I thought would have done so much more with his career.

I remember walking out for that first game at St Andrews; there were more than 12,500 fans there. The atmosphere was superb and this was in the third tier of English football. The crowd was bigger than Coventry's crowds for some Premier League games.

It is fair to say playing in front of such a big crowd gave me a real buzz and the adrenalin saw me through that first game – even if I was only half-fit.

Mark Cooper, Terry's son, put us ahead and then I remember the ball flashed across the box. I managed to knock it past their keeper to mark my debut with a goal.

That helped make me an instant favourite with the Birmingham fans and Louie capped a marvellous first game with the final goal in our 3–0 victory. Terry took me off with five minutes to go. I hardly had enough energy to walk off because I was totally knackered. My body was aching and my hamstring was about to ping but it was the happiest I had felt in months.

Terry Cooper and Birmingham had shown faith in me and I wanted to do everything I could to repay them for the gamble they had taken on me. This time there was gain from the pain.

The next match was another action-packed home encounter with Wigan Athletic. It ended all-square at 3–3 but I didn't even manage to get on the scoresheet. The next match was the big one for Birmingham. It was West Bromwich Albion at the Hawthorns. It was massive.

All the fans wanted to be there. The crowd was in excess of 26,000 and there was still another 6,000 or so locked outside. I remember arriving at the Hawthorns and being totally taken aback. It was like a tinderbox, which was night and day compared to playing in front of empty stadiums with Coventry reserves.

I had been used to derbies between Lincoln, Hull and Scunthorpe when I was at Grimsby and then there was the Old Firm game between Rangers and Celtic. These were games with a bit of edge but that wasn't really the case when I was at Coventry. We had games with Aston Villa but it wasn't quite the same.

I had missed the local derbies and being involved in this game had geed me up again and whetted my appetite. I had become a bit disillusioned with the game because of what had happened at Coventry. This sort of game is what football is all about.

West Bromwich Albion were also struggling. Their manager Bobby Gould was under a fair bit of pressure and also needed the win. It was a match he couldn't afford to lose. It was a typical all-action derby game with no quarter asked or given. Thankfully I managed to score early in the first half. I got on the end of a cross and headed it past their goalkeeper for the only goal of the game.

That increased my popularity with the Birmingham fans and after only three games I had built up a really good rapport with the Blues faithful. They were chanting my name in most games and that gave my confidence a massive lift. I always went out to give my all for them. Scoring the winner in a derby game always helped.

After the game it was carnage but thankfully it was the West Bromwich fans who were going mental. They had staged a protest and there must have been more than 6,000 who refused to leave the ground and stood there chanting for Gould to get the sack. It was madness as we made our way on to the team bus and it had even spilled over in front of the ground.

The West Bromwich fans eventually got their wish at the end of that season when Gould was fired for failing to win promotion. Little did I know my derby winner would come back and haunt me at the end of that season. Our next match was a 3–0 win over Torquay and my final game was away at Brentford. It

was a 2–2 draw, I remember it because it was my worst performance in a Birmingham jersey. It was a midweek game and we had
travelled all the way down for the game and, if I am being honest,
I was totally done in. I had played five games in the month and
I had absolutely nothing left in the tank.

I was disappointed because that was the final game of my loan
spell although I was still hopeful an extension could be agreed.
Cooper tried everything in his power to get the deal done. He
had initially wanted to extend it by another month but Coventry
refused. They knew I had done quite well and were trying to
squeeze as much money as they could out of Birmingham.

So they knocked the loan deal on the head and said they wanted
£100,000 for me and Birmingham would have to pick up my
wages – which was more than they could pay.

They couldn't afford to do the deal and pay the transfer fee as
well, so it was back in the balance. Birmingham then tried to push
for the loan deal, which suited everyone, but Coventry just wouldn't
entertain it.

I still had left 18 months left on my contract and I wasn't prepared
to walk away from that to help Coventry out. I was still hoping
an agreement could be reached, even after I went back to Coventry,
because it was soul destroying going back to Highfield Road after
a great month at Birmingham.

I went back and that Saturday afternoon I was back playing in
the reserves in front of a handful of people – just weeks after
playing in front of 26,000 in the Second Division.

I wanted to go back to Birmingham. They might have been
playing in the lower leagues but they were playing good football
and going for the title. They had a good squad and there were
exciting times ahead.

I was still hankering over the move but I knew within a couple
of weeks it wasn't going to happen. I was back at Coventry even
though I knew I was never going to play for their first team.

Butcher used to make us all come in at noon and then he would
announce his squad at 1.30pm. I was always made to come in

even though I knew my name was never going to be read out. I used to go to the ground with one of my mates and ask him to keep the car running. Then when I was told I wasn't involved I would get him to drive me up to St Andrews to watch Birmingham, when they were at home.

I decided I would rather be amongst people who appreciated me. I used to get slapped on the back and asked, 'When are you coming back to the Blues?' I longed to be involved with the action, especially as Birmingham went on to win promotion. The Blues finished second going up behind Brentford. I would like to think I played a small part in their success. I still have a great fondness of Birmingham from my short time there and it is great to see Birmingham City back where they belong in the Premier League.

When I was at Coventry I even started to get stick from our fans. I remember I was actually getting booed in the warm-up before a game against Liverpool when my name was read out over the tannoy. It wasn't a nice thing to hear but the club had spent a lot of money and I hadn't got the goals either of us had hoped for. It was something I just had to accept although it wasn't down to a lack of effort on my side. I actually have to take my hat off to my old manager Souness that day. By that time he had left Rangers to take over at Liverpool and he actually waited for me at the tunnel. He put his arm around me and walked up the tunnel with me. He said, 'Forget about them, they know nothing. They obviously don't know a good player when they see one.' I thought it was a nice touch from Graeme and it really helped to lift my spirits.

Unfortunately it may have boosted my self-confidence but I was still in the same position at Coventry but then things were to take another turn when Terry Butcher was sacked. The team were hovering just above the drop zone.

I have to say, at the time, I had very little sympathy when Terry did get the boot. Terry had arrived as a friend and I thought he would help me get out of Coventry but I was still stuck there rotting in the reserves long after he was gone.

In my opinion, Terry's biggest problem at Coventry was that he just wasn't strong enough with his players. As a player and captain he would give everything for his team and would go through brick walls for club and country. The picture of him in the England shirt with his head bandaged and blood all over his shirt is now pretty iconic. If he had gone about management in the same way then he wouldn't have had to fall on his own sword at Coventry.

He bent over backwards for his players and was too nice for his own good. I felt he was too soft at times and allowed certain players to have too much influence on team matters. He tried too hard to get everybody onside. If he had been his own man and just got on with things then I think he would have been a success. I was surprised Terry went down that road because he had worked under top managers like Souness and Sir Bobby Robson for most of his career. Souness had been successful because he had always run his dressing room with an iron fist. If Terry had done that, then I think his spell at Highfield Road would have been far more successful.

I didn't even see Terry again until a couple of years after that. He had bounced back and got the Sunderland job. We ended up playing them in a pre-season game with Falkirk and that was when I bumped into him again but we never spoke. It was disappointing because we had become quite close at Rangers but what happened with Coventry seemed to sour that friendship.

It was a few years later before we actually broke the ice again when we met at a Rangers dinner.

Terry has gone on to have a few jobs in management but he has made more of an impact north of the border with Motherwell and now Inverness, where he has done an excellent job in leading them back into the SPL at the first attempt.

It was funny because he was assistant manager of Scotland to George Burley and that is something I found quite amusing. He was the guy who used to wind up the Scottish guys when we were at Ibrox and so it was rather bizarre to see the former England captain as part of the Scotland set-up.

At Coventry I was left working under a new manager and this time it was Don Howe. Yes, the same man who had helped John Fashanu and Dennis Wise to break into the England set-up.

He came in as a caretaker and once again told me I would get my chance but I told him all I wanted was out. Howe did throw me on as a substitute against my old side Norwich, in a goalless draw, and then we beat Chelsea at Stamford Bridge. I must have done something right because I was handed only my second Coventry start of the season. It was at home against Oldham but proved frustrating, as we drew 1–1. That was to be my swansong in Sky Blue. I didn't feature again for the rest of that season. We won one game of that final eight and only managed to avoid relegation after a nail-biting final few weeks. We finished in 19th place, two points ahead of Luton who were relegated, along with Notts County and West Ham United.

That summer a certain Mr Gould was brought in as joint manager to assist Howe. That was to be the grand 'master plan' but before the new season kicked off Howe quit, leaving Gould to become the main man.

I told Gould I wanted out but he insisted I could still do a job for Coventry and he wanted me to give it another go. But I had heard it all before from his predecessor and it never really happened. My Coventry career was over and I knew it. I told Bobby that I needed to move on. He could see there was no point in trying to persuade me to change my mind and told me he would do all he could to help me find a new club. He said he would speak to the chairman but I wasn't about to hold my breath. I was fully expecting to have to sit out the final year of my Coventry contract in the reserves.

21

THIS NEW BAIRN HASN'T
LOST THE PLOT!

I HAVE to say, after my Coventry hell, anywhere was more appealing than Highfield Road. I hadn't played too often in the previous season, so I thought my options would be limited, but I was pleasantly surprised I still had a few suitors for my signature.

I thought I might have to drop down the leagues, but a few interesting proposals were brought to the table. Malaga or Groningen? Both opportunities came via agents when I was out of the picture in my final few months at Coventry.

The prospect of playing in Spain with Malaga, who were in the Second Division, was quite appealing. They sent a couple of representatives over to hold talks. It wasn't long after Michael Robinson had been out at Osasuna and John Aldridge at Real Sociedad, so there seemed to be a demand for British players at that time.

The lifestyle was certainly appealing, but my biggest problem was always the heat. I struggled badly with Rangers during our pre-season trip to Italy with heat exhaustion, so could you imagine what sort of state I would have been in if I had tried to play an entire season in Spain?

I knew I would be no use playing in the scorching heat. I mean, Malaga wasn't exactly Grimsby and so I decided to knock it back. I'm sure Andrea and the kids would have loved it, but they never got the chance. Maybe looking back it was a lack of adventure on my part, but it just didn't feel right and I wanted everything to be 100 per cent right after the way Coventry had ended.

I was also sounded out about Groningen. That was early in the summer and I still had a year left on my Coventry deal. Malaga had been appealing, but it was night and day compared with Groningen. It may be an impressive Dutch city famed for its university life, but it was an education I felt I could do without at that stage of my career.

Call me a creature of habit but I felt I would have been as well at Walsall or somewhere of that ilk, than moving to Holland. I was 31 and could have gone out there for a year or two. But then I would have had to move back to England at the end of that deal to consider my options again. Andrea and the kids had been through enough and it was unfair to move them for a couple of years. Going to Holland wasn't ideal either if I wanted to get into coaching or management.

I was settled in England and was ready to drop down the divisions when I took a call out of the blue asking me if I would consider coming back to Scotland.

Falkirk came calling. It was down to the influence of one of my former mentors, David Holmes, who had moved to Brockville and was helping them out on the corporate side.

He had mentioned my situation to their manager Jim Jefferies and he decided to follow things up. Jim phoned and asked me up for a chat.

I had planned to use his invitation to come and catch up with my old pals, Hunter Fletcher, Stuart McKenzie and the rest of the boys. Stirling wasn't too far away so it was a chance for me to go and say hello to some old friends. If I am being honest, that is all it was. I had no intention of joining Falkirk.

I came up and met Jim and he tried everything in the book to convince me to sign. To be fair, he put up a really good case and gave me something to think about. He felt I could help the team kick on and progress.

They were in the SPL and the other big hook was that he wanted to involve me in the coaching side with the reserves. That would give me the chance to put my foot on that particular ladder.

I went away and met my friends for lunch with everything spinning around in my head. I still felt it was a big commitment to uproot the family and return to Scotland. Meeting the guys actually helped swing my decision in Falkirk's favour. Alan Beaton dropped me some inside information about a plot of land only 500 yards away from where I had built my previous house in Stirling.

He took me round to this plot in the King's Park. Right away I could see the potential, especially after Alan produced a set of drawings from the boot of his car. It looked like an interesting proposition and so we decided to go and speak to the owner. He wasn't exactly too keen on selling because he had earmarked it for his dream home. But within half an hour I had made an offer and convinced him to shake hands on a deal. This was unbeknown to Andrea and the kids and, once again, I had to call them to get the suitcases packed. I felt guilty about making the decision without speaking to Andrea first. I eventually plucked up the courage to phone Andrea and tell her I would be home tonight and I had also bought a plot of land and we'd be moving back to Scotland! She was more than a little bit taken aback but the good thing was at least she was going back to somewhere where we both had friends and had been previously. The downside was she was settled in our house in Kenilworth and I was uprooting her and the kids again.

Socially our life was great and the kids were settled, but Andrea knew football-wise I needed to get out of Coventry.

It might have been slightly different if it had been somewhere completely alien to us like Newcastle or Bournemouth and she would have put her foot down and said no.

I thrashed out terms with Falkirk and Jefferies, and the only thing I had left to do was to straighten things out at Coventry. They had demanded a transfer fee, but eventually I managed to get a free transfer and a few bob off them to cover my removal expenses.

The Coventry chairman Derrick Robins wasn't keen on doing it. He still wanted money but it took Bobby Gould to come in and smooth things over for my release.

I eventually secured my release when Coventry terminated my contract and I could finally complete my move to Falkirk.

I thought I could put Coventry behind me, but there was to be one final twist before I headed north.

That year there was a collapse in the housing market and I ended up losing £100,000 when I sold our property in Kenilworth. It just summed up how much of a disaster my time had been there. Nothing had gone right, but now it was time to look to the future rather than wallow in the past.

I had to take a substantial drop in wages to join Falkirk but, by that stage, it wasn't about the money anymore.

My first meeting with Jim was at Brockville. The surroundings were terrible, but it wasn't an issue for me. I just wanted to go out and enjoy my football again and to pass my experience on to others round about me.

My career was never about personal gain. I just wanted to try and improve the teams where I played and, at the same time, try to gain the respect of the supporters.

Okay, Brockville was rundown, but it was the same as most SPL grounds of that era, outside of Ibrox. Easter Road was rough, Aberdeen was odd with its four differing stands and Tannadice was simply awful. I knew that was part and parcel of Scottish football.

When I was at Rangers I used to room with Mark Walters and I knew that the state of the grounds was one of the things that drove him out of Scottish football. He loved playing at Ibrox but used to hate playing away. It used to depress him so much, in the end he had to return to England. If we had played every game at Ibrox then I don't think he would have ever moved but, unfortunately, that particular luxury wasn't on offer.

Some of the grounds and dressing rooms we visited were archaic. Brockville fell into that crumbling category. We didn't even have a training ground and it was a case of throwing balls and goals into the back of a van and trying to find a patch of grass to train. More often than not we had to clear up dog dirt before we could even get a five-a-side game going. Who said top-flight football is all glamour?

That may have put a lot of people off. It wasn't a place for prima donnas. They wouldn't have survived because we were all prepared to roll up our sleeves and fight for each other.

That helped with the camaraderie and brought us closer together. It is fair to say the Coventry boys could have learned a thing or two from the Falkirk guys.

I knew a few of the team. Guys like Brian Rice, Tommy McQueen, Kevin McAllister, Richard Cadette and Joe McLaughlin and I had all crossed paths down south.

I knew Ian McCall from Rangers and his love of late-night room service. I had also played against Ian Westwater and Fraser Wishart when I was at Rangers. Tony Parks also joined later that season. I got friendly with McAllister when I stayed at the Leapark Hotel in Grangemouth. I would often meet him for something to eat or a quick pint.

As I said, it was a great dressing room. With the likes of John 'Yogi' Hughes and McCall you would expect nothing less. Both these guys are characters in their own right and have gone on to show that in management. I knew Yogi had the passion but I am surprised that Ian went in that direction.

He was always madcap and as a player was never short of confidence. Even when he wasn't playing at Rangers he still walked around as if he was Diego Maradona. He also liked to have a laugh even if it did mean pushing things to the limit.

We had a good mix of differing personalities. Amongst the big characters were some of the quieter guys, like Neil Oliver. Neil was the brunt of most of the jokes. I don't think his wages were as good as they maybe should have been, because he was a big player for us. Neil was always trying to find ways of saving money. Whether that came from petrol or clothes, he would always try to scrimp and scrape.

Even at that time Mr Wishart was banging the union's drum, but they never had the same power as the PFA down south. Fair play to Fraser, though, he has gone to carve out a decent career for himself since he hung up his boots.

In general, we had a good bunch of lads, mostly from working-class backgrounds.

In the midst of all that was young Forbes Johnston. He was a good, good player. A very quiet, educated boy, he kept himself to himself but was always up for a laugh. He was 20 or 21 and as well as holding down a first-team place at Falkirk he was also doing his law degree.

It was a five- or six-year course and he was still managing to be a standout for Falkirk. It was amazing the way he was able to juggle both. He was doing well in his studies and was also selected for Scotland's under-21 side. He really was an exceptional talent. I always wondered how far he would have gone had he concentrated solely on his football.

In the end, he was really unlucky when it came to injuries and had to retire early with a knee problem. He ended up emigrating to Australia. He was always the guy in the Falkirk dressing room who seemed to have it all. To see what happened was really, really sad. Hearing he had taken his own life at the age of 35 was a real tragedy. I still find it hard to believe.

Inside Brockville the tiles might have been hanging off the walls and it was always freezing but it didn't really bother us. It brought us closer together.

I was never a big-time Charlie. I grew up in Grimsby so for guys like 'Yogi' and myself it was a good place to play professional football.

Brockville also worked to our advantage, especially on match days. It was an intimidating atmosphere. The fans were more or less on your back and the pitch was so tight. It really wasn't a very welcoming place for the opposition. Nobody enjoyed playing there. I think pulling into that back car park was sometimes enough to put some players off. They probably arrived thinking, 'Do I really want to get off this bus?'

I ended up making my Falkirk debut at Dundee's Dens Park. Graham Rix had just signed for Dundee. I remember doing the warm-up and going across to speak to him. He joked I had played for Rangers and he had been at Chelsea – what were we doing here? I wasn't of the same opinion. I was just glad to be back playing football on a Saturday afternoon again.

Thankfully, I had a debut to remember. Tommy Sloan scored and then I grabbed the winner. It was a great start, but I soon realised that it wasn't going to be like that every week. We struggled badly. We only won one game in eight and were up to our necks in it from an early stage.

We did get a bit of a lift when we beat Motherwell in the League Cup. We had been drawn at Fir Park in the third round, where I grabbed the only goal of the game. As a striker I claimed for everything although that wasn't one of my best. In the next round we were paired with SPL opposition in Aberdeen. We were easily thumped 4–1.

At that stage there were still more downs than ups, although we also had a few hard-luck stories along the way. We lost 5–4 to Celtic at Brockville before a Sloan goal saw us beat Motherwell. We managed to draw with both Dundee teams but lost to Rangers and Aberdeen.

We had slumped to the bottom of the table by this point and we desperately needed to put some wins on the board. We did that by beating Partick at Firhill and then we thumped Airdrie 5–1 at home, where I grabbed a couple.

We were knocked back again when we lost to Hibs and came out on the wrong end of a five-goal thriller at Parkhead against Celtic.

Going back as a former Rangers player was always an experience. I didn't help my case either when I scored a goal. Gary

Gillespie, the Celtic centre-half, loved to pass the ball out of defence. I knew he would never launch the ball because it was against the Liverpool ethos he had been brought up with. So, I anticipated the pass into the midfield, I stole the ball, went through and rounded the keeper to score. That, as you could imagine, caused some fury amongst the Celtic fans.

I took a lot of stick after that. It started to snow and the next thing the referee asked for an orange ball to be thrown onto the field. I picked it up and kidded on I was polishing the ball and played a bit of keepie-uppie in front of the old Jungle stand.

Unfortunately, Celtic came back to win 3–2 and their fans had the final laugh.

I got a fair bit of stick from most opposition fans, but especially at Parkhead, Hearts and Aberdeen. It was all down to my time at Rangers which, as an Englishman, I found strange because that had been two or three years earlier.

The opposition fans had long memories and their hatred of Rangers was there for all to see. I was experienced and thick-skinned enough not to let it affect me. I was always of the opinion if they were focused on me then they were leaving my team mates to get on with things. Anyway, I was at Falkirk to win points and not popularity contests.

We drew with St Johnstone and then I hit a winner against Hearts. But it was the next game against Motherwell that was to prove season-defining.

We were a few points ahead of them and had a chance to put real daylight between them if we had won at Fir Park.

That was the game where circumstances conspired against us. Our keeper, Tony Parks, got sent off and I had to go in goal. Eric Martindale was the referee. Tommy McQueen tried to run the ball out of play and Motherwell's Stevie Kirk came across and shoved him in the back. It should have been our free kick; even a blind man could have seen that. At worst it was our throw in.

So everyone was amazed when my old team-mate Davie Cooper picked up the ball and took the throw – even though Tommy was still on the ground. 'Coops' threw the ball to Kirk and he didn't need a second invitation to roll the ball into the net.

Tony came out like a raging bull. He shouted it should have been our ball, but Martindale ignored him and let the goal stand. Tony, by this point, was incandescent with rage and, in his fury, he ended up taking his protests too far and got himself sent off.

Coops was like that. He would take advantage of anything to help his team gain an edge. It was the winning mentality he had. It was more of a general cheekiness, but he would do anything to come out on top.

He went on to take the piss even more when I had to replace Tony in the goals. He kept firing shots at me and I was scrambling about my box trying to keep them out. That was an experience because I had never played in goal before apart from mucking about in training.

Coops was a genius, as everybody knows, and he did me in with his deliveries into the box. He spent half the game giggling at me. He would shout: 'See if you can catch this one, Kev.' I had no chance. It was a nightmare.

I let in a couple of goals although I still managed to get the man-of-the-match award in the *Sunday Post*. I don't know if that was a sympathy vote but I knew I wasn't going to prolong my career as a goalkeeper.

The Motherwell game really hit us hard, but our already brittle confidence was smashed to smithereens the next week at home to Rangers.

During the game, a cross came in and I ran from behind a defender to side-foot the ball into the corner of the net. I was behind the player who had crossed it and the defender. There was absolutely no way I was offside, but the linesman flagged and the referee disallowed it.

That would have made it 2–2 and would have given us a point, but we ended up on the end of another defeat.

It was a very frustrating afternoon. One most non-Old Firm fans know all about. The Old Firm tend to get the big decisions.

I had played for Rangers and have been back there, and to Parkhead, with Stirling and Falkirk, and there is no doubt some officials are frightened to give decisions against the Old Firm. That is just the harsh reality of the Scottish game.

The officials are under more pressure when they take charge of Rangers and Celtic games because 80 per cent of the football fans in Scotland follow the Old Firm. That is why it is easier to give decisions for them than against them.

Look at some of the hassle former referee Hugh Dallas had to put up with. Sometimes you can understand why they take the easy way out, but, on the other hand, you are just looking for consistency and fairness.

Consistency was something we were struggling to find ourselves, in the league, although we took Celtic's scalp in the Scottish Cup. We had beaten Berwick Rangers in the third round and were handed a home draw against Celtic at Brockville.

I remember it because we really fancied our chances of winning. We had run them so close in the previous two league games and this time we felt we could beat them, especially at Brockville.

Celtic weren't really the force they are today because Rangers were the dominant force and were in the middle of their nine-in-a-row run. That season Celtic ended up finishing behind Aberdeen, but it was always one of those games I relished playing in.

You were always guaranteed a big crowd because it was Celtic and the Scottish Cup. I also knew from my previous experiences of playing with Falkirk that I would once again be Public Enemy No. 1. I wasn't to be disappointed.

At Brockville you could hear every shout and insult. It was the usual obscenities from 'You Orange so and so' to 'You dirty Proddie bastard'. A lot of them probably hadn't forgiven me for winding them up at Parkhead.

Anyway, when the game started, Neil Duffy took some of the pressure off me when he put us in front. There were a few close things at both ends before Eddie May made sure of a famous win, when he netted our second.

For Falkirk it was – and still is – a big thing to beat one of the Old Firm. It is for the rest of the SPL even today. It is great for the players, but it really is massive for the fans. They always have to live in the shadows of Rangers and Celtic and so it always makes it more special when you do beat them. It certainly lives long in the memory.

Unfortunately, any dreams of lifting the Scottish Cup were brought to an abrupt end in the next round when we were drawn against Hearts at Tynecastle.

We were capable of beating them but we never really got going and lost 2–0.

Back in the SPL, survival remained the name of the game.

By the end of February we were back at the bottom. We had lost to Dundee, Dundee United, Aberdeen, Rangers, Hearts, Motherwell and Celtic. Within that run we drew with Hibs and beat Airdrie and Hibs.

We beat Dundee and I scored in a 2–2 draw at Aberdeen. I still felt we had more than enough in our ranks to stay in the SPL. Yogi was solid at the back while Parks was a decent goalkeeper. I also felt we had better players than the likes of Motherwell and Dundee.

We also had Kevin 'Crunchie' McAllister, who could always produce some magic and the likes of Richard Cadette would sniff out a chance. Big Davie Weir had also broken into the team and looked a real prospect.

The big man has gone on to have a great career at the very highest level and it is all credit to him. He is a great guy and a damn good player into the bargain.

I first got to know Davie when I was taking the reserves. Getting the chance to help young players like Davie was a big factor in my decision to join Falkirk. I ended up taking the team, along with the former Falkirk player Peter Houston. He had retired and although he was working in the club's commercial department he was keen to get back involved in coaching.

Peter has since taken charge of Dundee United and done an exceptional job since taking over from Craig Levein. He was always seen as a No. 2 after his spells under Levein at Hearts, Leicester City, Dundee United and Scotland. Peter has certainly served his apprenticeship and is now making a name for himself. He deserves a lot of credit for the success he has had at Dundee United, winning the Scottish Cup and leading them back into Europe. Peter is also continuing as assistant to Levein in the Scotland set-up. Peter was a bit of a cult-hero at Brockville with the fans and he was also held in the same high esteem by his team mates. He is a real 'people person'. Everybody liked him and I think that has been a major factor in his success at Dundee United. The players all respect him and all love playing for him.

It is amazing to see how far he has come since we both stepped on the coaching ladder together with the Falkirk second string. It was a decent place to cut our teeth because we had a good group of experienced players at the club. That made it easier because although we didn't have any managerial experience the players were great. They certainly did all they could to help us.

It was during the nitty-gritty of the relegation fight that my hip problem really began to flare up. I had hardly played for Coventry for a year so I didn't really know the full extent of the injury.

At first, the medical staff at Falkirk couldn't find out what was causing the distress. I had taken a couple of cortisone injections in the groin to numb the pain but what had become apparent at my Coventry medical was now catching up with me.

I tried to take some of the strain off and threw more of my weight on to the left leg, but my general mobility was starting to be affected. Just being fit enough to play in the games was becoming a challenge.

I was pretty much in pain after every training session and game. I couldn't play because my thigh muscles kept going into spasm and I could hardly move the leg. I knew my career was coming to an end, but I still thought I would get another couple of years out of it.

I actually thought it might be a form of arthritis. I went and got some X-rays done. Our physiotherapist, John Sharp, who is now at Aberdeen, came in and said there was something showing up on the X-ray. There was a shadow over my femur bone. I remember John was looking pretty seriously at me. I was thinking I'd broken a bone; he thought it could be a cancerous tumour.

I had to wait a few days for the results. I started to worry but I never told Andrea or the kids about it.

Cancer wasn't as high profile amongst sportsmen as it is now, with what happened to Alan Stubbs and the tragedy that took Tommy Burns' life so prematurely.

At that time, you either had it or you didn't. If you had it, you were likely to be on your way out. That was the turmoil I had spinning around my head for three or four days.

Fortunately, my results came back clear but, to this day, they are still unsure what caused the shadow. I think it was some sort of scarring. The only thing I can think of was an accident I had when I was a youngster. I had been hit by a car and had hurt that leg. Maybe it had left an indentation on the bone. I don't know.

It was a relief that it wasn't cancer or something else life-threatening, but it did show that I had done a fair bit of damage to my right hip.

Jim Jeffries had done a lot of work to bring me to the club and I was desperate to make a contribution. That was why it was so frustrating that I was forced to sit out our last six games of the season.

My last appearance was a 1–1 draw at Easter Road. That was a decent result and we still believed we could dig ourselves out of trouble. We lost at home to Dundee United but an away win at Partick Thistle gave us hope. Unfortunately, we couldn't keep it going when we drew with St Johnstone and lost to Celtic.

We got thumped 6–0 by Hearts. By then we knew the writing was on the wall. We ended up being relegated, along with Airdrie who had finished bottom. We lost our final two games against Motherwell and Rangers.

There was a real sense of disappointment because we felt we

should have been good enough to stay up but for one reason or another it just didn't happen.

I had been through a similar thing when I joined Norwich after their relegation from the top flight. I tried to put the positives across that it could actually benefit the team and the club. Eventually that is what happened.

The team went down but I think became even stronger and better prepared as a result.

22

MORE PAIN BUT PLENTY
OF BROCKVILLE GAIN

JIM JEFFERIES was determined to bounce back at the first attempt. We made our intentions clear as we won seven of our opening nine games of the First Division campaign.

Cadette was scoring goals for fun and helped us to get some big wins over our main promotion rivals Dunfermline and Airdrie. All was going well for the team, but the same could not be said about myself.

I felt I was falling apart. I had struggled to get through pre-season because of my hip and the pain was getting more and more intense.

It took me even longer to get fit. When I eventually got myself into contention, I needed a run of games to get my match fitness. When I did get into the team my injury concerns started to catch up with me again.

The only bonus was the fact I could concentrate and focus a lot more on the coaching. If that was a side I was going to go into when I hung up my boots then I had to start learning the trade.

I was lucky because Falkirk was a great place to kick off. My time working with the reserves proved to be an invaluable experience.

Working with individuals on set-plays and different formations also let me see the game from a different angle. I continued to work with Peter Houston and we were left to get on with things, apart from team selection.

Jim would always come down and give us the team and tell us how he wanted us to line up. We would shape things and go through different routines.

Working for an experienced management team of Jefferies and his assistant, Billy Brown, was also a big help. Jim had started off in the lower leagues with Berwick and then got the Falkirk job. They were seen as a yo-yo team in and around the SPL, but Jefferies was determined to stabilise them and eventually he did.

He has this knack of signing good, experienced professionals who would come in and do him a turn, like myself. I am sure even Jim would admit that a big factor in his success is down to the part played by his No. 2, Brown. It was 'good cop, bad cop'.

Billy was always the calmer one who would organise the training sessions and put the players through their paces. Jim was more of the motivator but was also a decent coach.

You get what you see with Jim and Billy. If the team wins then we were all great and if we lost then we were all rubbish and he would threaten the axe.

To be fair to Jim when he blows he blows. If we believe what we hear, Sir Alex Ferguson can be pretty formidable when he loses it.

I wouldn't actually be surprised if Jefferies would be more than a match for him in the half-time rant stakes. When it came to the hairdryer treatment or letting teacups fly then Jim is in a league of his own.

Jim was also intuitive. I would be in the office on a Friday where he would name his team and set out his tactics. But, by the time Saturday lunch-time arrived, he would have completely changed things around because he had a premonition the night before.

Once it actually cost me my place in the team. I left the park on the Friday thinking I was playing. By the time I had returned at 1pm on the Saturday, I was out on my ear.

Jim pulled me aside and said he was leaving me out and bringing

Eddie May in. Eddie then went out and scored the winning goal. After the game, Jim went in and told the press how he thought about leaving Eddie out but decided to play him because he had had a dream the night before. You would have thought he was making it up, but he wasn't.

Jim and Billy both did really well and eventually got their move to Hearts first time around. That was always the job Jim wanted. They helped to turn Hearts around. They did precisely that in some difficult financial conditions and played a major part in helping them to lift the club out of the doldrums with their Scottish Cup win.

They got their chance to manage in the Premier League with Bradford City, although things didn't go that well for them. The odds were pretty much stacked against them from the day they arrived. Bradford were in freefall and were already all but relegated and they had to try and weed out the big earners.

He came back up the road and did a decent job at Kilmarnock before he returned to his first love at Hearts.

I now represent a few boys at Kilmarnock and Hearts and from the stories they have told me I don't think he has changed too much over the years. But why should he, because he has been successful wherever he has been?

I started to learn the managerial ropes under Jim and Billy, but to progress professionally I knew I needed to start taking my badges. I wasn't sure whether to do them through the FA or SFA, but, against my better judgement, I decided to go through the Scottish coaching system.

I had wanted to do my B badge, but the problem was I was still playing. Trying to find a week between the end of the season, family holidays and pre-season to do the course was damn near impossible. The summer was always short enough to fit your summer holiday in without having to squeeze in another week to sit your badges.

Thankfully that season the SFA organised a staggered course over a couple of months where previously you had to do the entire thing over a week. That allowed professional players to go. It lasted for seven or eight Thursday afternoons.

The likes of John Philliben, Stevie Kirk and myself went on the Hampden course, which was taken by Andy Roxburgh and Craig Brown.

What stuck out for me was not their coaching or training methods, but the emphasis they put on appearance. It really was staggering.

It is even more baffling because Roxburgh and Brown had both taken Scotland to the finals of the World Cup and European Championships.

As part of the course's introduction they stuck us all in the main stand at old Hampden and sent the under-16 Scotland team out onto the pitch and put them through their paces.

The coaching drills were thorough but I was taken aback by the emphasis they put on the importance of the youngsters having their socks pulled up and shirts tucked in.

Craig also insisted that all their bibs were on the right way round.

Stevie Kirk and I just looked at each other in disbelief. We were both wondering what this had to do with coaching?

The emphasis that was put on these minor details was really unbelievable over the duration of that course. They kept going back to it and seemed to want some kudos for bringing it to the fore.

Another example Brown used still makes me laugh to this day. He explained that my former Rangers team mate John Brown had caused him a headache because he used to wear white tape round the bottom of his socks.

Craig told us they had tried to experiment with different tapes and tried to dye them the same colour as Scotland's socks to see if they could get round the problem.

That was how much emphasis the SFA put on presentation.

But, in the end, it didn't matter because he never got the call from his country.

I don't care what anybody says, 'Bomber' should definitely have played for Scotland. Bomber performed at a really high level with Rangers at home and abroad and was as good as anybody in his position.

The course did help me but there was a lot of rubbish thrown in as well. Where it did help was on the organisational front, where you had to stand in front of your peers and give out instructions and organise passages of play.

I eventually got my badges and the practice side of it was great, but a lot of the theory I didn't agree with at all.

I was concentrating on the coaching side when I got my first-team recall at Falkirk. It also came when I least expected it.

It was against Airdrie, one of our rivals, who were also looking to bounce back into the SPL. I didn't think for one minute I would be involved so I had stupidly agreed to play in the local pub's golf outing at Falkirk's Tryst on the Friday.

I went into training that morning and I was left totally flabbergasted when Jim told me I was playing. You could imagine my surprise, especially as I was due to play golf an hour or so later. He also had strict rules which stated we couldn't play golf 48 hours before a game.

I shouldn't have played, but I knew I would drop my mates in it if I didn't. But, on the other side, I knew Jim would go right through me if he ever found out.

I decided to take the gamble and play. Anyway, when it comes to golf, I need all the practice I can get. I am a rotten golfer, but that day I had started unbelievably. We were playing Stableford rules and I scored 21 points over the first nine, which I was normally lucky to register over the entire round.

I played out of my skin, but then, at the turn, a group of Falkirk fans recognised me and asked if I would be starting against Airdrie? The rest of the day I didn't even bother about the game because I was too worried about getting caught. I was too busy hiding behind bushes and trees to rival Tiger Woods.

Thankfully Jim or Billy didn't find out. I was still a bit concerned when I took to the field the next day, but I managed to score the winner, with a late header from outside of the box, which beat John Martin all ends up to give us a 2–1 win. At least that got me back into the swing of things on the pitch.

We had stumbled a bit after drawing with Hamilton and losing to Clydebank, so that goal got us back to winning ways and me back in the team.

We got another run going by beating Ayr, Dumbarton and St Mirren, where I scored both the goals. That game is still one where I slag my mate Rab Dawson about his marking because there is a photograph of me towering above him for one of my goals.

That run left us at the top of the table as we switched our attentions to our glory run in the B&Q Cup.

We started the competition with a convincing 3–0 win over Cowdenbeath. The big one for the Falkirk fans was the quarter-final clash with Dunfermline. I was told as soon as I signed for Falkirk that this was the big derby.

There's only 20 miles or so between the two teams and so the rivalry is huge. The fans dislike each other and there is a real niggle when they meet. It was our supporters who were smiling that day. Cadette was on fire and scored a hat-trick while I chipped in with the other.

I seem to be quite lucky because I always had a knack of scoring in big derby games, like for Rangers against Celtic, Coventry against Aston Villa and Birmingham against West Bromwich Albion.

That always helped endear me to the fans of most of the clubs I played for, maybe with the exception of Coventry.

We played Meadowbank Thistle in the semi-final. We had been expected to win that one quite easily, but they pushed us all the way before we eventually came out on top in a five-goal thriller, thanks to a double from Cadette and another from Eddie May.

That ensured our cup final place against St Mirren. We weren't going to Hampden and none of the SPL clubs were in the competition, nevertheless we were still desperate to land the trophy.

· I certainly didn't expect to be in another final. Even though I was into my 30s it was still a big thing for me. There was even a bit of a buzz in and around the town in the build-up to that game.

St Mirren and Falkirk have both spent time in and out of the SPL, but when both are going well they certainly have the potential to boost their crowds.

That was shown at Fir Park for that final. Around 12,000 fans turned up. That was amazing because it must have been one of the coldest days in memory. There was sleet and snow, and the temperatures plummeted to sub-zero. It was that bad I expected to see Eskimos and polar bears in the stands.

I had some friends up from Grimsby, John 'Killer' Croft, Brian Snell, Roger Morgan and Malcolm Hammond, who used to come and watch me play all over Britain. They would pick a few of my games a season and would make the trip north.

When they heard Falkirk had made the cup final they decided to come up. So I left match tickets and players' lounge passes for them to come in and we could meet up after it.

After the match I walked into the lounge to find my pals but they were nowhere to be seen. I thought something was up so I phoned them. They said it had been that cold in the stands they had left with 25 minutes to go. They had got back in the car, stuck the heater on and had decided to hit the road and drive all the way back to Grimsby.

Fortunately, when it came to the final itself, we didn't freeze.

The game was won quite convincingly. Duffy, Cadette and Yogi scored our goals. We played really well and scored at just the right time to knock the wind out of St Mirren.

I remember standing frozen solid just willing the referee to blow the whistle because it was so cold. It was amazing because Yogi was the exact opposite. He was charging about with his short-sleeved shirt like it was a beautiful, sunny day; I was standing there freezing to death. You have to remember I am a Grimsby boy and I am used to the cold but that day was something else.

I just didn't enjoy the game at all even though we had lifted the cup. It was great picking up the trophy and doing a lap of honour in front of the fans, but the match was just a nightmare, even if it did mean another medal.

We went back to Brockville after the game to celebrate with our fans. There were 2,000 or so supporters back at the stadium, waiting to see us parade the trophy. It was great and after that we went back to the Park Hotel for the reception. It was some party. As you can imagine, it went long into the Monday morning. Let me say, quite a few of our team knew how to enjoy themselves.

Of course, we had had the disappointment of relegation, but the club was definitely on the way back up. We were top of the First Division and had lifted the B&Q Cup.

We knew we were never going to win the SPL, or the Scottish or League Cups, at that stage and so it made our B&Q win even more special.

We continued to push in the league, but my own fitness was starting to decline and I found myself in constant pain. I wasn't able to train every day and I was in agony after every game. It became that bad it was affecting me off the field.

That was around December and January.

I was having sleepless nights. Anyone who has had an arthritic hip problem will tell you how painful it is. My hip really started to get me down.

The one thing I was always able to do, no matter what was going on around me, was go out on a football pitch and give my all. Suddenly I wasn't able to do that and it was difficult to take.

I took a couple of cortisone injections, but I was reluctant to take any more because I had seen the long-term effects it had on the health of former players.

I also tried to avoid taking painkillers, although it was diffi-cult. I did take anti-inflammatory tablets to take away some of swelling and reduce some of the tissue damage, but after that it was all about trying to grin and bear it.

I continued to make myself available for selection, while

continuing to take the reserves. I also took the odd first-team session as well, whether it was keep-ball or the warm-up.

I tried to soldier on but I knew the end was near. I netted in a 3–0 win at Ayr United on 18 December; little did I know at that time that was to be my last goal for Falkirk.

By the end of the next month it had become too much and I had to hold my hands up and say it wasn't worth it. My final appearance for the Bairns was a 1–1 at Morton's Cappielow.

I had to make a decision: Hang up my boots or drop down the divisions and play at a lesser standard?

I had reached the point where my body could no longer react as quickly as I wanted to. I was disappointed but I knew there was no point in trying to kid my team mates or, more importantly, myself.

Jefferies started to look for a replacement and brought in the Yugoslavian, Dragutin Ristic. I don't think many of the boys in the dressing room could understand why Jim had signed him.

He had lost his place at Dundee and didn't look any better than the boys who were already at the club. Maybe Jim thought Ristic would help the team during the final run-in.

His impact was minimal, but, in the end, Falkirk managed to finish the job and seal their return to the SPL.

I might have moved on a couple of months before the end of the season but the boys definitely deserved to win the title. We had been the best team all season and, over the course of the campaign, had played the best football. I received a championship medal and it is still something I look very fondly on.

It was also another double in Scotland. Okay, it might not have been at the same level as when I was at Rangers, but, for me, what we achieved at Falkirk was just as important.

23

THIS BINO SEES RED

I HAD thought about dropping down the leagues and playing at a lower level but questioned if it was going to be worth all the pain and discomfort.

My local club, Stirling Albion, were aware of my predicament but were still desperate to sign me. Their chairman, Peter McKenzie, used to live across the road and would constantly chap at the door and ask if I would give it one more crack at Forthbank. Stirling were a good part-time club with decent facilities but I still wasn't convinced.

I was mulling over Peter's offer when my Falkirk boss Jim Jefferies threw a curve ball at me. Inverness Caledonian Thistle wanted to know if I would be interested in becoming their player-manager. They wanted a so-called big name to help them enter the Scottish Football League.

Jefferies felt it was a good opportunity and planted the seed. I was flattered they had even considered me but geographically it was just too far north. It was only a part-time position and I felt it would have been wrong to uproot the family again.

I asked Jim what he thought about me going to Stirling. He just looked at me and said: 'Would you not be better going to Inverness to be your own man rather than going to Stirling just to play?' I knew he had a point.

Jim tried to guide me the way of Inverness but it just didn't feel right. You have a gut instinct and I knew from the off it wasn't for me. Looking at the way Inverness have progressed through the leagues in recent seasons I sometimes sit back and wonder what might have happened if I had taken up their offer. They have played in the SPL and are a really good, solid and friendly club. It pleases me to see them do well because I have represented quite a few of their players throughout the years.

With the Inverness job out of the equation it left me with one final decision to make: do I hang up the boots or go to Stirling for one final farewell? I knew the clock was ticking and this was going to be my swansong. It was also better to be playing than sitting up in the stands or walking round the shops on a Saturday afternoon. With that in mind I decided to join Stirling. They were still in the First Division but only had 10 matches in the season to go. The manager, John Brogan, believed my experience could help Albion stay up. His other big signing of that time was midfielder Billy Reid from Hamilton. I think they paid something like £20,000 for Billy. Brogan had asked Peter to put up the money for us as one final gamble to save the club's First Division status and possibly his own job.

Right from the start I knew it was going to be a struggle because all the boys were part-time. They were out doing day jobs and we were up against teams who were still full-time and not long ago had been playing in the SPL, sides like Morton, Hamilton, Falkirk, Dunfermline and Ayr United.

I scored against Ayr United but chances were few and far between and eventually I dropped back to help in the midfield. I arrived in the March and we still hadn't won a game by mid-April. The team were giving their all but there was just such a gulf in class.

The patience of the chairman finally snapped after we drew at home to Airdrie. Brogan was sacked. It was harsh on John because even the very top managers would have struggled to keep Stirling afloat in that league. The decision to remove John didn't go down well with the fans.

I was stuck in the middle because Peter asked me to take over the team on a temporary basis until he found a replacement. I reluctantly agreed and took charge of the game at Hamilton. We managed to get a win thanks to an Ian McInnes goal. It was our first league win in over two months. It helped lift spirits but it didn't provide the springboard for survival we had hoped. I saw out the season but believed in my heart of hearts the club would bring somebody else in now we were down in the Second Division.

A few weeks went before Peter asked me if I would stay on as manager. He told me the aim was to win promotion and asked me if I thought I could achieve that goal. I knew we had a decent side and playing at a level against other part-time teams I believed we had a chance of winning promotion, although there were a lot of other things I also had to weigh up.

There was no contract and the salary on offer was only £300-a-week but in the end I decided to take the plunge. I wanted to go into management and saw it as the first step on the ladder.

I kept the majority of the squad together and only signed two players in those opening weeks. I took in Andy Paterson, a right back, who had been on trial with us during that summer, and persuaded the chairman to sign Craig Taggart from Falkirk. I knew Craig from my own time at Brockville. He was a good midfield player who I felt could do us a real turn.

I went to my old boss Jim Jefferies, who didn't want to stand in Craig's way. We agreed a deal where we could sign him for a nominal fee of £8,000.

I told my chairman the deal was done but Peter said: 'Leave it with me because I am friendly with Falkirk chairman George Fulston and I can get them down a bit.'

I left it in his capable hands and within a couple of days Taggart duly arrived. I have to admit it took Craig a few games to settle in but I was left gobsmacked when the chairman turned to me during that initial period and said: 'Signing Taggart has been a right waste of £20,000.'

I just looked at him and said: 'I agreed a deal for £8,000 – how did you end up paying £12,000 more?' He didn't even respond. I just looked at him again and shook my head in disbelief. I don't think Peter could explain it either! It wasn't as if we were rolling in cash. I also could have brought in another couple of players with the additional money he had needlessly spent.

Things were so tight I couldn't even afford to bring in an assistant manager, although I desperately needed somebody to help share the burden. It was too much trying to play and organise everything else off the field as well.

I'd heard that Ray Stewart, a former adversary from my playing days at West Ham, had been released by St Johnstone. He had been in charge of the McDiarmid Park youth set-up. I didn't really know him that well but had heard good things about his coaching and so I decided to arrange a meeting with him. We hit it off straight away because we both have similar philosophies on how the game should be played. We appeared to complement each other in much the same way as the successful Graeme Souness-Walter Smith or Ken Brown-Mel Machin partnerships that I had worked under at Rangers and Norwich respectively.

I managed to wangle it so Ray could come in on a part-time basis by scraping together £100-a-week in expenses for him.

I think the chairman also saw the logic in the appointment and after five or six games gave Ray a guaranteed wage of £150-a-week. It proved to be one of the best signings I ever made.

I knew I had somebody I could rely on on the sidelines, especially if I was going to continue playing. I was still in a lot of pain with my hip but I felt I could contribute, especially in the Second Division. I knew my problems were arthritic and I would have to eventually get things sorted out later in life.

I was confident in the players even though we made an indifferent start. I wasn't helped by other factors outwith my control. Billy Reid, our experienced midfielder, walked out and disappeared off the face of the earth. He didn't turn up for training and nobody knew where he had gone. I think he was having problems in his private life and we couldn't get hold of him.

He eventually re-appeared for a training session three weeks later. He came in, picked up his wages and disappeared again. His outstanding wage packets had mounted up and I had 10 weeks' money waiting for him.

I had to phone the players' union and the Scottish Football League to ask what I should do. I was informed I needed to find him and give him his money or he could sue us – even though he hadn't turned up! How mad was that?

We finally tracked Billy down and sent him his cheque for the remainder of his money and that was it. Billy never returned to Forthbank as a player again. I think he became so disillusioned with the game and everything else that was happening in his life that he decided to chuck it. The next time I saw Billy was a couple of years later when he appeared as a youth coach at Clyde. Since then he has gone on to make a decent name for himself in management, taking the main job at Clyde and now with his old team Hamilton, who he memorably led into the SPL.

His decision to become the invisible man hardly helped my cause. Billy was one of our better players and he just upped sticks and left.

I knew I had to make changes if I wanted the club to progress. Ideally I would have loved the club to go full-time but we didn't have the finances. I felt unless we moved in that direction then the club would continue to yo-yo between the First and Second Divisions. It was all down to ambition and I wanted to take the club forward.

The fans were also at me to attend their supporters' meetings. It wasn't really my scene but I knew Brogan had gone to them and so I reluctantly agreed to attend. I didn't want to alienate them before I had even got my feet under the desk. I should have stuck with my initial instincts because it proved to be a massive mistake. It was the one and only supporters meeting I attended and I ended up falling out with half the fans. They felt, because it was their club and they followed them home and away, that they should have an influence on team selections. They knew a lot of the players but only as personalities and at times that tainted their views. They didn't see them in training or their attitudes before the game but they still wanted to have an input. I politely declined their advice and decided to get on with things in my own way. Let's just say my way didn't go down too well but I knew I would be judged by results and nothing else. I would stand or fall by my decisions.

In that first season I also seemed to be at war with one director or another, although the chairman was always first class. The biggest bugbear of our directors was the fact I wasn't really a big fan of the lesser cup competitions, especially the local Stirlingshire Cup.

We were well represented in the Stirlingshire FA but I saw their competition as more of an inconvenience than a tournament of any real worth. I didn't give the Challenge Cup and the Stirlingshire Cup much credence at all and that often got me into trouble with the local blazers.

Nobody was interested in these competitions. The attendances were rubbish and nobody really cared, so why should I bother? That was my view and one that caused more than a few waves of discontent.

The board felt I devalued these competitions by putting out weakened teams. The Stirlingshire Cup was the worst because you couldn't play trialists, it had to be signed players.

We were drawn against Alloa and I was determined not to risk injuring any of my first-team players. That left us so short of players that I registered Danny Cunning, our kitman, and his 15-year-old son. I also handed a shirt to a trainee doctor from Africa, who had been helping us out on a part-time basis. I fielded them along with Stevie Nicholas who was only 15 at the time. There was no financial reward or kudos in winning the cup but there was always the risk of suspensions and injuries so what was the point of taking any risks?

I got so much stick for that that I actually decided to help organise the competition the following season, although it was in a manner that suited me, i.e. a five-a-side competition that was done and dusted in one day.

My priority was always promotion but in the league we hit the rocks. I came out of the team but Ray argued I should get the boots back on. I didn't want to but I was left with very little option. We didn't have a big squad and I didn't think the kitman was quite ready for league duty.

I agreed to go on the bench for a game at Dumbarton. I watched from the dugout and again everything that could go wrong did go wrong. We went 2–0 down and Ray told me I had to put myself on. I did and we ended up fighting back for a 2–2 draw when I grabbed the equaliser. I continued to soldier on before I decided enough was enough. I was in too much pain and couldn't go on, so my final senior appearance ended in a 3–0 defeat to Morton at Forthbank on 11 February. My playing career spanning 18 years was at an end. What a way to bow out!

It didn't help that we were struggling to live up to our 'promotion contenders' tag and the fans started to turn. I didn't think we were too far away and only one player away from being a really good team. The missing part of the jigsaw, for me, was a big, dominant centre half.

We didn't have the money to go and buy anyone but I conned the chairman a wee bit. I went to Dunfermline and spoke to their manager Bert Paton about a centre half and he offered me Gary Paterson for nothing.

I spoke to the player and everything was agreed until I got a phone call from Paul D'Mello, the secretary at Dunfermline. He insisted they wanted money and the reason was one of the most bizarre I have ever heard in my football career. He said Gary was a really tall guy and they had spent money on buying him a special club blazer and training kit, which was too big to give to anybody else, so they wanted to recoup some of that expenditure. In the end, I persuaded Peter to give them £500 to get the deal done.

I put him right in the team and we won seven and drew three, so I felt it justified my decision to sign Gary.

We rocketed from sixth up to second and suddenly looked a good bet to win promotion. Another bargain basement signing, Paul Deas, who we picked up from St Johnstone for nothing, helped strengthen our charge.

It was a big boost because when I first took over half the team couldn't even make it to training. The part-time/full-time mix did cause a few problems, which I had to address. Some of the part-timers felt I favoured the other lads but that was never the case. Our keeper Mark McGeown was always part-time and my captain, Tommy Tait, was the same. I could have given Gary or Taggart the armband but I deliberately left it with Tommy to dispel the accusations of favouritism. Tommy was a good, honest professional who was well respected by all the players. He could see both sides and knew what I was trying to achieve at the club.

Things clicked and it came down to a final day shootout between third-placed Dumbarton and ourselves for the final promotion spot. A draw was all we needed to go up behind Morton. It was a big game for the club and more than 3,000 crammed into Forthbank. Murdo McLeod was Dumbarton's manager but I felt really confident we would do it. We were on a great run and the boys were really buzzing until disaster struck 20 minutes into the game. Big Gary was carted off on a stretcher and his game was over. Half an hour later, a long throw into the box, which Gary would have mopped up with ease, opened up our old Achilles heel. We failed to clear and Dumbarton scored through Hugh Ward. They went on to grab their decisive second thanks to Charlie Gibson. In the end we lost and our promotion hopes had been cruelly crushed. It was heart-breaking because I honestly believe that if it hadn't been for Gary's injury then we would have won promotion.

We came up the tunnel after the game and Dumbarton's players were jumping for joy. I opened our dressing-room door to let our players listen to the Dumbarton celebrations. I waited for a quiet moment and stood up from the gloom and told my players that is what winning sounds like. We need to wipe the slate clean and to start working to make sure we are the ones celebrating next season.

I believed in my team and I knew we were heading in the right direction, despite all the criticism that had come my way. There were, however, the financial headaches of our failure to win promotion.

Some fans were also concerned the club were spending money we didn't have but that was never the case. We had full-time players but I was never in danger of bursting my playing budget; never mind the bank. Even when I speak to some fans today they say I left Stirling in a right financial mess but that is utter rubbish. If you look at the facts I actually made the club more money than I cost them.

You only have to look at some of the boys I took on through the YTS system. They included promising youngsters like Eddie Forrest, Stevie Nicholas and Paul Mortimer.

My judgement was proved right as all three went on to make a name for themselves in the first team. Eddie and Stevie both moved on for decent transfer fees and made Stirling more than £130,000 between them.

You can then add the £100,000 profit we made from selling Alex Bone to Ayr United and the £30,000 we got from Dundee for Steven McCormack.

I don't think anyone can argue with the job I did and the figures speak for themselves.

24

WE ARE THE CHAMPIONS
AND ROCKING RANGERS

AT THE END of the season we had been short of players and I had turned out as sweeper for the reserves. I played against Queen's Park and was up against this big striker who was a real handful. I found out it was a guy called Steve McCormack. He ran me all over the place and that was something I was no longer capable of.

I spoke to the Queen's Park coaching staff and they told me McCormack wasn't in their plans but because of their amateur status I would have to wait until the new season to sign him. I believed he could do a job, even though his career had been somewhat chequered. He had failed to win contracts at St Johnstone and Alloa, but I felt he was worth the gamble.

I decided McCormack would be my main striker but it didn't go down too well with the locals. I signed him as a replacement for Willie Waters, who to the supporters was God. The fact McCormack didn't have the greatest of CVs didn't help and it was fair to say his playing style was anything but conventional, although I was still confident he would score goals.

I was delighted when he scored on his debut against Montrose but then he went another six without hitting the net. That was when the Willie Waters campaign really kicked in. McCormack wasn't helped by the fact the team had also been slow to click.

The one silver lining during that period was our League Cup win over Hamilton. That saw us hit the jackpot when we were drawn against Rangers at Ibrox. The tie brought a lot of media attention because it was against my former club but, for me, it was all about the players. I wanted it to be an occasion that would live with them forever.

The club were going to make a fair bit of money out of it, so I persuaded the chairman to take us to the Moat House, on the River Clyde, for our pre-match meal. I'm sure Peter and the board saw it as a waste of money but I felt it would help the boys and set us up nicely for the match.

Everybody was treated really well and the staff made a right fuss of us all, from the directors right down to the players and backroom staff.

Rangers then organised a police escort for the team coach. We travelled to Ibrox with three outriders on either side. It brought a real touch of class, as we zoomed through the city like we were Real Madrid or Barcelona not tiny little Stirling Albion.

Ibrox was a new arena for many of the players and a lot different from the grounds we had been used to in the Second Division. I also found it strange returning as a manager for the first time. I've always had a great relationship with the Rangers fans and they were brilliant as I walked out to take my seat in the dugout.

I had hoped Walter Smith might rest some of his players for their league campaign but was left disappointed when I was handed their team sheet. He had put out all his big guns, like Ally McCoist, Trevor Steven and Mark Hateley, with Andy Goram in goal.

It was going to be an experience playing against top-drawer opposition like that. Rangers knocked the ball about for fun and quickly charged into a 3–0 lead.

I was just hoping that things weren't going to get too embarrassing, although I remained heartened by our battling performance, if not the scoreline.

We nicked a goal through Craig Taggart and started to cause

Rangers a few problems. Big McCormack got another 10 minutes from time to set up a grandstand finish. You could sense the panic round Ibrox. The carnival atmosphere had disappeared and more than a few of the Light Blue legions were left biting their nails.

The problem was Rangers had dropped down the gears, thinking the job had been done and when you do that, no matter who you are, it is very difficult to kick back into life.

Suddenly we were on the front foot and there was a belief amongst my players we could get a result. I think the Rangers fans also feared the worst and the backslapping and friendly banter turned to abuse and panic. The shouts turned to 'Drinkell get to f***!' because they knew we were on the verge of causing a potential embarrassment.

I always felt we would get another chance to score and we did. Joe McLeod, the former Dundee United and Motherwell winger, burst clear and had the option to go himself or square it for Taggart. If he had passed it, Taggart would have rolled the ball into the empty net but McLeod went for glory and flashed his shot narrowly past.

The dream was over and Rangers stumbled over the finishing line. I was disappointed we hadn't got more for our efforts but I was as proud as punch with my players. They had given me everything and had pushed the mighty Rangers all the way. They took a lot of credit from their dogged display and rightly so.

I shook Walter's hand after the game but one of the nicest touches was being invited up to have a drink with Willie Waddell and Willie Thorton, who I had regular chats with when I first arrived at Ibrox. They congratulated me on my team's performance and that was a gesture of class that showed what true gentlemen they were.

We may have lost the game but financially we still walked away as winners. Peter collected a cheque for something like £115,000. For a club like Stirling that was the equivalent of winning the lottery. Suddenly spending the extra money on the pre-match meal looked like peanuts.

Big Stevie's goal at Ibrox also did his confidence the power of good. He went on to net a hat-trick at Forfar, as we hit them for six. From that day we never looked back. We went on an amazing 23-game unbeaten run. It put us within touching distance of the top. A couple of weeks later we hit the front and there was no catching us. Our one and only league defeat at the back end of that campaign came against Stenhousemuir. We won our last five games of the season and clinched the title up at Montrose. What a relief!

From Links Park I drove down to Sheffield for the World Snooker Championships, which had become a regular occurrence through my friendships with the Doyle's, Lee and his dad Ian. I am a big snooker fan and I go down every year to watch the final couple of days at the Crucible. That allowed me to get away from the madness for a few days, before I returned to see us presented with our trophy following our league game with Berwick Rangers at Forthbank. It sparked another wild and well-deserved celebration.

We had finished the season with the Second Division trophy, above more fancied teams like Alex Smith's Clyde and Steve Archibald's East Fife. The most pleasing fact for me was that our title success was a real team affair, although McCormack had played a major part with his 25 goals. Not bad for a player nobody rated! His strike partner Alex Bone had also weighed in with 18 goals in 26 games, which wasn't too shabby either. Paul Deas went on to lift the supporters' Player of the Year award, so all my major signings had made a significant contribution.

I was also rewarded for the team's success when I was named as our division's manager of the year. I was presented with my Bell's trophy along with fellow league winners Walter Smith of Rangers and Allan McGraw of Morton. Maybe I wasn't so bad at this management game after all.

25

DOWN AT THE ALBION

NOW we were able to look forward to our First Division return. I knew it was going to be a real battle because although we had a few full-timers a lot of our squad were still part-time.

We were up against the likes of Airdrie, Partick Thistle, Morton, Falkirk, St Johnstone and St Mirren. I knew we had to strengthen but my biggest challenge was trying to keep Stevie McCormack. Not surprisingly after his debut season heroics, there was a fair bit of interest in him.

Luton, in particular, were keen to sign him, so we agreed he could go down there on trial. He did well and they asked to take another look at him when they headed to Scotland for pre-season. Big Stevie was going to play two games for Luton and then against them in the final match for Stirling.

We agreed the fee would be £100,000 if they wanted to sign him. Luton were always a good passing team under Lennie Lawrence but that wasn't really McCormack's game. I went to watch him when he played against Livingston in the second game. He didn't play well but in typical Stevie style he still scored.

Lawrence tried to knock the price down but I said no. I told him to wait and see what he does in the game against his team. Lennie could then judge him against his own defenders. We won and Steve scored a hat-trick. I thought if that doesn't cement the deal then nothing will. After the game Lawrence was still swithering and claimed Luton couldn't afford to meet our asking price.

Our chairman was adamant we would get the money elsewhere and pulled the plug.

We certainly could have done with the money because I still had to go round my pals and scrape together additional sponsorships. Not only did I have to go out and rustle up the money, Ray Stewart and I had to get the boards made and put them up around the ground. We certainly couldn't be accused of not getting our hands dirty!

We were also responsible for introducing corporate facilities to Forthbank. Before we arrived, the guests had to make do with a few drinks in the boardroom and a platter of sandwiches; we took the commercial side of things up a notch. I saw it as a way to generate some extra money. I organised three-course meals with a match ticket thrown in so people could make a day of it. It enabled us to tap into another potential market. Who said football management is all about the team?

On the pitch we were still the poor relations compared with the big hitters in the First Division. We didn't get much luck in the cups either. In the Coca Cola and Scottish Cups we were paired with SPL side Dundee United. We were always able to run top-flight teams close but never seemed to have enough to pull off that headline-grabbing shock.

We lost 2–1 to goals from Robbie Winters and Owen Coyle in the League Cup and our Scottish Cup exit was more straightforward with Winters and Gary McSwegan giving United a 2–0 win.

The gate receipts brought in a bit more money and allowed us to concentrate on survival. We still had the core of our championship squad and I managed to add another couple of bargain-basement signings.

Neil Bennett came in from Alloa. They had wanted £12,000 but I ended up giving them Willie Waters and one of our youngsters and got another £2,000 in return. It wasn't a bad bit of business even if I do say so myself.

There was also the Icelandic teenager called Gretar Hjartarsson. He had good ability and pretty much landed in our lap. He was

227

recommended to us by the former Celtic and Motherwell player Johannes 'Shuggy' Edvaldsson. Hjartarsson proved to be a good signing and went on to play for the Icelandic national team.

He played his part in our wins against St Mirren and Clydebank, which sparked an impressive nine-game unbeaten run that took us up to the dizzy heights of seventh going into our final game at Dundee.

We probably could have finished as high as fifth if we had won at Dens Park but that was never going to happen because I decided to rest four of our top players to avoid unwanted suspensions.

The boys were all one booking away from a ban and the last thing I wanted was to start off the new season with an instant handicap. The fans were fuming and gave me pelters for not putting out my strongest XI. They couldn't see the bigger picture.

The real achievement was remaining in the First Division. It should have been seen as a success for a club like Stirling to finish seventh. We really had punched above our weight.

The new season saw the team evolve again. I started to bring in youngsters like Eddie Forrest and Paul Mortimer, who had come through our YTS system. They had got their taste at the end of the previous season, while I also gave young Stevie Nicholas his competitive chance. I knew, given time, they would all make an impact but some of my other major stalwarts were causing me unnecessary headaches. McCormack was out of contract and told me Raymond Sparkes had become his agent. He informed me the offer we had made him was derisory and he would be leaving. Big Stevie went on trials in Norway, France and England before he eventually ate humble pie and came back to Stirling at the end of November, but by then he was no longer the main man and he was unable to walk straight back into the team.

He started to complain but guys like Gavin Price and Alex Bone had come in and done a decent job. They had also shown their team mates and me loyalty and deserved their chance. McCormack never got back to the levels he had previously and a few months later I sold him to Dundee.

228

We kicked off the new campaign in hope rather than expectation because it was becoming increasingly difficult to maintain the full-time element of the squad.

Players like Craig Taggart, Ronnie McQuilter and Joe McLeod had all decided to move on because they could earn more elsewhere, or by getting a job and playing football on the side. Those three, in particular, were with me when I first started laying the foundations and had taken a big gamble to remain full-time on a pretty low, basic salary. But after three years it became apparent that Stirling Albion, with our financial restrictions, would never be able to meet their own growing expectations.

Joe departed that summer and within months of the new season Taggart and McQuilter followed him out the door. Add to that McCormack's disappearing act and a huge chunk of the successful team I had built up had been ripped apart.

It was all about limiting the damage. We yo-yoed between ninth and 10th although our fortunes in the cup were slightly better. In the Coca Cola Cup we beat Partick and got another SPL team as our reward. This time we did get the scalp we craved when we thumped the Scottish Cup holders Kilmarnock. They came up to Forthbank and we battered them 6–2.

I remember the game because it wasn't long after Bobby Williamson had been given the Kilmarnock job on a permanent basis. This defeat was a real embarrassment for him. We were a small club, with part-time players and we had hit his SPL team for six. He was a bit down after the game and I invited him in for a beer and tried to cheer him up and console him. I had been in the same position after many games that season myself so I knew how he felt.

Our reward was another crack at the top flight with Aberdeen. But this time there was to be no glory, as the Dons had too much for us. Aberdeen had a strong side, which included Brian Irvine who I had found to be one of my toughest opponents during my own playing days in Scotland.

He might not have been as technically gifted as some of his

229

more glamorous team mates but I found him a real tough nut to crack. He reminded me a lot of the former England and Arsenal star Martin Keown, who I played against in England. He was another strong out-and-out defender and they both had similar personalities. It didn't matter how many times you crashed into them they never seemed to get fazed. They were totally focused on their games.

I would say big Brian was always under-rated, due to the fact he was living in the shadows of Willie Miller and Alex McLeish. But as a fellow professional I knew what a good player he was.

Our cup campaigns were over but the New Year brought a bit of hope in the league when we toppled Partick Thistle at Firhill. That took us, temporarily, out of the relegation zone but we were always swimming against the tide. In the end we were unable to survive and that left the club and myself at a crossroads.

26

STOOD UP BY ST MIRREN

A FEW weeks before our relegation I was at an Old Firm game at Ibrox, where I was approached by a businessman called Stewart Gilmour. He told me he was fronting a consortium to buy St Mirren and said they wanted me to become their new manager.

I took it with a pinch of salt but a few hours later Ray Stewart called me to say he had bumped into Gilmour in a Glasgow bar. He had told him of our discussion and his plan to take us both to Love Street. I had never hidden my desire to go into full-time management but at the same time, I didn't want to do the dirty on Stirling. I was also aware the consortium had still to buy St Mirren, who had a manager in Tony Fitzpatrick

In the meantime our relegation left the Stirling chairman, Peter McKenzie, in a bit of a panic. He was concerned about the finances and the direction of the club. He pulled me in and said: 'Things aren't really working out? What can we do?'

I wasn't really in the mood for arguing. I said to Peter: 'What do you want me to do?' Peter stuttered and stumbled and then made the excuse that relegation meant the club could no longer afford full-time football or myself.

I could have sat there and said: 'No way, I have been here four or five years and I am not leaving unless you give me money to go.' I knew previous managers had been squared up but I wasn't really bothered about the financial aspect of things. So I did the honourable thing and walked away. I knew money was tight at Stirling and didn't want to take finances that would be taken out of the new manager's budget.

The thing that disappointed me about old Peter was where he turned next. I had no problems with him asking my assistant Ray to replace me. I thought he would make a decent manager but when I was in charge Peter was always at me to get rid of Ray, especially when one or two stories from his private life hit the newspapers.

I refused because I knew Ray was a good coach and he was a really close friend. That was why I found it rather ironic that hours after I quit Peter offered him the job.

Ray was as surprised as anyone and out of loyalty to me he turned it down. He said he would take the team for the final game at Morton but after that he had to find a new manager.

After my departure from Stirling had become common knowledge I took a call from Gilmour inviting me to be his guest for St Mirren's final game of the season against Dundee.

He said it would be the ideal opportunity for me to see the team and to start making plans for the new season. I asked him what the situation was with regards to Fitzpatrick and he told me that Tony would be in charge for the final time.

That was something I was far from comfortable with. There was no way I was going to sit in the directors' box like some sort of vulture hovering over Fitzpatrick's back. I told Gilmour I would leave it until he had resolved the matter and didn't think it would be right for me to attend the game.

Gilmour said: 'You need to come to the game because we only have a couple of weeks to do our retained list and we need to sort it out. We need to know what players you want to keep or release.' He then agreed to fax me a list of the St Mirren playing staff. They would indicate on it which players they thought we should keep and then I could give my thoughts. We also discussed terms and what I would be looking for in terms of a contract for Ray and myself.

Everything was agreed and thrashed out during that final week of the season. I went off on a family holiday expecting to return as manager of St Mirren.

Tony had his detractors on the St Mirren board but there were others who quite liked him. In that final match they put on a decent showing and beat Dundee.

Fitzpatrick was a St Mirren legend, having helped them to win the Scottish Cup, and after that match there was a swell of fans who had heard Tony was going to be sacked. Apparently they began chanting his name outside the main stand, demanding he keep his job.

Gilmour assured me everything would be okay and it was still their intention to bring me in. But when they finally took charge a big problem had emerged. During their due diligence they had failed to look into Tony's contract. They thought it was up that summer but it still had another 12 months to run. It was going to cost them a substantial five-figure sum to pay him off but Gilmour was adamant he would sort it out.

The problem was they didn't have the money to pay Tony off and things kept dragging on. So much so that Tony was still in charge for the start of the new season while I was left sitting in the house. This went on for several weeks until it got to the stage where I knew it just wasn't going to happen. What disappoints me, looking back, is that Gilmour and his fellow directors didn't just come out and say the deal was off. I would have thought a lot more of them if they had. They strung me along and left me in the lurch while I didn't have a penny coming in.

I didn't see Gilmour again for a year after it. He said hello but never had the decency to explain what had happened. I have since spoke to Fitzpatrick and even he was aware what had been going on behind his back.

At least Tony kept himself in a job but for me I was left waiting for the phone to ring, hoping somebody else would take a chance.

A lot of people thought I would have got the Falkirk job when it went to John Lambie, while I was also heavily linked with the Kilmarnock position but nothing came of that either.

In that final season at Stirling I was also approached by a Grimsby director, Dougie Everett, and asked to put my CV in for their manager's post. My former club were a bit up and down during that time and seemed to change their boss every season or so. I was certainly up for it and didn't need to be asked twice. It was not long after Brian Laws left and they had put Paul Groves, one of their players, in charge. I sent my CV to Everett's house but the next morning the chairman took his own decision and appointed the former Charlton, Middlesbrough and Cardiff manager Lennie Lawrence. The appointment was a shock to everyone because it had come straight out of left field. It was a bit of a blow because my CV had never even got to the board-room even though there had been strong rumours in the local press and around the town that I was going to get the job. I started to get the feeling I was never going to get my chance at a higher level.

27

THE GABLE END
OF MANAGEMENT

THERE were opportunities for me to get back into the dugout but they were with other smaller, part-time clubs, who wanted me to replicate the job I had done at Stirling Albion. But I didn't have the desire or drive to drop back down to that level again. I had proved myself at Stirling and I couldn't motivate myself to go down that road again. I had dedicated so much time and effort into Stirling and to go somewhere else and start from scratch again was just a non-starter for me. That left me sitting around the house, feeling sorry for myself, wondering if the phone would ring or I would finally have to call time on my managerial career.

Then one afternoon I took a call from John Paton, who was the chairman of the Scottish Third Division side Montrose. I knew John because he had been a director at Rangers.

He had also, rather ironically, been the one who had been ousted by Gilmour when he took over at St Mirren. John had decided to return and re-invest to his hometown Angus club.

John asked if I would do him a favour and take over the manager's job. He knew I wasn't the sort of guy who liked to be sitting around doing nothing and pitched heavily on that point.

Montrose were a good family club and despite vowing that I wouldn't go back to part-time football again I decided to buckle and help them out. It was back to basics again, much like when I first arrived at Stirling.

It was a club where everybody mucked in both on and off the pitch. I was no different. Sometimes I would go up and stay overnight so I could paint a few walls, take training or help push the commercial side of things.

There were good people up there but it always seemed like I was flogging a dead horse. I was a part-time manager and no longer had the pulling power of being in charge of a club in the central belt. It became near impossible to entice good players up to Montrose. The better players would take less money to play locally or would drop down to the juniors rather than travel up to Angus. It was hard. I couldn't even get some of the young boys I knew from Stirling to come up and play because they felt it was too far away.

I still thought I could bring in some decent signings who would enhance the squad and more than hold our own in the Third Division. But it became quite clear that luck wasn't going to be on my side at Links Park.

I brought in David Muirhead but within weeks he had broken his metatarsal, while Tommy Harrison, a former Hearts youngster who I had high hopes for, snapped his Achilles on his debut and would never play again.

Everywhere I turned I seemed to hit a brick wall and I finally decided enough was enough. I met with John and told him I couldn't carry on. He was as good as gold and understood my situation and we mutually agreed a parting of the ways.

28

SPECIAL AGENT
TO THE RISING STARS

I HAD to accept my managerial dream was over and I wondered what the future was going to hold. Did I still have a future in the game in some other capacity?

Not long after that, two of my old Stirling protégés Stevie Nicholas and Eddie Forrest got in touch to ask for my advice. They had both moved on from Albion but had seen their dream of playing in the Scottish Premier League crushed when Motherwell were plunged into administration.

Their chairman John Boyle ripped up the contracts of a clutch of their players, mainly the big-earners and the fringe players he no longer wanted. The shocking thing was that Motherwell were able to ring-fence their top young players, like James McFadden, Stephen Pearson and Steven Hammell.

They were allowed to rip up the contracts of the players they no longer wanted while protecting the others who might have had a potential sell-on value.

Eddie and Stevie were two of those victims and needed help. I started to make a few phone calls to managers in a bid to find them new clubs. I then took calls from several irate agents telling me I shouldn't be operating without a licence. It hadn't really crossed my mind to be an agent. I had been basically making calls as a favour to help the boys out. It was only then I thought about actually becoming a full-time agent.

Being the belligerent type, I decided to look into the requirements. I was given a lot of advice from Ian and Lee Doyle, who had successfully run the Cuemasters snooker management company, which looked after top stars like Stephen Hendry. I knew the service the Doyles provided to their clients and that was something I was keen to replicate on the football front. I didn't want to become 'Johnny 10 per cent' who signed up a player, did the deal and then walked away with a quick buck. If I was going to do the job then I was determined I was going to do it properly.

The Doyles looked after everything for their snooker players from the table, financial advice, mortgages, sponsorship or media support. They took care of everything and let their players get on with their snooker. The Doyle family eventually sold off their company before they came back under the 110 Sport umbrella. That was when Lee asked me to come on board because they wanted to diversify into other sports, like football, golf, snooker, rugby, cycling and athletics.

It was an offer I was more than happy to take up and it allowed me to take my first steps in the agency game. I still had my manager/scout hat on and it enabled me to go out and build for the long term. I didn't go and knock on the doors of the big stars to make some quick cash. I went out and identified young players who I thought could really progress and make a name for themselves in the game. I took on guys like Darren Barr and Iain Turner and you can now see these guys really fulfilling their potential. Darren was a young player coming through the ranks at Falkirk but now he is a Scottish international and is playing for Hearts, while Iain, who had been a promising young goalkeeper at Stirling Albion, has in recent seasons been getting a first-class education while earning good money in the English Premier League with Everton.

It is the same today because I have guys like Jamie Murphy

and Steven Saunders at Motherwell and Jamie Hamill and Craig Bryson at Kilmarnock.

I would always look at the lower leagues to try and find a diamond in the rough, similar to what I did with Stevie McCormack when I was manager of Stirling.

That was when I came across Kenny 'The Flying Doc' Deuchar. The big man came to my attention when he was scoring goals for fun at East Fife in the Third Division. He was earning something like £30-a-week while continuing to study to become a doctor.

Kenny, who had been released by Falkirk, had the potential to play in a higher league but he was only going to get better if he was given the chance to go full-time, so he could concentrate on his football. Otherwise he was always going to be up against it as he trained to become a doctor. There were some Friday nights he would work nightshift, finish at midday on a Saturday, get a shower and then head straight to Methil to play for East Fife. It wasn't exactly the ideal preparation. It was hardly surprising when he stepped out and there was nothing left in the tank.

The Godsend for Kenny was what was being created at Gretna. They had come into the Scottish Football League and started to make a few ripples with the financial backing of the English businessman Brooks Mileson.

Kenny went to Gretna and scored goals for fun at Raydale Park. He became 'Doctor Goals' and a cult hero all over Britain with the help of Jeff Stelling on Sky Sports. Kenny became a big favourite and that helped me cement my relationship with Gretna and Brooks.

I went on to do quite a few deals at Raydale, bringing in guys like Bryan Gilfillan, Derek Townsley, Davie Nicholls and Dene Shields. They all made a real impact at Gretna, to such an extent that Brooks asked me to become the official agent for the club and I also took on Rowan Alexander, their manager, as a client.

I engineered moves to bring in experienced players like James Grady and other big names. These guys weren't my clients but I was told to go and strike a deal with their agents and then pass it on to Brooks to sign off.

The one thing about Brooks is that all of the players who met him took an instant shine to him because he was such an infectious individual. I remember the night Gilfillan was called up to the Northern Irish under-21 squad. It was a massive thing for a club like Gretna to get international recognition. He went out and bought 50 seats to fly all the staff, from the management and players to the office staff, out to Belfast to watch Bryan play for Northern Ireland. He saw it as a celebration for Bryan and Gretna.

The club also went out and signed good, established players like David Bingham, Stevie Tosh, Chris Innes and Alan Main. They were mainly players at the other end of the age scale. They were offered a bit more security to drop down the leagues.

We had two or three great years when they won the Third and then Second Division titles and got to the Scottish Cup final, where they eventually lost bravely to Hearts on penalties. I was asked to deal with all the club's media preparations on the day and I was even in the dressing room at half-time, listening to the team talk and doing the little things like trying to get the players sorted out for the after-match drugs test. It was a great day and a real fairytale for Gretna and Scottish football. It is just a shame they couldn't go all the way and beat Hearts on penalties.

People can say what they like about Rowan Alexander and Brooks Mileson but getting Gretna to a Scottish Cup final was a real achievement.

On the back of that Gretna qualified for the UEFA Cup. It didn't help that they went into Europe and were thrashed by the Irish League side Derry City.

I think that, and their domestic success, made a lot of people in football wary and a bit jealous of Gretna. They were no longer seen as this friendly club because other chairman now saw them as a threat. There was even jealousy within the SPL because they were paying more than some top-flight clubs. I couldn't understand it because everything Brooks did was to the benefit of Scottish football.

The club had a core of experienced players and started to look more towards the longer term and that was when the likes of Martin Canning came in. He was a decent player at Ross County, and a few SPL clubs, including Aberdeen, were looking at him but it was only Gretna who could afford to pay his £50,000 asking price.

I was sent to look at players and to offer my professional advice. I watched guys like the Northern Irish international Peter Thompson, who was scoring goals for fun for Linfield. Gretna bid something like £100,000 but still couldn't get him.

I also scouted the young English winger Gary Roberts, who was playing for non-league Accrington Stanley. I thought he was a really good prospect who would have done a decent job for Gretna but Rowan knocked it on the head because he was desperate to bring in Jim McAlister from Morton. In the end Roberts went on to play in the Championship with Ipswich and is still making a name for himself in the lower leagues of England, so, for me, that shows his quality.

It was not long after the club won promotion to the First Division when Brooks' health began to fail. By the Christmas he was in a bad way and the experienced Mick Wadsworth was brought in to assist with the running of the club. As Brooks' health deteriorated Wadsworth took greater control of the footballing operation and, in the end, he was given total control of the club. That ended up driving a wedge between Rowan and Brooks because everyone knew that Wadsworth wanted an input when it came to first-team matters. Brooks and Rowan had been like father and son over those first few years but their relationship deteriorated so much that they couldn't even look each other in the eye. It was all rather sad the way it ended and I still feel for Rowan and the way he was treated. He was put on gardening leave and unfounded accusations started to fly about. I think that was wrong because what Rowan achieved at Gretna was unbelievable. People say he only had success because he had Brooks' financial backing but having money doesn't necessarily guarantee you success. Look at Manchester City. They might have all the money in the world but have they come close to winning the English Premier League yet? Rowan deserves respect and shouldn't have been treated the way he was because what happened has certainly tarnished his professional reputation. That was wrong because his record was top-drawer and he merited another crack at management.

Rowan should also have been there that day at Motherwell when Gretna played their first game in the SPL. Even if he hadn't been in charge, he more than played his part in helping Gretna get there. I was criticised for taking Rowan to Fir Park on that day. It was claimed it was a publicity stunt but we were advised by our lawyers that Rowan should turn up for work. He was still on gardening leave although the club were adamant that Rowan was still the manager. Our lawyer told us if that was the case then Rowan has to turn up for work to fulfil his own contractual obligations. He ended up losing his job and it all turned pretty ugly and headed for the courts before Gretna eventually went to the wall and he got nothing. It left Rowan without a penny and everything he had worked for disappeared when his beloved Gretna went out of business. I still believe that if Brooks' health had been okay then he would have looked after Rowan. Things might have been scaled down with a bit of dignity rather than the cost-cutting approach that was adopted by Wadsworth.

When the club looked like it was going to fold I had to go and find new clubs for the likes of Deuchar and Canning. I had always had an eye on getting Kenny out of Gretna by that time anyway because people, including Rowan and Wadsworth, didn't think he could score goals at First Division level never mind in the SPL. His goal record in the Second and Third Divisions was second to none but they didn't really fancy him when they took the step up. They sent him off to Northampton on loan but Northampton couldn't afford to buy him.

Wadsworth then sent him packing on loan to St Johnstone, where his goalscoring record was phenomenal and he helped them to win the Challenge Cup.

Then suddenly Gretna hit the skids and lost half their team as they slumped into administration, and suddenly Wadsworth had no option but to throw him in.

Kenny came in and played half a dozen games and managed to score goals, including two against Rangers, which brought about his move to America.

We knew Gretna wanted to move him on and I had been in talks with a few teams in the MLS. A few teams had been impressed with his statistics and asked for some further DVDs.

Real Salt Lake were one of the teams but they pushed things further and came and had a look. Their officials came across for the Rangers game and also planned to watch him again the following midweek against Kilmarnock.

But Kenny did that well against Rangers that the Real Salt Lake officials wanted to get the deal done there and then. We spent half the night finalising the deal, before Kenny took them for something to eat at his restaurant at the Falkirk Wheel.

He went out to America and did reasonably well and came back to the SPL where he has had spells with Hamilton and St Johnstone, where once again he has shown he is more than capable of cutting it at the top level.

I have sat at many of Kenny's games with his family and it gives me a great deal of delight to see him come up the hard way. Kenny has worked for his success and has proved a lot of doubters wrong to achieve what he has in the game. He could still easily be playing in the SPL but took the decision to drop down to the First Division with Falkirk, where he feels he has unfinished business, so he could continue his doctoring. He knows his football won't last forever and will be well set when the day comes when he finally decides to hang up his boots.

I feel an enormous amount of pride watching guys like Kenny and Mark Brown, who nobody in the SPL would touch when he was released by Motherwell but he went up to Inverness and ended up getting his dream move to Celtic. Mark showed his quality there and is now making a name for himself in the SPL with Hibs.

Another is Charlie Mulgrew. He bounced back from the disappointment of not making it at Celtic and Wolves. There was never any question about his talent but after some real hard graft he is now back at Parkhead.

I can no longer play and so helping my players to make their way in the game is the next best thing. It gives me as much of a buzz seeing my boys do well as it used to when I hit the net.

Unfortunately that isn't always the case in football agency because there are too many agents – and too many bad agents. You just have to go out and do your best and hope your reputation and professionalism come to the fore – in the same way they did in my own playing days.

29

RAISING A GLASS
TO DRINKS

TREVOR WHYMARK
(Grimsby Town 1980–1984)

KEVIN DRINKELL was a top-drawer striker and I still find it hard
to believe he never got the chance to play for England.

I had the great honour of representing my country and I definitely believe 'Drinks' was good enough to follow in my footsteps.
I think he got an England B call-up but apart from that was pretty
much overlooked. I know it was a big disappointment because his
form at Norwich and Rangers was definitely good enough to force
him onto the international scene.

Kevin had to make do with his club career and, to be fair, he didn't
do too badly on that front. He was hugely popular at most of the
clubs he played for and that shows you what a good player he was.

Kevin was a big, big favourite with us at Grimsby. He was the
local lad and rising star. Not only was he a good footballer, but
he also gave nothing less than 100 per cent and helped to inspire
others around him. He was a real crowd pleaser.

When I joined Grimsby the bulk of the squad had taken the
team from the Fourth Division into the Second Division (the current
Championship). They were beginning to struggle and that is why
they turned to me for my top-level experience.

I didn't know many of that current team and I have to say Kevin wasn't really a guy I knew much about. I was aware he had been the club's top scorer but I didn't really see him at close quarters until I joined Grimsby.

He was quite quiet and never really asked for advice or guidance but you could see he was taking everything in and used anything he could that would help improve his game.

He scored goals for fun but was really unlucky with back and hip problems because if he hadn't been then I am sure he would have moved on a lot sooner than he did.

Even when I was moved up to become assistant manager there was a lot of interest in Kevin from some really big top-flight teams. I know that my old team, Ipswich Town, were one of several teams who thought seriously about signing him. I took a phone call from one of their scouts working for Sir Bobby Robson but for one reason or another, things never came off.

But it was only going to be a matter of time before he got his move and eventually Norwich came calling. He never looked back and showed everybody that he could more than hold his own in England's top tier.

I now live quite close to Norwich and I used to take my kids to watch them. We used to go and see Kevin and we were all delighted to see him do so well. Even after I left Grimsby to join Southend, Kevin and Andrea called and asked if my wife and I would become Godparents to their oldest daughter, Alexandra. It was a lovely touch and a decision we didn't have to think twice about. That sums up Kevin. He was a great player and a top guy, with a really lovely family.

PAUL WILKINSON
(Grimsby Town 1982–1985)

I USED to clean Kevin Drinkell's boots but it is fair to say it was his guidance that helped polish me into a half-decent centre forward. I was the young apprentice at Grimsby Town, looking to make my way, and 'Drinks', as a fellow local boy, was a guy we all looked up to. He had come through the ranks to become the main No. 9 and that was something I certainly aspired to. I used to look after Kevin's kit and boots but he probably did a bit more for me than I did for him. As one of Grimsby's top stars, Kev always used to have the top make of boots and so when he was finished with them he would hand them over to yours truly. Thankfully there was still plenty of goal dust in them by the time they were handed down.

Kevin was a bit of a nightmare when you cleaned his boots because he was always pretty pernickety but that was because he always wanted the best in whatever he did. I also have to say he was always very generous when it came to handing out the Christmas tips.

'Drinks' also took me under his wing. He was a top professional and player from whom to learn my trade. Kevin was good in the air, had great feet and was also a real physical force.

He used to stay back with me in the afternoons and help me practise my heading. It must have worked because that was something my own game became famed for.

He also helped with the physical and mental side of things and that got me ready to make my own first-team bow.

We went on to play together in the Grimsby first team and we had some great times. There were quite a lot of local lads at that time playing in the old Second Division, which is the current Championship, so, looking back, that was some achievement.

I went on to play for Everton, Nottingham Forest, Middlesbrough and Watford but I have to say I owe a lot of what I achieved in my career to 'Drinks'. I would just like to say thank you for everything you did for me.

KEN BROWN
(Manager of Norwich City from 1980–87)

KEVIN DRINKELL was a rare breed. Not only was he a great footballer but one of the most loyal players I have ever come across in the game.

There aren't many players who wouldn't make a song and dance about things or kick off if they were told they were not getting their move to Manchester United. But that is precisely what happened with Kevin. We received an enquiry from Sir Alex Ferguson when I was manager at Norwich but he was my top striker and there was no way I was going to let him go. I immediately said: 'Thanks but no thanks. Kevin is not for sale,' and that was pretty much the end of the conversation.

I was always honest and up front with my players and, out of courtesy, I pulled Kevin in and told him about Manchester United's interest and the fact we weren't prepared to sell him.

I was a bit concerned he might try to force the move because Manchester United are a big team with a massive history. I thought I might have a fight on my hands and was prepared to fight tooth and nail to keep him at Carrow Road but I needn't have worried.

I told Kevin how desperate I was to keep him and how he was going to be my main man and that was enough to keep him at Carrow Road. For me, that showed the loyalty of the man.

Not bad for a player who we had been left sweating on when I signed him on a tribunal from Grimsby. But we had been watching him for a while and believed he would be a real asset to Norwich. Even after we signed him we ended up getting relegated and lost our place in Europe because of the Heysel disaster. I said to Kevin and my other new signings: 'You can go if you want.' But nobody took me up on my offer and they all played their part in getting Norwich back into the top flight.

And, to be fair, in his three seasons at Norwich Kevin proved to be worth every penny. He was a great player and servant for the club and thoroughly deserves his place in Norwich City's Hall of Fame.

'Drinks' was terrific for us. He was a typical bustling centre forward. He gave everything on the pitch and enjoyed life to the maximum off it.

Looking back I know I cost him a move to Manchester United but I am surprised he never went on to play for one of England's top clubs like United, Liverpool or Tottenham. He had the chance, I know, to go to Spurs after I left but unfortunately it didn't happen because they couldn't agree a fee with Norwich. He did eventually get his big move to Rangers and once again showed what a top striker he was.

STEVE BRUCE
(Norwich City 1984–87)

IT IS with great pleasure that I have been given the opportunity to write a few words about Kevin who I had the honour to play alongside and room with whilst we both played for Norwich City FC in the '80s.

Kevin was a quality footballer and excellent goal scorer but a poor room mate. He smoked in those days and I hate to think how much cigarette smoke I inhaled during my time rooming with him – I am sure he is more health conscious now!

CHRIS WOODS
(Norwich City 1981–86 and Rangers 1986–91)

YOU knew that whenever the pressure was on and you needed a big result that 'Drinks' would deliver. He was a top striker and great team mate into the bargain. I was lucky enough to play with Kevin at Norwich and Rangers and he was a great guy to have by your side.

It was fair to say Kevin was your old-fashioned centre forward. He was big, powerful, great in the air and with a real eye for goal. The one vision of Kevin, for me, was seeing Ian Andrews flap as Kevin challenged him for the ball on his Old Firm debut. Kevin scored in that famous 5–1 win and gave Celtic and Andrews a real battering that day.

Watching that game and most of his other performances for Norwich and Rangers I was just glad I was in his side. He was a real handful and for goalkeepers and defenders Kevin was the ultimate nightmare. If he wasn't scoring goals or battering defenders he was chasing after lost causes. He would never give the opposition a moment's peace.

You can always measure a player's success by the popularity he has with the fans and at Norwich and Rangers Kevin was a big, big favourite. That shows the job he did for both clubs.

He also played his part in the success of both clubs. At Rangers he was part of the team that went on the road to nine-in-a-row and at Norwich he was part of the side that helped Norwich back into the top flight. He finished top scorer in both those seasons so the part he played in both those title wins can't be underestimated.

I also came across Kevin when he kicked off his career at Grimsby and he was a hero down there. Kevin had a really good career and he deserves enormous credit for what he achieved.

It was even more surprising because you knew away from the pitch Kevin could be found with a pint and a cigarette in his hand. The point is that it didn't affect his performance on the pitch and who knows, they probably helped to make him the great player he was.

ALLY McCOIST
(Rangers 1983–98)

'DRINKS' was part of the Rangers team who kicked off our nine-in-a-row charge. He helped us win the SPL and the League Cup and definitely deserves his medals – then again you would give anybody a medal if they had to play upfront with Scott Nisbet!

Kevin finished that season as our top scorer and played a massive part in our success although I have to keep reminding him that he only finished on top of the scoring charts because I was out for half the season. What I would say is that if we had both been fit then we would have scored a lot more goals. Kevin certainly played a massive part and did brilliantly to take on the main burden himself.

Kevin was a great strike partner to play alongside. He was a very unselfish player, unlike myself! He made a lot more goals for me than I made for him. A lot of it went unnoticed but I can assure you it was appreciated by his team mates. What you saw is what you got with Kevin.

The fans loved guys like Kevin, Nigel Spackman and Terry Hurlock because they were whole-hearted and really grew to love the club.

He scored in some big games like the Old Firm derby. I also got one later that season and big Kevin insisted I never got a touch and that it was Ian Ferguson's goal. I can now assure everyone that I did. It was a belter. I got the slightest of touches and if I hadn't then I am in absolutely no doubt Packie Bonner would have got back and saved it.

We nicknamed Kevin 'Chi-Chi the Panda'. A typical day at Ibrox for Kevin was he eats, shoots and leaves! That was 'Drinks'.

There was one day that really sticks out for me. Kevin had been up all night and was struggling to be fit for a midweek game. He came in to see the doctor in the morning and 20 minutes later the doctor came out and said: 'There is absolutely no chance of Kevin playing tonight. You should see the bags under his eyes.' I turned to the doc and said: 'Is that any different to any other day?'

Finally, can I just sign off by saying that your hotel tab at the Holiday Inn had nothing to do with me. I don't want to drop anybody in but the main culprit has the initials ID and can be found under the phone book as I. Durrant.

STEVE OGRIZOVIC
(Coventry City 1984–2000)

THE first time I ever came across Kevin he made a big impression on me – so much so that he left me concussed. I was still at Shrewsbury Town when he was making a big name for himself at Grimsby Town. Kevin, quite literally, gave me a real battering. His all-action style sent fear down the backs of most defenders and goalkeepers and I saw at first hand why. I went out to challenge him for a high ball and let's just say I came off second best, so much so that I ended up with concussion. There was no malice or intent on Kevin's part but his bravery knew no limits. I played on and although I knew I was playing for Shrewsbury I had to ask one of our defenders where we were and what the score was. They thought I was having a laugh but I was being deadly serious.

I also came across Kevin a few times when he was at Norwich and he continued to score goals there and in Scotland for Rangers. So I was delighted when I heard we had managed to persuade him to move to Coventry.

Kevin wasn't the quickest but they say the first yard is up in the head and it was clear that he was no slouch there. He might have been all-action but he was a very intelligent player with a great touch.

I also knew I would be a bit safer on a Saturday afternoon with Kevin on my side although I knew, for my own safety, I would need to keep my distance in training.

Kevin was bought by John Sillett after the FA Cup success to try and move Coventry forward. Kevin fell into that category of Coventry 'no longer shopping in Woolworths we are now shopping in Harrods'.

Throughout his career he was always a goal scorer and he showed that as he netted quite a few early in his career but the team started to struggle and the chances began to dry up. Kevin didn't get as many goals as he had hoped and then after we had a change of manager he found himself on the sidelines. I don't

252

know the reasons why Kevin was frozen out but I remember thinking that he was being unfairly treated. He would always come in and train hard and you knew that there was always the chance he could get you a goal. I couldn't understand it because he was still good enough to be playing in our first team and yet for whatever reason he would be left in the stands. It was a shame for Kevin and Coventry but the good thing was that Kevin moved on and continued to show what a good player he was when he returned to Scotland with Falkirk.

I still see Kevin in his work as an agent and it is good to catch up with him because he is a great guy and was also a decent team mate to have by your side.

KEVIN GALLACHER
(Coventry City 1990–93)

KEVIN, all I can say is thank you very much for nearly blowing my move to Coventry City. Just as well John Sillett is a better judge of a player than yourself. If he had listened to you then John Colquhoun would have been at Coventry and I would still have been a Dundee United player.

All joking aside, Kevin was a player who I knew and had played against when he was at Rangers. He was a good striker and a real predator, so I was more than happy to come down to Coventry and provide him with the ammunition to try and fire us up the table.

I used to play down the right and Kevin's other good friend and neighbour, Dave Smith, would play down the left.

Unfortunately we were at Highfield Road at a very difficult time and it was more about keeping things tight and hitting on the counter attack than going for goals.

It was also at a time when the famous FA Cup winning team of 1987 was starting to dwindle and the money was starting to dry up.

Kevin, to be fair, would never shirk a challenge and you knew even if the ball wasn't in the box he would still put in a decent shift. I later moved into the centre and he proved a decent foil for me.

I remember one game against Nottingham Forest where I scored a hat-trick and Kevin played a major part in my success that day, giving the Forest rearguard a real hard time.

It was amazing because Kevin used to love a cigarette and a pint but he never let that get in the way of his football. That is more than can be said for Dave Smith. He lived near him at Coventry and he tells me his liver is still recovering.

Kevin later moved on to make a name for himself back in Scotland, where he is now an agent.

He actually nearly helped broker a deal for me to go to Motherwell at the end of my career. The move was dependent on James McFadden going to Preston North End. I took the call from Kevin and I was invited to come up and play in a trial game for Motherwell but I was halfway up the road when Terry Butcher said he could no longer go through with the deal.

McFadden's Preston move had collapsed and he no longer had the funds. It was a pity but I appreciated Kevin's efforts then the same way I did when I played alongside him in the sky blue of Coventry.

JIM JEFFERIES
(Manager of Falkirk 1990–95)

WHEN I signed Kevin it was a major coup for Falkirk. I have to say when I first made my move I honestly didn't think there was a snowball's chance in hell of him moving to Brockville. He was still with Coventry in the English top flight and although he wasn't really getting a game there I made my pitch more in hope than expectation.

Fortunately, thanks to a visit to the Open at Muirfield and a few gentle words of persuasion I managed to pull it off. Kevin was still a big name in Scotland from his time at Rangers and there was a real buzz around the place when we landed him. Kevin was a real handful when we had come up against him at Rangers and the one thing he guaranteed every team was a real presence and goals.

Kev might have been coming to the end of his career but we got a real shift, like Mo Johnston and Frank McAvennie, out of him for the two seasons he was at Falkirk. Kevin wasn't the tallest but he was terrific in the air, scored goals and was a great at holding the ball up, which was important for us in the SPL. Even after we got relegated Kevin played a big part in helping us win the First Division and the B&Q Cup. I know he is still highly thought of by the Falkirk fans. That shows the job he did for us.

At Falkirk we allowed him to start coaching and to take his badges. He did very well on that side of things. He had the chance to become manager of Inverness but I think it was just too far away and he decided to join Stirling instead, where he later went on to become the boss at Forthbank. He did a good job there and now he is using his expertise in the field of football agency. Even there he is making an impact and has pulled me out more than a few favours over the years at Kilmarnock and now Hearts.

DAVID WEIR
(Falkirk 1992–96)

KEVIN DRINKELL was one of the more experienced players at Falkirk and was a player we all looked up to. He had played at the highest level in England and with Rangers. He was a player we knew we could all learn from. He was a great guy to have in the dressing room.

Kevin always spoke well and you knew if he had something to say it was worth listening to. I was a defender and it was always an experience to come up against Kevin, even in training. He was a very clever player and a great target man.

He was coming towards the latter stages of his career when he was at Brockville. He maybe wasn't as mobile as he had been at his peak but he was still a major part of our team. Kevin was very good when you played the ball into his feet. He scored goals but he was always great linking up the play and bringing others into things. He was a very good team player and he played a major part in Falkirk winning the First Division and B&Q Cup when he was there.

Kevin also started to cut his coaching teeth at Falkirk and the manager (Jim Jefferies) was more than happy to give him a platform to progress his career. He certainly led by example every time he stepped on to the park or the training pitch. If you can't learn from top players like Kevin then who can you learn from? I have always tried to learn from the more experienced players in the teams I played in and now I am in a position where I try to pass on my own experiences to my team mates.

RAY STEWART
(Stirling Albion 1994–98)

KEVIN gave me my big break in management and for that I am eternally grateful. I initially came in and worked for nothing and I have to say it was worth it because working with Kev was a great experience. I would go as far as saying he is up there with the best managers I have worked with throughout my football career.

I have worked with Jock Stein, John Lyall, Jim McLean, Billy Bonds, Lou Macari and Paul Sturrock and Kevin is definitely up there with the best of them.

The job he did at Stirling was truly exceptional and I don't think he got the credit he deserved for his time at Forthbank. Kevin really deserved to get a bigger job. There was no doubt he could have managed in the Scottish Premier League or even in the higher leagues in England, but for whatever reason he never got the chances he should have.

Maybe he was too honest and straight talking for his own good. There was no rubbish or lies. He was as straight as a die and I think that is important in football, and life.

He was a good manager. He would let me get on with the training and then would come in and work on the set pieces, tactics and formations. We were a decent partnership and I think Kevin's record speaks for itself.

You also have to take into consideration the financial constraints we were working under because Kevin had to fight tooth and nail to get every penny he could for players.

We would often have to pull on our boots just to make up the numbers and there was one game we were that short I had to go in goal after our keeper had been sent off. It was between me and Kevin but as gaffer he pulled rank and I had to pull on the gloves. I think he is still scarred from the time he had to play in goal for the first team at Falkirk, when they lost to Motherwell! It was difficult but we juggled things and did everything we could to bring success to the club.

I was just disappointed that I never got to play alongside Kevin in his prime. I played against him a few times when he was at Norwich and I was at West Ham. It is fair to say I always came off second best. I think he scored two or three goals against me through the years just because of his movement and his ability to peel away and find space at the back post.

He was a nightmare for opposition defenders and I know there would have been a lot more than myself who Kevin would have haunted throughout the years with his goals and all-action play.

BILLY REID
(Stirling Albion 1994–95)

'DRINKS' and I signed for Stirling on the same day. We were both quite big signings for the club and the one thing that struck me about Kevin was how down-to-earth he was. He had played for some big clubs like Rangers and Norwich but he was just one of the guys. Kev might have played at a higher level than most of us but the one thing he was always prepared to do was roll up his sleeves and put his shoulder to the wheel.

There were no airs or grace about Kevin. He was a team player and would go out and give his all for his team. He was a real 100 per center and I think every professional really appreciates a team mate like that. Kev was coming to the end of his playing days and he maybe wasn't as quick as he had been at his peak but he was still a good out at our level.

We knew with Kev up there he was more than capable of leading the line even if it was at a time when Stirling were struggling.

Kevin eventually took over the manager's job at Forthbank from John Brogan but unfortunately I didn't really get the chance to work with him on that side because my own playing days were cut short by injury.

It was disappointing because Stirling was probably the only club in my career who I felt never got value for money for me but back problems and sciatica meant I had to hang up my boots. It was a pity because I would have liked to work under Kev but I never really got the chance.

Fortunately I have kept in touch with Kevin and now he has moved into the sports management side and he has done a fair bit of business, bringing in one or two players during my time in charge of Hamilton. The good thing about Kevin is he has played the game at the top level and also managed at the other end. He knows all the pitfalls and his experience will go some way to helping the players he now represents.

30

GLORY, GLORY

GRIMSBY TOWN

1978–79 – Grimsby win promotion to Division 3.

1979–80 – Grimsby win the Division 3 championship.

1981–82 – League Group Cup winners (The current Football League Trophy).

NORWICH CITY

1985–86 – Norwich City win the Division 2 title.

1985–86 – Kevin wins the Golden Boot for finishing top scorer in Division 2.

2001–02 – Kevin is inducted into the Norwich City FC Hall of Fame.

RANGERS

1988–89 – Rangers win the Skol Cup.

1988–89 – Rangers lift the SPL title.

1988–89 – Kevin finishes the season as the top scorer in the Scottish top flight.

FALKIRK

1993–94 – Falkirk win the B&Q Challenge Cup.

1993–94 – Falkirk claim the Scottish First Division title.

STIRLING ALBION

1995–96 – Kevin manages Stirling Albion to the Scottish Second Division title.

1995–96 – Kevin is named as the Bell's Second Division Manager of the Year.

OTHER ACHIEVEMENTS

1986–87 – English League Select XI call-up.

1985–86 – England B call-up for international match with Malta.

KEVIN'S PLAYING CAREER

Season	Club	Appearances	Goals
1976–77	Grimsby Town	4	2
1977–78	Grimsby Town	30	6
1978–79	Grimsby Town	29	7
1979–80	Grimsby Town	42	17
1980–81	Grimsby Town	33	9
1982–83	Grimsby Town	45	20
1983–84	Grimsby Town	41	18
1984–85	Grimsby Town	39	15
1985–86	Norwich City	47	22
1986–87	Norwich City	48	19
1987–88	Norwich City	42	12
1987–89	Rangers	45	20
1989–90	Rangers	7	–
1989–90	Coventry City	27	7
1990–91	Coventry City	15	–
1991–92	Coventry City	4	–
1991–92	Birmingham	5	2
1992–93	Falkirk	35	7
1993–94	Falkirk	20	6
1993–94	Stirling Albion	11	1
1994–95	Stirling Albion	10	2

(Career statistics include league, major domestic cups and European appearances only.)

KEVIN'S MANAGERIAL CAREER

1994–1998   Stirling Albion
1998–2000   Montrose

AFTERWORD
BY TERRY VENABLES

KEVIN DRINKELL was a striker I liked immensely and one I would have loved to have signed. Believe me it wasn't through a lack of trying. I tried to sign Kevin when I was manager of both QPR and Tottenham but I was left disappointed because we were unable to agree a deal with his club at the time, Norwich.

It was a real disappointment for me especially when I went to Tottenham. I had started to rebuild my Spurs team and Kevin was one of the names who was high up my wanted list. The problem was that Kevin had just finished as Norwich's top scorer and we couldn't afford to meet Norwich's asking price.

It was a big blow to me because I would have loved to have worked with Kevin. I felt he would have brought a lot to both QPR and Tottenham.

He always scored goals but the thing I liked about Kevin was his strength and the way he could hold up the ball and bring his team mates into play. He could link up well and was a great asset for Norwich at that time.

Kevin had a great career on both sides of the border and I am just disappointed I never got the chance to work with him. He made a decent name for himself but I honestly believe if I had been able to sign him I would have been able to make him an even better player and maybe even a full England international. But the one thing is that Kevin still made a real name for himself and can look back on his career and his achievements with a great deal of pride.